Praise for *Geekonomics: The Real Cost of Insecure Software*

"The clarity of David's argument and the strength of his conviction are truly inspiring. If you don't believe the world of software affects the world in which you live, you owe it to yourself to read this book."

—*Lenny Zeltzer, SANS Institute faculty member and the New York Security Consulting Manager at Savvis, Inc.*

"*Geekonomics* stays with you long after you finish reading the book. You will reconsider every assumption you have had about software costs and benefits."

—*Slava Frid, Gemini Systems, CTO, Resilience Technology Solutions*

"Information Security is an issue that concerns governments, companies and, increasingly, citizens. Are the computer systems and software to which we entrust our sensitive and critical information, technologies that are out of control? David Rice has written an important and welcome book that goes to the heart of this issue, and points to solutions that society as a whole needs to debate and embrace."

—*Nick Bleech, IT Security Director, Rolls-Royce*

"If you are dependent upon software (and of course, all of us in the modern world are) this book is a fabulous discussion of how and why we should worry."

—*Becky Bace*

GEEKONOMICS

GEEKONOMICS

THE REAL COST OF INSECURE SOFTWARE

David Rice

↞Addison-Wesley

Upper Saddle River, NJ • Boston • Indianapolis • San Francisco
New York • Toronto • Montreal • London • Munich • Paris • Madrid
Cape Town • Sydney • Tokyo • Singapore • Mexico City

Many of the designations used by manufacturers and sellers to distinguish their products are claimed as trademarks. Where those designations appear in this book, and the publisher was aware of a trademark claim, the designations have been printed with initial capital letters or in all capitals.

The author and publisher have taken care in the preparation of this book but make no expressed or implied warranty of any kind and assume no responsibility for errors or omissions. No liability is assumed for incidental or consequential damages in connection with or arising out of the use of the information or programs contained herein.

The publisher offers excellent discounts on this book when ordered in quantity for bulk purchases or special sales, which may include electronic versions and/or custom covers and content particular to your business, training goals, marketing focus, and branding interests. For more information, please contact:

U.S. Corporate and Government Sales
(800) 382-3419
corpsales@pearsontechgroup.com

For sales outside the United States please contact:

International Sales
international@pearsoned.com

This Book Is Safari Enabled

The Safari® Enabled icon on the cover of your favorite technology book means the book is available through Safari Bookshelf. When you buy this book, you get free access to the online edition for 45 days.

Safari Bookshelf is an electronic reference library that lets you easily search thousands of technical books, find code samples, download chapters, and access technical information whenever and wherever you need it.

To gain 45-day Safari Enabled access to this book:

- Go to http://www.awprofessional.com/safarienabled
- Complete the brief registration form
- Enter the coupon code RZQG-33UQ-AY9J-A3PZ-6YB5

If you have difficulty registering on Safari Bookshelf or accessing the online edition, please e-mail customer-service@safaribooksonline.com.

Visit us on the Web: www.awprofessional.com

Library of Congress Cataloging-in-Publication Data is on file.

ISBN-13: 978-0-321-73597-3
ISBN-10: 0-321-73597-8

This product is printed digitally on demand. This book is the paperback version of an original hardcover book.

Editor-in-Chief
Karen Gettman

Acquisitions Editor
Jessica Goldstein

Development Editors
Sheri Cain
Chris Zahn

Managing Editor
Gina Kanouse

Senior Project Editor
Kristy Hart

Copy Editor
Language Logistics, LLC

Indexer
Erika Millen

Proofreader
Williams Woods Publishing

Publishing Coordinator
Romny French

Cover Designer
Chuti Prasertsith

Senior Compositor
Gloria Schurick

Author Photo
Heidi Borgia

For my family.

CONTENTS

PREFACE

You may or may not have an inkling of what insecure software is, how it impacts your life, or why you should be concerned. That is OK. This book attempts to introduce you to the full scope and consequence of software's impact on modern society without baffling the reader with jargon only experts understand or minutia only experts care about. The prerequisite for this book is merely a hint of curiosity.

Although we interact with software on a daily basis, carry it on our mobile phones, drive with it in our cars, fly with it in our planes, and use it in our home and business computers, software itself remains essentially shrouded—a ghost in the machine; a mystery that functions but only part of the time. And therein lies our problem.

Software is the stuff of modern infrastructure. Not only is software infused into a growing number of commercial products we purchase and services we use, but government increasingly uses software to manage the details of our lives, to allocate benefits and public services we enjoy as citizens, and to administer and defend the state as a whole. How and when we touch software and how and when it touches us is less our choice every day. The quality of this software matters greatly; the level of protection this software affords us from harm and exploitation matters even more.

As a case in point, in mid-2007 the country of Estonia, dubbed "the most wired nation in Europe" because of its pervasive use of computer networks for a wide array of private and public activities, had a significant portion of its national infrastructure crippled for more than two weeks by cyber attacks launched from hundreds of thousands of individual computers that had been previously hijacked by Russian hackers. Estonia was so overwhelmed by the attacks that Estonian leaders literally severed the country's connection to the Internet and with it the country's economic and communications lifeline to the rest of the world. As one Estonian official lamented, "We are back to the stone age...." The reason for the cyber attack? The Russian government objected to Estonia's removal of a Soviet-era war memorial from the center of its capital, Tallinn, to a military cemetery.

The hundreds of thousands of individual computers that took part in the attack belonged to innocents: businesses, governments, and home users located around the world unaware their computers were used as weapons against another nation and another people. Such widespread hijacking was made possible in large part because of insecure software—software that contains manufacturing defects allowing, among other things, hackers to hijack and remotely control computer systems. Traditional defensive measures employed by software buyers such as firewalls, anti-virus, and software patches did little to help Estonia and nothing to correct software manufacturing practices that enabled the attacks in the first place.

During the same year, an experienced "security researcher" (a euphemism for a hacker) from IBM's Internet Security Systems was able to remotely break into and hijack computer systems controlling a nuclear power plant in the United States. The plant's owners claimed their computer systems could not be accessed from the Internet. The owners were mistaken. As the security researcher later stated after completing the exercise, "It turned out to be the easiest penetration test I'd ever done. By the first day, we had penetrated the network. Within a week, we were controlling a nuclear power plant. I thought, 'Gosh, this is a big problem.'"

Indeed it is.

According to IDC, a global market intelligence firm, 75 percent of computers having access to the Internet have been infected and are actively being used without the owner's knowledge to conduct cyber attacks, distribute unwanted email (spam), and support criminal and terrorist activities. To solely blame hackers or hundreds of thousands of innocent computer users, or misinformed—and some might say "sloppy"—power plant owners for the deplorable state of cyber security is shortsighted and distracts from the deeper issue. The proverbial butterfly that flaps its wings in Brazil causing a storm somewhere far away is no match for the consequences brought about by seemingly innocuous foibles of software manufacturers. As one analyst commented regarding insecure software as it related to hijacking of the nuclear reactor's computer systems, "These are simple bugs [mistakes in software], but very dangerous ones."

The story of Estonia, the nuclear reactor, and thousands of similar news stories merely hint at the underlying problem of modern infrastructure. The "big problem" is insecure software and insecure software is *everywhere*. From our iPhones (which had a critical weakness in its software discovered merely two weeks after its release) to our laptops, from the XBOX to public utilities, from home computers to financial systems, insecure software is interconnected and woven more tightly into the fabric of civilization with each passing day and with it, as former U.S. Secretary of Defense William Cohen observed, an unprecedented level of vulnerability. Insecure software is making us fragile, vulnerable, and weak. It is difficult to overstate the seriousness of the situation.

The threat of global warming might be on everyone's lips, and the polar ice caps might indeed melt but not for a time. What is happening *right now* because of world-wide interconnection of insecure software gives social problems once limited by geography a new destructive range. Cyber criminals, terrorists, and even nation states are currently preying on millions upon millions of computer systems (and their owners) and using the proceeds to underwrite further crime, economic espionage, warfare, and terror. We are only now beginning to realize the enormity of the storm set upon us by the tiny fluttering of software manufacturing mistakes and the economic and social costs such mistakes impose. In 2007, "bad" software cost the United States roughly $180 billion; this amount represents nearly 40 percent of the U.S. military defense budget for the same year ($439 billion) or nearly 55 percent *more* than the estimated cost to the U.S. economy of Hurricane Katrina ($100 billion), the costliest storm to hit the United States since Hurricane Andrew.[1] Disturbingly, $180 billion may be an exceptionally low estimate.

Since the 1960s, individuals both within and outside the software community have worked hard to improve the quality, reliability, and security of software. Smart people have been looking out for you. For this, they should be commended. But the results of their efforts are mixed.

After 40 years of collaborative effort with software manufacturers to improve software quality, reliability, and security, Carnegie Mellon's Software Engineering Institute (SEI)—an important contributor to software research and improvement—declared in the year 2000 that software was getting worse, not better. Such an announcement by SEI is tantamount to the U.S. Food and Drug Administration warning that food quality in the twenty-first century is poorer now than when Upton Sinclair wrote *The Jungle* in 1906.[2] Unlike progress in a vast majority of areas related to consumer protection and national security, progress against "bad" software has been fitful at best.

While technical complications in software manufacturing might be in part to blame for the sorry state of software, this book argues that even if effective technical solutions were widely available, market incentives do not work for, but *work against* better, more secure software. This has worrisome consequences for us all.

Incentives matter. Human beings are notoriously complex and fickle creatures who will do whatever it takes to make themselves better off. There is nothing intrinsically wrong with this behavior. Acting in one's best interests is what normal, rational human beings do. However, the complications arise because society is a morass of competing, misaligned, and conflicting incentives that lead to all manner of situations where one individual's behavior may adversely affect another. Nowhere is this more easily observed than how individuals conduct their everyday lives within free market economies. As such, *Geekonomics* is the story of software told through the lens of humanity and economics, rather than the lens of technology.

To see and to understand insecure software merely as a technical phenomenon to be solved by other technical phenomena is to be distracted from the larger issue. Software is a human creation and it need not be mysterious or magical. It also need not make us fragile, vulnerable, and weak. To understand software and its implications for society requires an understanding of how humans behave, not necessarily how software behaves. More specifically, this book looks at the array of incentives that compel people to manufacture, buy, and exploit insecure software. In short, incentives matter for any human endeavor and without understanding the incentives that drive people toward or away from a particular behavior, all the potential technical solutions that *might* help address the problem of insecure software will sit idle, or worse, never be created at all. After 40 years of effort with debatable improvement, this much is evident.

As with any complex issue, and especially with a complex issue such as software manufacturing, there are few "right" answers regarding how to fix the problem. However, there are ways of approaching complex issues more fruitful than others that are worth investigating. Protecting economic and national security from the effects of insecure software is as much an economic issue as it is a technological issue. We know software is as notoriously complex and fickle as the humans that create it, if not more so. But as a human creation, we need not understand insecure software in its entirety; we need merely to get humans to stop creating the stuff. And this is where incentives come in.

At base, economics teaches us, at least in part, how to get incentives right. Of course, economists are not always right when it comes to forecasting the expected effects of a particular incentive, but economics allows us to approach complex issues from a scientific perspective and make reasonable, better-informed decisions. By using and analyzing data—even imperfect data—economics allows us to view the world as it is, look back as it was, and to anticipate how it might be. Incentives help navigate the path to a desired future. The desired future of this author is a stable, secure, global infrastructure that propels humanity beyond its wildest dreams.

There are three primary themes in *Geekonomics*:

- First, software is becoming the foundation of modern civilization; software constitutes or will control the products, services, and infrastructure people will rely on for a wide variety of daily activities from the vital to the trivial.

- Second, software is not sufficiently engineered at this time to fulfill the role of "foundation." The information infrastructure is the only part of national infrastructure that is destructively tested while in use; that is, software is shipped containing both known and unknown weaknesses that software buyers are made aware of and must fix only *after* installation (or after losing control of your nuclear power plant). The consequences are already becoming apparent and augur ill for us all.

- Third, important economic, legal, and regulatory incentives that could improve software quality, reliability, and security are not only missing, but the market incentives that do exist are perverted, ineffectual, or distorted. Change the incentives and the story and effects of insecure software change also.

Because of the complexity of software itself and the complexity of manufacturing software, no single discipline, even one as powerful as economics, is sufficient for holistically addressing the topic at hand. As such, this book also contains a splash of psychology, physics, engineering, philosophy, and criminology that are mostly framed within the context of incentives. This book does not contain the complete story of insecure software, only those parts that a single author can realistically include in a book meant to inform, entertain, and enlighten.

I *like* software. I really do. Though the tone of my writing is often forceful and urgent regarding insecure software in general and software manufacturers in particular, I truly appreciate all the things I can do with software that I could not possibly do as quickly, efficiently, or cheaply without it. Writing this book was infinitely easier using a word processor than with a traditional typewriter (I haven't owned one of those for 20 years). But everything has a cost and not all costs are readily apparent at the time of acquisition. I had no less than three separate storage locations (laptop hard drive, USB key, network storage) for this book's manuscript just in case something should happen, which it inevitably did. My word processor application (which will remain nameless) crashed or froze roughly 40 times in the course of writing this book. Without software this book might not have been written as quickly compared to older methods. That is not in question. Without reliable backups, however, this book would not have been written at all.

Ironically, in writing this book I attempted to avoid providing a litany of software disasters in hopes of escaping claims that I might be promoting "fear, uncertainty, and doubt," a claim that so often pollutes and plagues discussions regarding software security; yet, many of my non-expert reviewers (the non-expert is this book's target audience) thought I was being unfair to software manufacturers because I did not provide the necessary probative evidence to establish why software manufacturers are partly to blame for threatening the foundation of civilization. "What was needed?" I asked. A litany of software disasters would be helpful, came the reply. And so my hope is that the litany of disasters provided in this book are seen as necessary to provide context and perspective for those unfamiliar with the subject and impact of insecure software, rather than the primary focus of the book.

ACKNOWLEDGMENTS

I would like to thank and acknowledge everyone who made this book possible: My first and deepest thanks is to my wife, whose patience, support, and feedback made this book possible in the first place. Ed Skoudis for connecting me with Addison-Wesley and for brainstorming the book title with me in San Diego. Thank you to Becky Bace, a dear friend and trusted colleague, Alan Paller, Howard Schmidt, Stephen Northcutt, Richard Salgado, Lenny Zeltser, Slava Frid, Randy Sabbet, Daniel Jackson, and the numerous contributors to the Workshop on the Economics of Information Security. Special thanks must go to Nick Bleech whose frank and candid comments and the tremendous amount of time he invested in reviewing the manuscript helped me immensely.

I must also thank all the researchers, authors, and journalists whose writings were invaluable in constructing the themes and explanations in this book. There are too many to acknowledge here but I have made my best efforts in crediting their words and ideas in the book's notes. Also there are many folks who must remain nameless by nature of their work. They gave me my start in the arts of information security and invested heavily in my skill and education. Without them, my knowledge of the issues surrounding software security would be sorely lacking. Thank you.

I would also like to thank my publishing and editorial staff. My first thanks is to Jessica Goldstein who kept me sane through a majority of the writing process and whose direction was invaluable in creating this book. It was a pleasure to work with you, thank you. Thank you to my developmental editors Chris Zahn and Sheri Cain whose insights on structure and flow were very helpful in maintaining my momentum. Thanks to Romny French and Kristy Hart.

ABOUT THE AUTHOR

David Rice is an internationally recognized information security professional and an accomplished educator and visionary. For a decade he has advised, counseled, and defended global IT networks for government and private industry. David has been awarded by the U.S. Department of Defense for "significant contributions" advancing security of critical national infrastructure and global networks. Additionally, David has authored numerous IT security courses and publications, teaches for the prestigious SANS Institue, and has served as adjunct faculty at James Madison University. He is a frequent speaker at information security conferences and currently Director of The Monterey Group.

The Foundation of Civilization

---

*"The value of a thing sometimes lies not in what one attains with it,
but in what one pays for it—what it costs us."*

—*Frederick Nietzsche*

For the city of London, 1854 was a dreadful year. An outbreak of cholera, the third in 20 years, claimed over ten thousand lives. Six previous city Commissions failed to adequately address London's growing sewage problem, leaving the entire metropolitan area—more than one million people—subject to the vagaries of overflowing cesspools, ill-constructed sewers, contaminated groundwater, and a dangerously polluted Thames River. Considering London was one of the most populated cities at the time and depended heavily on the Thames River, inaction had unfortunate consequences. Sadly, thousands of deaths could not properly motivate Parliament to overcome numerous bureaucratic and political obstacles required to address the crisis.

It was not until an inordinately hot summer in 1858 that the stench of the Thames so overwhelmed all those in close proximity to the river—particularly members of Parliament, many of whom still believed cholera to be an airborne rather than a waterborne pathogen—that resistance finally subsided. The "Great Stink" served as impetus to the largest civic works project London had ever seen.[1]

For the next ten years, Joseph Bazalgette, Chief Engineer of the Metropolitan Board of Works, constructed London's newer and larger sewer network against imposing odds. Despite Parliament's hard-won support and a remarkable design by Bazalgette himself, building a new sewer network in an active and sprawling city raised significant technical and engineering challenges.

1

Most obvious among these challenges was excavating sewer lines while minimizing disruption to local businesses and the city's necessary daily activities. Less obvious, but no less important, was selecting contracting methods and building materials for such an enormous project. Modern public works projects such as the California Aqueduct, the U.S. Interstate highway system, or China's Three Gorges Dam elicit images of enormous quantities of coordination and concrete. Initially, Bazalgette enjoyed neither.

Selecting suitable building materials was an especially important engineering decision, one that Bazalgette did not take lightly. Building materials needed to bear considerable strain from overhead traffic and buildings as well as survive prolonged exposure to and immersion in water. Traditionally, engineers at the time would have selected Roman cement, a common and inexpensive material used since the fourteenth century, to construct the extensive underground brickworks required for the new sewer system. Roman cement gets its name from Romans who used it in a vast majority of infrastructure for both the Republic and Empire. The "recipe" for Roman cement was lost during the Dark Ages only to be rediscovered during the Renaissance. This bit of history aside, Bazalgette chose to avoid Roman cement for laying the sewer's brickwork and instead opted in favor of a newer, stronger, but more expensive type of cement called Portland cement.

Portland cement was invented in the kitchen of a British bricklayer named Joseph Aspdin in 1824. What Aspdin discovered during his experimentation that the Romans did not (or were not aware of) was that by first heating some of the ingredients of cement—finely ground limestone and clay—the silica in the clay bonded with the calcium in the limestone, creating a far more durable concrete, one that chemically interacted with any aggregates such as stone or sand added to the cement mixture. Roman cement, in comparison, does not chemically interact with aggregates and therefore simply holds them in suspension. This makes Roman cement weaker in comparison to Portland cement but only in relative, not absolute terms. Many substantial Roman structures including roadways, buildings, and seaports survived nearly 2,000 years to the present.

It is the chemical reaction discovered by Aspdin that gives Portland cement its amazing durability and strength over Roman cement. This chemical reaction also gives Portland cement the interesting characteristic of gaining in strength with both age and immersion in water.[2] If traditional cement sets in one day, Portland cement will be more than four times as hard after a week and over eight times as hard in five years.[3] In choosing a material for such a massive and important project as the London sewer, Portland cement might have rightly appeared to Bazalgette as the obvious choice. There was only one problem: Portland cement is unreliable if the production process varies even slightly.

The strength and therefore the reliability of Portland cement is significantly diminished by what would appear to the average observer as minuscule, almost trivial changes in mixture ratios, kiln temperature, or grinding process. In the mid-nineteenth century, quality control processes were largely non-existent, and where they did exist were inconsistently employed—based more on personal opinion rather than objective criteria. The

> *Portland cement might have rightly appeared to Bazalgette as the obvious choice. There was only one problem: Portland cement is unreliable if the production process varies even slightly.*

"state of the art" in nineteenth century quality control meant that while Portland cement was promising, it was a risky choice on the part of Bazalgette. To mitigate any inconsistencies in producing Portland cement for the sewer project, Bazalgette created rigorous, objective, and some would say draconian testing procedures to ensure each batch of Portland cement afforded the necessary resiliency and strength. His reputation as an engineer and the success of the project depended on it.

Bazalgette enforced the following regimen: Delivered cement sat at the construction site for at least three weeks to acclimate to local environmental conditions. After the elapsed time, samples were taken from every tenth sack and made into molds that were immediately dropped into water where the concrete would remain for seven days. Afterward, samples were tested for strength. If any sample failed to bear weight of at least five hundred pounds (more than twice that of Roman cement), the entire delivery was rejected.[4] By 1865, more than 11,587 tests were conducted on 70,000 tons of cement for the southern section of the sewerage alone.[5] Bazalgette's testing methodology proved so thorough, the Metropolitan Board who oversaw the project eventually agreed to Bazalgette's request to construct sewers entirely from concrete. This not only decreased the time required to construct the sewerage, but eliminated the considerable associated cost of the brickworks themselves.[6]

Once completed, Bazalgette's sewer system saved hundreds of thousands of lives by preventing future cholera and typhoid epidemics.[7] The sewer system also made the Thames one of the cleanest metropolitan rivers in the world and changed the face of river-side London forever. By 1872, the Registrar-General's Annual Report stated that the annual death rate in London was far below any other major European, American, or Indian city, and at 3.3 million people (almost three times the population from the time Bazalgette started his project), London was by far the largest city in the world. This state of affairs was unprecedented for the time. By 1896 cholera was so rare in London, the Registrar-General classified cholera as an "exotic disease." Bazalgette's sewer network, as well as the original cement used in its construction, remains in use to this day. Given that Portland cement increases with strength over time, it is likely London's sewer system will outlive even some of Rome's longest standing architectural accomplishments such as the aqueducts and the Pantheon.

Software and Cement

While Bazalgette's design of the sewer network was certainly important, in hindsight the selection and qualification of Portland cement was arguably the most critical aspect to the project's success. Had Bazalgette not enforced strict quality control on production of Portland cement, the outcome of the "Great Stink of London" might have been far different. Due to Bazalgette's efforts and the resounding success of the London sewer system, Portland cement progressed in a few short years from "promising but risky" to the industry standard used in just about every major construction project from that time onward.

Portland cement's popularity then, is due not just to its physical properties, but in large part to Bazalgette's strict and rigorous quality tests, which drastically reduced potential uncertainties associated with Portland cement's production. At present, more than 20 separate tests are used to ensure the quality of Portland cement, significantly more than Bazalgette himself employed. World production of Portland cement exceeded two billion metric tons in 2005, with China accounting for nearly half of that production followed closely by India and the United States.[8] This works out to roughly 2.5 tons of cement for every person on the planet. Without Portland cement, much of modern civilization as we know it, see it, live on it, and drive on it would fail to exist.

Cement is everywhere in modern civilization. Mixed with aggregates such as sand and stone, it forms concrete that comprises roadways, bridges, tunnels, building foundations, walls, floors, airports, docks, dams, aqueducts, pipes, and the list goes on. Cement is—quite literally—the foundation of modern civilization, creating the infrastructure that supports billions of lives around the globe. One cannot live in modern civilization without touching, seeing, or relying on cement in one way or another. Our very lives depend on cement, yet cement has proven so reliable due to strict quality controls that it has to a large extent disappeared from our field of concerns—even though we are surrounded by it. Such is the legacy of Bazalgette's commitment to quality: We can live our lives without thinking twice about what is beneath our feet, or more importantly, what may be above our head.

Civilization depends on infrastructure, and infrastructure depends, at least in part, on durable, reliable cement. Due to its versatility, cost-effectiveness, and broad availability, cement has provided options in construction that could not otherwise be attained with stone, wood, or steel alone. But since the 1950s, a new material has been slowly and unrelentingly injected into modern infrastructure, one that is far more versatile, cost-effective, and widely available than cement could ever hope to be. It also just so happens to be invisible and unvisualizable. In fact, it is not a material at all. It is software.

Like cement, software is everywhere in modern civilization. Software is in your mobile phone, on your home computer, in cars, airplanes, hospitals, businesses, public utilities, financial systems, and national defense systems. Software is an increasingly critical component in the operation of infrastructures, cutting across almost every aspect of global, national, social, and economic function. One cannot live in modern civilization without touching, being touched by, or depending on software in one way or another.

> *Like cement, software is everywhere in modern civilization.*

Software helps deliver oil to our cities, electricity to our homes, water to our crops, products to our markets, money to our banks, and information to our minds. It allows us to share pictures, music, thoughts, and ideas with people we might meet infrequently in person but will intimately know from a distance. Everything is becoming "smarter" because software is being injected into just about *every thing*. Software has accelerated economic growth through the increased facilities of managing labor and capital with unprecedented capacity. Hundreds of thousands of people if not millions owe their livelihoods to software. With its aid, we have discovered new medicines, new oil fields, and new planets and it has given us new ways of visualizing old problems, thereby finding solutions we might never have had the capacity, time, or ability to discover without it. With software we are able to build bridges once thought impossible, create buildings once thought unrealistic, and explore regions of earth, space, and self once thought unreachable.

Software has also given us the Internet, a massive world-wide network connecting all to all. In fact, connectedness in the twenty-first century is primarily a manifestation of software. Software handles the protocols necessary for communication, operates telecommunications equipment, bundles data for transmission, and routes messages to far-flung destinations as well as giving function and feature to a dizzying array of devices. Software helps connect everything to everything else with the network—the Internet—merely a by-product of its function. Without software, the network would be just a bunch of cables, just as a human cell without DNA would be just a bunch of amino acids and proteins.

Software is *everywhere*; it is everywhere because software is the closest thing we have to a universal tool. It exhibits a radical malleability that allows us to do with it what we will. Software itself is nothing more than a set of commands that tells a computer processor (a microchip) what to do. Connect a microchip to a toy, and the toy becomes "smart;" connect a microchip to a car's fuel injector, and the car becomes more fuel efficient; connect it to a phone, and the phone becomes indispensable in life's everyday affairs. Connect a microchip to just about anything, and just about anything is possible because the software makes it so. Software is the ghost in the machine, the DNA of technology; it is what gives *things* the appearance of intelligence when none can possibly exist.

The only aspect of software more impressive than software itself is the people that create software. Computer programmers, also known as software developers or software engineers, write the instructions that tell computers what to do. Software developers are in large part a collection of extremely talented and gifted individuals whose capacity to envision and implement algorithms of extraordinary complexity and elegance gives us search engines, operating systems, word processors, instant messaging, mobile networks, satellite navigation, smart cars, advanced medical imaging; the list goes on. As such, software is a human creation, and as a human creation it is subject to the strengths and foibles of humanity. This is where the similarities of cement and software become most interesting.

Software, like cement before it, is becoming the foundation of civilization. Our very lives are becoming more dependent on and subject to software. As such, the properties of software matter greatly: quality, reliability, security, each by themselves accomplish very little, but their absence faults everything else. Like Portland cement, software can be unreliable if production processes vary even slightly. Whereas variations in kiln temperatures, mixture ratios, or grinding processes can detrimentally affect the strength and durability of Portland cement after it has been poured, there are a host of similar, seemingly trivial variations in producing software that can detrimentally affect its "strength" when "poured" into microchips. It is up to humans to get the production process right.

Unlike Portland cement, for more than 50 years software of all types and function has been continuously released into the stream of commerce plagued by design and implementation defects that were largely detectable and preventable by manufacturers, but were not. This has and does result in catastrophic accidents, significant financial losses, and even death. The trepidation over insufficient software manufacturing practices extends back to the late 1960s when the North American Treaty Organization (NATO) convened a panel of 50 experts to address the "software crisis." While the panel did not provide any direct solutions, the concept of a "software engineer" was developed as a means to more closely align software manufacturing with the engineering discipline rather than artistic creativity. The intent, as far as we can tell, was to remove the "rule of thumb" in the production of software and all the inconsistencies such approximation introduces. After 50 years, defining what actually constitutes the principles and practice of software engineering has not progressed far. What is clear, however, is that the unfortunate history of software blunders sullies the reputation of software in general and distorts the genius of software developers in particular.

> *What is clear, however, is that the unfortunate history of software blunders sullies the reputation of software in general and distorts the genius of software developers in particular.*

Perhaps most frustrating is the inconsistent use of quality control measures by such a wide range of software manufacturers for such an extended period of time. Software is infinitely more complex than cement to be sure, but complexity does not entirely account for systemic, reoccurring software manufacturing defects. Quality control measures—even in the absence of a clear definition for software engineering—have been and are available specifically to address problems with software production.

Software has its own modern-day equivalent of Joseph Bazalgette: his name is Watts Humphrey. Humphrey is a fellow and research scientist at Carnegie Mellon University's Software Engineering Institute (SEI) and is often called the "father of software quality" having developed numerous methodologies since the 1980s for designing quality and reliability into software products. In 2005, President George W. Bush awarded Mr. Humphrey the National Medal of Technology, the highest honor for innovation in the United States. The only problem in this story is that a significant portion of software manufacturers around the world still largely ignore or only superficially implement Humphrey's guidance. As a result, the Software Engineering Institute noted at the beginning of the twenty-first century that software was getting worse, not better. Such a proclamation augurs ill for civilization's newest foundation.

But if software quality were the only issue, perhaps we could discount the problem of low-quality software simply on the basis of "growing pains." After all, at 50 years old, some might argue software is still a relatively new phenomenon and that such failures in quality are understandable and even tolerable for such a young technology. When civil engineering was 50 years old, for instance, the brick had not even been invented yet.[9]

Yet when civil engineering was 50 years old, the profession was not building and connecting global infrastructure. Software's newness has not precluded it from being injected into nearly every aspect of modern civilization. That software connects everything to everything else magnifies even the smallest foibles in software production. This introduces a critical aspect of software vastly different from weaknesses in traditional building materials: once interconnected, even the smallest piece of insecure software may have global consequences. New or not, software needs to be worthy of its place.

Weaknesses or defects in software can not only result in a given software application failing for one reason or another (including no reason), but software defects can potentially be exploited by hackers, who, discovering or knowing the weakness exists, may use it to surreptitiously access and control a system from a continent away, stealing sensitive personal information such as credit cards or social security numbers or absconding with trade secrets or intellectual property. Such weaknesses could also be used to hijack computer systems and then turn those systems against their owners or against other nations and other peoples. In the end, insecure software is *right now* resulting in economic and social costs that are now well into billions of dollars per year with no sign of abatement. The trend is disturbing.

Understanding why this situation persists and seems to be only getting worse has important implications for modern civilization. In other words, new or not, society inevitably demands any technology used in the foundation of civilization, whether cement or software, should be given the time and attention foundations deserve. Bazalgette and his legacy expected no less; nor should we.

In the Shadow of Utility

The litany of documented software failures is extensive and tragic.[10] It does not take much effort to find examples of software failures resulting in loss of life, limb, money, time, or property. The trend only promises to become worse as software becomes more critical to almost every aspect of modern life; yet, software manufacturers enjoy an astonishing amount of insulation from government oversight, legal liability, consumer retaliation, and indeed, as some critics have observed, engineering skill. A proven record of significant, costly, and deadly failures with no significant decline in use by its victims is baffling. On top of—in fact, despite—these shortcomings, victims (consumers, corporations, and governments included) lavishly spend on acquiring and defending a clearly defective product. Why?

> *Software manufacturers enjoy an astonishing amount of insulation from government oversight, legal liability, consumer retaliation, and indeed, as some critics have observed, engineering skill.*

Why do software manufacturers continue to produce and consumers continue to purchase unreliable and insecure software?

Why do software users willingly and repeatedly accept licensing terms that absolve software manufacturers of most forms of liability for any design or implementation defects that might result in injury, harm, or damages?

Why do governments make so few demands on software manufacturers while placing onerous compliance requirements on software buyers, who are least qualified to address the problems associated with software manufacturing?

Why should software not be subject to the same public policy concerns applied to other critical elements of national infrastructure?

Why do chickens cross the road?

Each of these questions is answered in part by this simple response: *to maximize utility*. We all do things that might appear perfectly acceptable in our own eyes that might appear perfectly crazy to someone else. A chicken crossing the road in the presence of drivers who may be willing to flatten the poor thing simply to interrupt the monotony of driving might appear rather crazy to an outside observer. In fact, from an economist's perspective, this is perfectly rational behavior on the part of the chicken so long as the chicken believes it will be better off for the crossing. Jumping out of an airplane with a parachute might seem perfectly crazy to observers, unless the skydiver believes they are better off for the jumping. Likewise, software buyers continuing to accept software licensing terms that put them at a distinct disadvantage legally, financially, or personally should the software fail might appear perfectly baffling, unless buyers believe they will be better off for the accepting.

Economists use the notion of *utility* to help explain why people behave the way they do. The concept of utility is a little like the concept of "happiness" only more general. I explain the concept of utility in more detail in Chapter 2, "Six Billion Crash Test Dummies," but suffice to say, utility centers around the notion that most of us want to make our lives better, and that many of our life decisions are probably based on this desire. Software inarguably makes our life better, but like crossing the road or jumping out of an airplane or owning a swimming pool, everything has a cost.

It is not always the utility we get out of something or some activity that matters most, but how much it potentially costs us. Costs are not always obvious to the individual at "time of purchase" so to speak, and can be hidden or otherwise obscured. In general, cost can be measured in private terms, what it directly costs an individual to behave in a certain way, or measured in social costs, what it costs society for an individual to undertake a certain activity. The balance of private and social costs is the focus of many public policy efforts.

The private cost of smoking, for instance, is relatively low monetarily from an individual's view point, but can impose substantial social costs due to the prolonged medical services associated with caring for long-term chronic smokers. Imposing a cigarette tax is but one way to raise the private cost of an activity in order to deter the behavior, which thereby potentially reduces the social cost by reducing the total number of smokers in the population and how much they smoke.

People's evaluation of utility versus cost can lead to some fairly interesting situations. As a case in point, in the United States swimming pools kill or injure more children under the age of 14 than firearms. At 16 percent, accidental drowning was the second leading cause of injury-related death of children aged 14 and under in 2004 (car accidents ranked first); compare this with only 1 percent of children that died due to accidental discharge of firearms.[11] In fact, injury-related death due to accidental discharge of firearms ranks at the bottom of all other causes of death and injury among children including choking (17 percent), fire and burns (10 percent), and bicycle accidents, poisoning, and falls (each at 2 percent).

There are plenty of people, and parents in particular, who might forbid children playing at the home of a neighbor who possesses one or more firearms, but the likelihood of a child drowning at a neighborhood pool party is far higher than a child being injured or killed by the firearm of a neighbor. Yet few parents espouse an anti-swimming pool sentiment or join anti-swimming pool action groups as they would for firearms, even though statistics would certainly warrant such behavior. The rather simplistic answer to this incongruency is that a larger portion of the population sees the intrinsic utility of a swimming pool over and above the utility of possessing a hand gun. Yet a swimming pool incurs a much higher cost to both families and society than do firearms. Even things with obvious utility like a swimming pool can have a dark shadow.

Played out against this background of people's desire for utility (and not always recognizing the real cost), is the story of software. The questions at the start of this section really touch on the issues of self-interest and, more importantly, the incentives we have as individuals to undertake certain activities and the utility we derive. Understanding incentives also gives us a possible foundation to address the issues of why software manufacturing seems to be in the state it is in. If it is up to humans to get the production processes for Portland cement and software correct, then it is just as important, if not more so, to understand why humans behave as they do. Incentives are a good place to start.

As such, *Geekonomics* is not so much the story of software told through the lens of technology, but through the lens of humanity, specifically the incentives for manufacturing, buying, and exploiting insecure software. Economics is simply one way of understanding why humans behave as they do. But if economics is generally described as "the dismal science," then software engineering is economics' freakish, serotonin-deprived cousin. Economics is positively cheery and approachable in comparison. To date, the discussion regarding software has been largely dominated by technology experts whose explanations largely serve to alienate the very people that are touched most by software. *Us*.

Yet the congress of these two disciplines tells an important and consequential story affecting both the reader's everyday life and the welfare of the global community. The issue of insecure software is at least as much about economics as it is about technology. And so I discuss both in this book. This book is not intended to be a comprehensive economics text, a litany of software failures (although this is sometimes inevitable), a diatribe as to how the world is coming apart at the seams, or a prophecy that civilization's ultimate demise will occur because of "bad" software. Prophesizing disaster is cliché. Bad things happen all the time, and forecasting tragic events does not require an exceptional amount of talent, intelligence, or foresight. If anything, the world tolerates disaster and somehow still makes progress. This does not mean valid threats to economic and national stability due to "bad" software are illusory or should be minimized. On the contrary, the story of insecure software has not been readily approachable and therefore not well understood. We cannot manage what we do not understand, including ourselves. Software is a ghost in the machine and, at times, frustratingly so. But as software is a human creation, it does not need to remain a frustrating ghost.

My intent in this book is to give this story—the story of inse-cure software—a suitable voice so that readers from any walk of life can understand the implications. I promise the reader that there is not a single graph in this book; nor is there a single snip-pet of code. This story should be accessible to more than the experts because it is we who create this story and are touched by it daily. The consequences are too great and far-reaching for the average person to remain unaware.

The first task of *Geekonomics*, then, is to address the ques-tions presented at the beginning of this section as completely as possible within the confines of a single book. This means some aspects may be incomplete or not as complete as some readers might prefer. However, if anything, the story of software can be entertaining, and this book is intended to do that as well as inform and enlighten.

The second and more difficult task of *Geekonomics* is to ana-lyze what the real cost of insecure software might be. Swimming pools can have a high cost, but how costly is insecure software, really? This is a challenging task considering that unlike statistics regarding accidental drowning, good data on which to base cost estimates regarding insecure software is notoriously lacking and inaccurate for three reasons. First, there is presumed to be a sig-nificant amount of underreporting given that many organizations might not realize they have been hacked or do not want to pub-licly share such information for fear of consumer retaliation or bad publicity. Second, actual costs tend to be distorted based on the incentives of those reporting their losses. For some victims, they may tend to inflate losses in an effort to increase their chances of recovering damages in court. Other groups of victims might deflate costs in an effort to quell any uprisings on the part of customers or shareholders. Law enforcement and cyber secu-rity companies can tend to inflate numbers in an effort to gain more funding or more clients, respectively. Whatever the incen-tives might be for reporting high or low, somewhere within these numbers is a hint to what is actually going on. Finally, the real cost of something might not be measured in money alone.

The third and final task of *Geekonomics* is to identify current incentives of market participants and what new incentives might be necessary to change status quo. One alternative is always choosing to do nothing; simply let things work themselves out on their own, or more accurately, let the market determine what should be done. This book argues against such action. Any intervention into a market carries with it the risk of shock, and doing nothing is certainly one way of avoiding such risk. But intervention is necessary when a condition is likely to degenerate if nothing is done. The magnitude of the risk is great enough and the signs of degeneration clear enough that new and different incentives are needed to motivate software manufacturers to produce and software buyers to demand safer, higher quality, and more secure software.

Fragile Analogies

Writing a book is far easier than writing software. If the text in a book should have "bugs" such as ambiguities, inconsistencies, or worse, contradictions, you the reader might be annoyed, even angry, but you will still have your wits about you. Simply shrug your shoulders, turn the page and read on. This is because, as a human, you are a perceptive creature and can deal to a greater or lesser extent with the paradoxical and ambiguous nature of reality. Computers are not nearly so lucky. As Peter Drucker, a legendary management consultant, pointed out in *The Effective Executive* more than 40 years ago, computers are logical morons. In other words, *computers are stupid*. This is the first important realization toward protecting modern infrastructure. Computers are stupid because logic is essentially stupid: logic only does what logic permits.[12] Computers do exactly as they are instructed by software, no more and no less. If the software is "wrong," so too will be the computer. Unless the software developer anticipates problems ahead of time, the computer will not be able to simply shrug, turn the page, and move on.

Computers cannot intrinsically deal with ambiguity or uncertainly with as much deft and acumen as humans. Software must be correct, or it is nothing at all. So whereas humans live and even thrive in a universe full of logical contradictions and inconsistencies, computers live in a neat, tidy little world defined by logic. Yet that logic is written primarily by perceptive creatures known as software developers, who at times *perceive* better than they *reason*. This makes the radical malleability of software both blessing and bane. We can do with software as we will, but what we *will* can sometimes be far different than what we *mean*.

The radical malleability of software also poses additional explanatory complications. Software is like cement because it is being injected into the foundation of civilization. Software is also like a swimming pool because people opt to use it even though statistics tend to show the high private and social costs of its use. In fact, in this book, software is described to be like automobiles, DNA, broken windows, freeways, aeronautical charts, books, products, manuscripts, factories, and so on. Software might even be like a box of chocolates. You never know what you're going to get. With software, all analogies are fragile and incomplete.

Cement is an imperfect analogy for software, but so too is just about everything else, which means analogies used to understand software tend to break quite easily if over-extended. The radical malleability of software means any single analogy used to understand software will be somewhat unsatisfying, as will, unfortunately, any single solution employed to solve the problem of insecure software. As a universal tool, software can take far too many potential forms for any one analogy to allow us to sufficiently grasp software and wrestle it to the ground. This challenge is nowhere more obvious than in the judicial courts of the United States, which reason by analogy from known concepts.[13] This does not mean that software cannot be understood, simply that significantly more mental effort must be applied to think about software in a certain way, in the right context, and under the relevant assumptions. As such, this book may liberally switch between analogies to make certain points. This is more the nature of software and less the idiosyncrasies of the author (or at least, I would hope).

Finally, there are many different kinds of software: enterprise software, consumer software, embedded software, open source software, and the list goes on. Experts in the field prefer to distinguish between these types of software because each has a different function and different relevancies to the tasks they are designed for. Such is the radical malleability of software.

A fatal flaw of any book on software, therefore, is the lack of deference to the wild array of software in the world. The software in your car is different than in your home computer, is different than the software in space shuttles, is different than software in airplanes, is different than software in medical devices, and so on. As such, one can argue that the quality of software will differ by its intended use. Software in websites will have different and probably lower quality than software in airplanes. And this is true. There is only one problem with this reasoning: Hackers could care less about these distinctions.

At the point when software is injected into a product and that product is made available to the consumer (or in any other way allows the attacker to touch or interact with the software), it is fair game for exploitation. This includes automobiles, mobile phones, video game consoles, and even nuclear reactors. Once the software is connected to a network, particularly the Internet, the software is nothing more than a target. As a case in point, two men were charged with hacking into the Los Angeles city traffic center to turn off traffic lights at four intersections in August 2006. It took four days to return the city's traffic control system to normal operation as the hackers locked out others from the system.[14] Given that more and more products are becoming "network aware;" that is, they are connected to and can communicate across a digital network, software of any kind regardless of its *intended* use is fair game in the eyes of an attacker. As William Cheswick and Steven Bellovin noted in *Firewalls and Internet Security*, "Any program no matter how innocuous it seems can harbor security holes...We have a firm belief that everything is guilty until proven innocent."

This is not paranoia on the part of the authors; this is the reality.

Therefore, I have chosen to distinguish primarily between two types of software: software that is networked, such as the software on your home computer or mobile phone, and software that is not. The software controlling a car's transmission is not networked; that is, it is not connected to the Internet, at least not yet. Though not connected to the Internet, weaknesses in this software can still potentially harm the occupants as I illuminate in Chapter 2. But it is only a matter of time before the software in your transmission, as with most all other devices, will be connected to a global network. Once connection occurs the nature of the game changes and so too does the impact of even the tiniest mistake in software production. That software has different *intended* uses by the manufacturers is no excuse for failing to prepare it for an actively and proven hostile environment, as Chapter 3, "The Power of Weaknesses," highlights.

Finally, the radical malleability of software has moved me to group multiple aspects of insufficient software manufacturing practices such as software defects, errors, faults, and vulnerabilities under the rubric of "software weaknesses." This might appear at first as overly simplistic, but for this type of discussion, it is arguably sufficient for the task at hand.

Six Billion Crash Test Dummies: Irrational Innovation and Perverse Incentives

This [software vulnerability] list acutely scratches at the top of an enormous iceberg. The underlying reality is shameful: most system and web application software is written oblivious to security principles, software engineering, operational implications, and indeed common sense.

—Dr. Peter G. Neumann
Principal Scientist, SRI International Computer Science Lab

Y ou are a crash test dummy for software manufacturers and are paying extravagantly for the privilege. In 1986, an Alabama driver lost his seven-year-old grandson due to defective software that failed to correctly control the flow of fuel to the vehicle's engine. This failure caused the vehicle to stall in the middle of an intersection and, as a result, was struck by a logging truck. The vehicle was purchased two days prior and had been driven less than 200 miles.[1] The jury awarded $15 million to the family based on evidence that General Motors had known of the software defect in their cars for some time but did not take prompt action to resolve the problem.

In 1996, a software defect in the flight systems of a Boeing 757 caused the airplane's flight computers "to go crazy," causing the pilots to become disoriented and crashing the plane into the Pacific, killing seventy. "This is not the first time that one of these planes has had this kind of fault," said an official. "We have to find out why the computers went crazy."[2]

In 2003, the northeastern United States experienced the largest power outage in decades. A software defect was identified as the cause of alarm failures that contributed to the scope of the blackout. The estimated cost for this event was between $6 billion and $10 billion.[3]

In 2004, a 22-year-old hacker exploited a known weakness in a software application used by the mobile phone carrier T-Mobile. The hacker was able to access T-Mobile customer account information such as passwords, social security numbers, and dates-of-birth as well as gain access to sensitive government documents, private emails, and private customer photos (such as the famous collection of Paris Hilton's pictures of herself that ended up on a public website). The hacker attempted to sell customers' private information to fraudsters and identity thieves.[4]

That same year, a software defect in the air traffic control system at Los Angeles International Airport caused the voice communications system to crash, cutting off all air traffic controllers with the planes they were directing in and around the airspace, which included most of the southwestern United States. The emergency backup system also crashed within a minute after it was turned on.[5] Controllers had no way of directing planes to keep them safely apart.

In 2005, more than 23,900 Toyota Prius owners were sent notice their cars had a "programming error" that might potentially cause the car to stall or shut down while driving at highway speeds.[6] Owners were instructed to bring their cars to dealerships for an hour-long software upgrade. Unlike the General Motors incident in 1986, no fatalities were reported.

In 2006...

The list goes on and on. These are not isolated incidents. Peter Neumann, Principal Scientist at SRI International, maintains a growing list of more than 400 separate incidents in which software defects caused or threatened injury to individuals or caused significant financial loss. In 2006 alone, more than 7,000 software vulnerabilities were discovered in a dizzying array of software applications, any of which were used or could have been used (in addition to the 12,000+ vulnerabilities from previous years) by hackers to gain illicit access to private sensitive information. This activity contributes to the estimated $48 billion in business losses due to identity theft.[7] Year on year, cyber intrusions cause billions of dollars in damages for individuals, governments, and commercial ventures. What was true for software in 1967 was true in 1986, in 2003, in 2006, and so on. The failure to reduce the number of preventable software defects is a systemic problem for software manufacturers.

Typical software engineering practices, as one observer noted, "encourage programmers to produce, as quickly as possible, large programs which they know will contain serious errors."[8] And these "mistakes" are released into the global stream of commerce in products that might control a fuel injection system, an aircraft flight system, an x-ray machine, national telecommunications systems, oil pipelines, financial systems, or a mobile phone. Software engineering practices and the results they produce have been regularly described by industry observers as "shockingly sloppy,"[9] "grossly inadequate,"[10] "deeply flawed,"[11] "oblivious...[to] common sense," and less elegantly, "beyond crappy to shitty."[12]

Software manufacturers immediately contend that software actually does work *most of the time* and that by focusing on the smaller number of failures compared to the larger number of successes, reality is unfairly distorted. This argument has some merit. But like DNA, software that works most of the time can still cause a great deal of harm, and even kill. The inarguable "successfulness" of DNA in keeping organisms alive for billions of years does not deter nations around the globe from spending billions of dollars combating defects in DNA, yet nations have yet to demonstrate the same level of concern for the "DNA of technology" that they are becoming ever more dependent upon.

> *Typical software engineering practices, as one observer noted, "encourage programmers to produce, as quickly as possible, large programs which they know will contain serious errors."*

The worrisome aspect of this inattention is that many preventable defects go undetected by software manufacturers during production and therefore remain latent in the products and services we use; that is, defects are present but not visible...until it is too late. Some unfortunate soul, at some unknown point in time, will experience the effects of a latent software defect. It might cost them their data if their software crashes, their identity if a hacker exploits the defect, or their life if the software "just goes crazy." It might also cost a lot of money. The estimated cost in 2002 to the United States due to lack of adequate software testing was estimated between $20 billion and $60 billion.[13] But this is just one small part of the cost because it was based on a handful of industries. The cost of cyber crime enabled by insecure software is even higher.

When a software defect is discovered, a "patch" may be issued by the software manufacturer, fixing, or at least attempting to fix, the problem. This certainly may improve the software for other users in general, but the damage has already been done by the time the patch is released. Worse this cycle is repeated for every single newly discovered defect. Damage is being done repeatedly and the frequency is increasing. The high, unremitting number of preventable software defects continuously released into the global stream of commerce makes the world's population nothing more than crash test dummies.

Why do software manufacturers expend so little effort (or not *enough* effort, depending on your perspective) on designing "good" software as well as discovering defects before releasing software into the marketplace? And why do software buyers seem to tolerate defect-ridden software even though they do not tolerate the same level of deficiency in any other products?

As it turns out, software manufacturers and software users are behaving quite rationally. Squeezing out a majority of defects during production of a software application can be considerably expensive for a software manufacturer. While software manufacturers certainly test their applications to some extent, software manufacturers must decide, just as any other type of manufacturer would have to decide, how much expense to endure and remain competitive in the marketplace. More testing drives up the production cost of the application, which in turn drives up the retail price of the product. Manufacturers that test less can offer products at much reduced prices, even sometimes offering their product for free.[14] This in turn places pressure on other manufacturers to reduce production costs and therefore reduces the incentive to conduct thorough testing.

Software buyers, on the other hand, as savvy consumers, shop on value and price: "What am I getting, and how much will it cost me?" To determine value, software buyers often look at the number of features or functionality offered by a given software application just as they would when considering the number of available options in a new car, or upgrades in a new house. This is understandable. The greater the number of features and the greater possibility of possessing desired utility at a "reasonable price" will compel users to choose one product over another. In other words, is the purchase perceived as a "good deal" by the buyer?

But additional features and functionality increase software's complexity. Increased complexity makes software harder to test. Software that is harder to test increases the cost to the manufacturer of producing the software. Increased manufacturing costs increases the retail price, which brings us back to the buyer's propensity of seeking out a "good deal." If the price is too high, a buyer can simply opt *not* to buy one product and choose another less-expensive product.

What pollutes this equation is the historic glitchiness of software. A vast majority of software buyers, as high as 77 percent, do not trust their software to behave as expected or protect them from exploitation by hackers.[15] In which case, users might not be willing to purchase higher-priced software for fear and uncertainty that the purchase is not a "good deal." This fear and uncertainty reduces the price software users are willing to pay, which puts competitive price pressure on software manufacturers, further driving down the incentive to test software thoroughly because the additional production cost will not only make the product more expensive to the user, but will cut into any potential profits of the manufacturer. A death spiral ensues. Purchasers seek more features but at a lower cost; manufacturers add more features but invest less in production processes. As a result, software quality and security fail to improve and can indeed decline (as it has as observed by the Software Engineering Institute).

> *A vast majority of software buyers, as high as 77 percent, do not trust their software to behave as expected or protect them from exploitation by hackers.*

When so many perfectly rational people act in a perfectly rational manner but create a perfectly dangerous situation, there is a problem. In fact, there are numerous incentives, not just the ones summarized here, that work against the notion of high-quality software. In many instances, the software market is subject to economic, financial, and legal incentives directly opposed to trustworthiness and security. These disincentives mix to form a powerful cocktail, inebriating the software market to the point of failure; that is, even though software usage increases and software companies continue to thrive, market forces are aligned in such a manner that individual self-interest adversely affects the public good. Without correction, this makes software increasingly dangerous for all of us.

This chapter investigates the lessons of crash test dummies and the factors that brought about regulation of auto manufacturers. The automobile industry and crash test dummies are used as both analogy and as a heuristic device to outline similarities with software manufacturers and the contours of the problem at hand. Intertwined with all this is a discussion of market failure and the incentives of software manufacturers and software buyers that make market failure possible.

The Story of Crash Test Dummies

Crash test dummies—anthropomorphic simulations of human bodies—were first used in 1949 by the U.S. Air Force to evaluate human tolerance to injury and were later adopted—some would say reluctantly—by the automobile industry in the 1960s. Put simply, crash test dummies allow engineers to assess situations and equipment without endangering human welfare. Crash test dummies are our surrogates for survival.

The inception of crash test dummies was significant. Over the decades, crash test dummies saved hundreds of thousands of lives, improved vehicle safety standards, and validated a wide range of safety features that are now required in almost all automobiles including seatbelts, airbags, crumple zones, and side impact protection. The U.S. Department of Transportation popularized crash test dummies in the 1980s with a series of public service announcements featuring two talking dummies called Vince and Larry. Their slogan was simple: "You can learn a lot from a dummy." Or so one would hope.

In 1967, the United States enacted legislation giving mandate to the National Highway Transportation Safety Administration (NHTSA) to require car manufacturers to conform to Federal Motor Vehicle Safety Standards and Regulations. The requirements ensure that "the public is protected against unreasonable risk of crashes occurring as a result of the design, construction, or performance of motor vehicles and is also protected against unreasonable risk of death or injury in the event crashes do occur."[16]

Part of protecting the public included standardizing methods by which manufacturers tested vehicle safety features such as seatbelts and airbags. This was not an easy task. Early crash test dummies were primitive, offering little in durability and even less in repeatable and measurable results. This had three significant consequences. First, without standardized tests for occupant safety features, effectiveness of these features was questionable at best. Second, without consistency, the NHTSA could not properly compare safety devices from different manufacturers. In the truest sense, without repeatability and measurability, NHTSA would be comparing apples to oranges with little gain for the effort. The third consequence was litigation.

As would be expected, the newly regulated automobile industry fought back in the courts. For years, American automobile manufacturers blamed the epidemic of car-related injuries on driver error, bad roads, or anything else to deflect attention away from design defects in the vehicles themselves.[17] In keeping with this practice, some car manufacturers, namely Chrysler Corporation and Ford Motor Company, took the United States government to court over standardized testing, stating that it was "unenforceable as standards imposed upon automobile manufacturers did not meet required criteria for objectivity due to the inadequacy of anthropomorphic test dummies for testing purposes."[18] General Motors, on the other hand, after finally abandoning their less-than-noble technique of harassing public safety advocates such as Ralph Nader, decided to take an alternative route to litigation and do the right thing: improve the testing process by improving the crash test dummies, thereby improving automotive safety. General Motors set out to address issues of durability, repeatability, and measurability.

The more closely a crash dummy emulates the human body, the more accurate the data collected about the effectiveness of safety devices. Of course, the most realistic data is collected from human bodies, and that is, in fact, what the industry first used, cadavers. Though morbid, exact bio-fidelity was invaluable. The use of cadavers led to much advancement in determining the amount of force the human body could withstand. However, cadavers have limitations. Besides low durability (cadavers could only be used once), data about impact forces could not be easily collected, hampering measurability, nor was data consistent (no two humans are perfectly alike), thereby reducing repeatability.

After years of research and many versions of artificial crash test dummies, Dr. Harold Mertz, a biomechanics expert at General Motors North American Operations Safety and Restraints Center, unveiled the Hybrid III in 1976. The Hybrid III test dummy simulates "average" males, females, and children using components closely imitating the motion of human joints as well as body structures most prone to injury such as the neck, knee, and chest cavity.[19] Besides accurately simulating the human body, the Hybrid III could be mass produced and widely deployed, giving the industry the consistency it so desperately needed. Dr. Mertz openly shared the Hybrid III design with competitors and governments and actively lobbied to get the Hybrid III globally adopted. Beginning in 1998, twenty years after its inception, Dr. Mertz's Hybrid III is the only recognized crash test dummy for both United States and European car safety regulations.

The story does not end with better dummies, however.

Five Stars and Rising

In 1978, the National Highway Transportation Safety Administration started openly publishing crash test information based on the data collected from crash test dummies.[20] While openly publishing crash test information was invaluable to the industry and its government overseers, ultimately this information needed to be translated and distilled for the consumer for it to have meaning in the marketplace.

A crash test rating system was created by NHTSA, employing a scale of one to five stars reflecting the chance of injury to vehicle occupants. An NHTSA five-star rating awarded to a particular vehicle model correlates with a 10 percent chance of serious injury to vehicle occupants in a 35 mile-per-hour head-on collision. In contrast, a one-star rating represents a greater than 46 percent chance of serious injury.[21] In other words, if you were driving a one-star rated vehicle and got into an accident, you would have roughly a 50/50 chance of walking away without injury; whereas, in a five-star rated vehicle your chances of non-injury increase to 90 percent. The difference between a good crash-test rating and a poor one is significant.

Interestingly, in the United States safety rating information is widely available everywhere—libraries, the Internet, Consumer Reports, consumer advocacy groups—everywhere, that is, except at the point of sale. While automakers exuberantly advertise four and five-star ratings in marketing campaigns, safety information is not required on the showroom sticker, even though much of the sticker information, such as suggested retail price, features, and EPA fuel economy for city and highway, is federally mandated.

Auto manufactures are conspicuously silent regarding cars that score less than a four-star rating. This means car buyers must be sufficiently self-motivated to investigate safety ratings of potential purchases *before* going to the showroom. As most auto buyers have probably experienced at one time or another, the showroom is not the fairest or most appropriate place to engage in rational analysis. It is an emotional, biased place with all the objectivity of a casino. Not posting crash test information on a showroom sticker is tantamount to forgoing warnings on cigarettes or alcohol simply because information about related health issues is available from a primary care physician.

To address this imbalance, Ohio Senator Mike DeWine introduced legislation known as the *Stars on Cars Act of 2005*, making crash test ratings compulsory on showroom stickers. Senator DeWine stated, "Most consumers care about safety. They will make better choices and, in all likelihood, they are going to choose safer vehicles and more lives will, in fact, be saved. It just makes good common sense to do this."[22]

Consumers care about safety, reliability, or security of any product affecting their welfare, whether the product contains petroleum, pesticides, saccharine, or, in our case, software. But "caring" largely depends on whether consumers are aware of the issues and to what extent information is readily available about those issues. In modern society many threats to health and well-being are hidden or obscure (like hoof and mouth disease, obesity, or chronic smoking), and unless someone informs consumers about the danger, it is likely consumers will continue with behavior that endangers their

> *Consumers care about safety, reliability, or security of any product affecting their welfare, whether the product contains petroleum, pesticides, saccharine, or, in our case, software.*

well-being and the well-being of others, even though the behavior might sometimes appear rather innocuous.

As such, the five-star rating system is actually a simplified warning system that informs buyers about the risks related to their purchases. Warning labels on alcohol and cigarettes are far less subtle and simply give users the choice between use and non-use. The five-star rating system for cars, in contrast, is more granular, allowing users to choose from a spectrum of risk regarding their potential purchases. Consumers will purchase a vehicle based on the level of risk they are willing to assume and the price they are willing to pay.

The five-star rating system also acts as a strong incentive for auto manufacturers to improve vehicle quality. It could be reasonably assumed that a majority of car drivers value their personal safety and would therefore opt to select a five-star rated vehicle over a lower-rated vehicle. Lower-rated cars would presumably sell less often than higher-rated cars. To increase car sales then, auto manufactures would be motivated to design and manufacture a larger number of safer cars rather than less. And even though safer cars are more expensive to produce, consumers have considered the additional cost worthwhile. This has proven to be accurate. With vehicle sales on the rise, nearly 95 percent of 2006 vehicles sold in the United State received four or five -star ratings in frontal impact tests, and 87 percent received four or five stars in side crashes involving the driver.[23] The five-star rating system has proven so effective in raising car safety that NHTSA is considering introducing new, more stringent requirements to better differentiate among vehicles considered "safe."

A criticism of the five-star rating system espoused by the few auto manufacturers whose cars score poorly has been that the rating system does not accurately portray or predict performance in real-world conditions, and therefore the five-star rating system is flawed. A 2007 study conducted by the Virginia Commonwealth University School of Business shows this argument to be inaccurate. The study looked at the relationship between crash-test scores of various vehicles over a 20-year period. For vehicles with a five-star rating, fatalities increased 7 percent over the 20-year period; whereas, fatalities increased 36 percent for vehicles with a two-star rating.[24] The study appeared to conclusively demonstrate that vehicles with a five-star rating did in fact do a better job of protecting passengers and drivers in real-world conditions than lower-rated cars.

We have crash test dummies to thank for the five-star rating system because without them, the rating system would be difficult, if not impossible, to achieve, or worse, meaningless and irrelevant. Crash test dummies, therefore, might teach us something about the software market in general and software manufacturers in particular.

You Can Learn a Lot From a Dummy

Whereas the automobile industry has been forced and cajoled into transparency and accountability over the years, the software industry, though 50 years old, remains largely insulated, opaque, and unaccountable. As far as "hidden dangers" go, software ranks extraordinarily high, for software is essentially invisible and unvisualizable.[25] Everywhere software touches the user, but nowhere is the user able to touch software. How much to trust software, then, or how safe it is, is difficult to determine indeed.

Without a clear rating system, software buyers are left holding a massive bucket of unpredictability for any given software application they may decide to use. Software might work well, but only part of the time, and under bizarre circumstances. When software decides to work well or "just go crazy" remains rather arbitrary. Worse, software users face considerable uncertainty regarding the products and services they use for which they have literally no control over. The software could be embedded in a product or machinery, or used by public or private venture to manage their identity, benefits, or finances. Although a car might have a five-star safety rating, no such assurances exist for the vehicle's software-controlled fuel injection system, braking system, or navigation system for that matter. The same is true of software in home computers, mobile phones, or software running websites such as eBay, Google, or MySpace.

> *Whereas the automobile industry has been forced and cajoled into transparency and accountability over the years, the software industry, though 50 years old, remains largely insulated, opaque, and unaccountable.*

But to generate a rating system that is easily understandable by a software user requires, at minimum, the ability and requirement to test software extensively—and not only extensively, but *objectively*. Herein lies the first lesson of crash test dummies.

Although software manufacturers have the capability to test their software, the type and scope of testing efforts varies widely among software manufacturers and, as discussed in the introduction to this chapter, is highly dependent on competitive pricing pressures. This means that while Microsoft conducts testing on its software, these tests might have little to no relation to the depth, breadth, types, or number of tests conducted by Sun Microsystems, Red Hat Linux, Oracle, Mom and Pop's Software Tinkershop, or any of the thousands of software manufacturers around the globe.[26] Each manufacturer is its own measure, unrelated to any other. So a statement of "our product is secure" by one manufacturer cannot be reliably compared against any other manufacturer's claim.

Moreover, the type and amount of testing that *is* conducted, as well as the results produced, are not made public, leaving buyers to take the word of manufacturers regarding the thoroughness and completeness of the testing conducted as well as the overall quality of the manufactured good. Such opaqueness permits manufacturers to make whatever claim about their software they desire. And some manufacturers have done just that.

In 2002, Oracle, the most successful database software manufacturer whose software runs in nearly half the world's companies, proclaimed their database software "unbreakable." That is, Oracle's database software was impervious to unauthorized users that might want to break into a database and steal information. For enterprise customers such as Verizon Wireless, UPS, or the U.S. Census Bureau who rely on Oracle for storing information about shipping, invoicing, inventory, health, or personal details of employees or citizens, the security of Oracle's software is quite important. Larry Ellison, CEO of Oracle, boldly stated, "Bill Gates said he would devote the month of February to security [referring to Microsoft's moratorium on software production in 2002 to conduct security awareness and training]. February is a short month. We've devoted 25 years to security."[27] A bold statement indeed. However, within months, hackers, drawn by the challenge of unbreakability, discovered defect after defect in Oracle's software that can give attackers access to a database's contents. Hackers have been finding defects ever since.[28] Oracle has taken up to two years to fix the reported flaws.[29]

This unfortunate display of hubris was made possible in part by the complete lack of transparency, objectivity, or accountability across the breadth of software manufacturers, not just Oracle. While the claim of "unbreakability" was certainly extreme, lesser claims would be equally groundless. In the absence of an objective measure, software manufacturers can say and do as they please. Any claim can be made, even if it is without merit, as it many end up being. Software applications and websites declaring themselves "secure," "hacker safe," or "world-class, best-of-breed" have no comparative meaning. In the absence of transparency, no amount of assurances on the part of the manufacturer can be accepted with any confidence. And without any accountability, software manufacturers can drag their feet as Oracle and other manufacturers have done in fixing production defects.

Even in the extremely rare case where a manufacturer might allow the software's source code to be evaluated by the purchaser, there are no objective measures to make a proper risk assessment by the purchaser themselves. It is often merely one expert's opinion against another's. While arguably still helpful for an individual purchaser, it is not scalable, repeatable, objective, or comprehensive.

One possible answer to this situation is government purchasing requirements. The United States government employs an international security standard called the *Common Criteria*, which is used as a determining factor in purchasing decisions for Information Technology products.[30] A product is certified at an Evaluation Assurance Level (EAL), which is a numerical rating with seven levels. An EAL 1 rating is the most basic level, while an EAL 7 rating is the most stringent. Cost increases proportionally as the EAL levels increase, making the testing procedures to obtain an EAL 7 rating quite expensive. The requirements for certification at a certain Evaluation Assurance Level are clearly established and are tested by qualified laboratories, which means manufacturers can target very specific security objectives if their checkbook allows.

The shortfall with the Common Criteria, however, is the same criticism levied against the NHTSA five-star rating system; that is, it has no relation to the real world. But in this instance, unlike in the Virginia Commonwealth University study, no facts are available to defend the Common Criteria from this charge. In fact, empirical evidence undermines rather than supports the Common Criteria rating system.

For instance, Microsoft Windows 2000 was certified at an EAL 4+ level, which, to simplify this discussion, satisfies U.S. government purchasing requirements. However, even though certain security requirements are stipulated by an EAL rating, other important aspects are absent. Patches for discovered security vulnerabilities in Windows 2000 continue to be released. In fact, despite numerous patches, Windows 2000 still maintains its EAL 4+ rating. This is true of other operating systems such as Linux, which have received similar EAL ratings.

This discrepancy is made possible because the process of getting certified in the Common Criteria allows *the vendor* to specify certain assumptions about the environment the system will be operating in. The EAL rating system relates to those vendor-specific assumptions and only to those assumptions. This means the environment assumed by the vendor might have no relationship whatsoever to the customer's actual environment, making the EAL rating's assurances difficult to translate into the real world. Allowing a software manufacturer to specify assumptions about operating environment would be equivalent to a car manufacturer stipulating that the four-star rating awarded to their car is only relevant if the car is driven in snow, on a sunny day, uphill, with no ice, and no cross wind. Worse, the Common Criteria does not sufficiently account for the quality of the software itself, as the number of vulnerabilities in Windows 2000 (in excess of 100) attests.[31] So while the Common Criteria is helpful in some ways, it lacks in other important ways. In fact, many "security standards" do not relate to software defects at all but merely the configuration options and organizational processes required to protect software from exploitation due to the defects contained in the software itself.

Regardless of the inevitable debate the comments here will incite, unlike the Virginia Commonwealth University study that defended the NHTSA rating system, empirical evidence to date provides no such defense to Common Criteria's rating system for improving the "safety" of cyberspace. As an example, the NHTSA rating system has helped the United States enjoy a 4.7 percent per year decrease in the number of deaths per mile traveled despite an 80 percent increase in travel from 1980 to 2000.[32] In contrast, since 1998 14 nations have adopted the Common Criteria as their determining factor in IT purchasing only to see cyber crime and cyber intrusions skyrocket year on year with 2006 declared the "Year of Cyber Crime" because of the astronomical level of data theft.[33] In the end, security standards such as the Common Criteria are certainly helpful but miss by too wide a margin regarding the specific engineering foibles of software manufacturers.

To summarize the first lesson of crash test dummies, then, objective testing criteria and transparent reporting are crucial for developing a meaningful rating system. Standardized testing allows efficiency, consistency, and scalability in testing, potentially sidestepping unreasonable costs to manufacturers and polluting the market with ambiguous results or unsupported vendor assertions. Consumers should be able to easily distinguish between high and low -quality products. While the effectiveness of the NHTSA five-star rating system will certainly remain open to debate, in the end consumers need not be experts in vehicle safety or biomechanics in order to make a wise purchasing decision. Software buyers have no such luxury or assurance at this time.

The second lesson of crash test dummies is that drivers might be partly to blame in some accidents but are not entirely to blame for all accidents. In 1966, the Senate Commerce Committee stated, "For too many years, the public's proper concern over the safe driving habits and capacity of the driver (the 'nut behind the wheel') was permitted to overshadow the role of the car itself."[34] The Senate Commerce Committee's remarks were directed at auto manufacturers who insisted the high rate of vehicular fatalities was due to bad drivers, poor roads, and so on—any reason really instead of what the data was actually demonstrating: Design and manufacturing defects in cars were causing an unacceptably high number of injuries and fatalities. In the story of software, it appears software buyers might be in the same unfortunate predicament as car drivers were once in 40 years ago.

Current legislation regarding data breach notification laws, such as California Senate Bill 1386, penalizes organizations for failing to properly protect information relating to private details of customers, citizens, or employees against unauthorized access. In so doing, legislators have made the same mistake earlier legislatures made regarding automotive manufacturers and what the Senate Commerce Committee highlighted in 1966. Blame does not belong solely to the nuts behind the wheel; auto manufacturers share a good portion of the culpability for injuries and fatalities. Likewise, blame does not belong solely on the shoulders of software buyers, the nuts behind the keyboard; software manufacturers share a good portion of the culpability for the shambles of cyberspace. A vulnerability in Oracle, or any other software manufacturer's product for that matter, is a gateway for attackers to gain access to lucrative data repositories, as hackers repeatedly demonstrate.

> *Blame does not belong solely to the nuts behind the wheel; auto manufacturers share a good portion of the culpability for injuries and fatalities. Likewise, blame does not belong solely on the shoulders of software buyers, the nuts behind the keyboard; software manufacturers share a good portion of the culpability for the shambles of cyberspace.*

Penalizing users of software without demanding elevated software production standards is like punishing car buyers for purchasing unsafe vehicles even though the only vehicles available are unsafe. This would be humorous if it weren't so sad.

The arguments in support of data breach notification laws appear all too similar to the arguments used by 1960s auto manufactures to deflect attention away from the real problems of vehicular safety and to foist the consequences onto unsuspecting and unprepared shoulders—namely, that data breach notification laws "force companies to take responsibility for the data they own."[35] People certainly have the right to know when their personal information has been mishandled or stolen. This is not disputed. Data breach notification laws are necessary and important measures for protecting personal information. But the burden these laws impose is not shared proportionally to responsibility. Product liability laws regularly protect consumers against defective products, yet in the absence of equivalent product liability laws for software—of which there are none at this time—data breach notification laws essentially hold companies strictly liable for any breach whatsoever, including breaches due to latent defects in software.[36] Software manufacturers have contributed substantially to the problem by continuing to release software containing preventable defects into the global stream of commerce, yet share no burden whatsoever when weaknesses in their software allow data breaches to occur in the first place.

The third and final lesson of crash test dummies is that sometimes government intervention is required in a market no matter how distasteful government intervention might appear to some. The NHTSA mandate for protecting vehicle occupants was sound for a number of reasons. First, auto manufacturers lacked sufficient incentive to protect consumer safety. In the 1950s and 1960s, automobiles were not equipped with seat belts or crumple zones, nor were they designed to withstand foreseeable and likely accidents because auto manufacturers were concerned more with aesthetics than safety.

The focus of manufacturers on aesthetics was perfectly rational given that aesthetics, even to this day, entice buyers and sell a wide range of products, not just cars. But lack of car safety imposes far greater social costs on the rest of the populace through an increased number of injuries and fatalities than the social cost associated with unbecoming or unsightly vehicles. The social cost of injuries and fatalities is not directly paid by the manufacturer and therefore is not included in the manufacturer's equations for the costs of production. While auto manufacturers were certainly not *intentionally* creating unsafe cars, manufacturers had no incentive to make cars safer considering the increased production costs would diminish possible profits. Thus, the social cost of injuries and fatalities would be paid only by the populace unless the manufacturer was somehow required to include that cost of safety in the cost of production.

In the case of software, software manufacturers are focused on features, given that features offer compelling value propositions to the buyer. But lack of software security imposes a social cost on the rest of the populace. Software manufacturers are not intentionally creating defective software any more than auto manufacturers were intentionally creating unsafe autos, but the social costs associated with defective software—injuries, fatalities, communications disruption, identity theft, cyber crime, just to name a few—are not directly borne by software manufacturers; therefore, the cost of safety/security is not included in the cost of production.

The second reason why the NHTSA mandate was sound was consumers were insufficiently informed about important aspects of car design and car safety. As such, buyers could not make appropriate decisions about the real cost of a vehicle. Certainly a vehicle without crumple zones and seat belts is less expensive to produce than a car that contains these safety features, but the cost related to the *absence* of these features is hidden at the time of purchase and might only be paid at a later, unfortunate time by one or more of the vehicle's occupants. One way of making this hidden cost "visible" is with a rating system; hence, the creation of the NHTSA five-star rating system for new cars. That buyers were focused primarily on aesthetics rather than safety is perfectly rational, and in part, is what drove auto manufacturers to produce cars extensively decorated with chrome and festooned with tail fins. Manufacturers were simply responding to market demand. What was irrational was the result—beautiful, but deadly cars. Only after publication in the 1960s of Ralph Nader's book *Unsafe At Any Speed* did consumers realize the magnitude and consequence of design defects and the dangers posed by unregulated auto manufacturers. There was a large public outcry, and the NHTSA was created shortly thereafter.

In the case of software, buyers are equally uninformed about important aspects of software design and software security. As such, buyers cannot make appropriate decisions about the real cost of software. Certainly, software that has been released to market without adequate testing might be cheaper to produce just as a vehicle without safety features would be cheaper to produce, but either situation poses unacceptable risks to the buyer. The cost related to the absence of testing is hidden at the time of purchase. It is only at some later time that the cost is realized by the user or the user's customers.

The third reason why the NHTSA mandate was sound is derived from the first; the sclerosis of auto manufacturers toward promptly resolving automotive design defects was especially pernicious to national security. This sclerosis was exacerbated by the extensive use of legal doctrines such as privity as well as contract disclaimers (which I discuss in Chapter 5, "Absolute Immuity"), that disclaimed all meaningful warranties and excluded any consequential damages.

More to the point, an increase in driver deaths decreases a nation's labor pool, which in turn can detrimentally affect the economic productivity of a nation. For 1950s and 1960s America, competition with and the threat posed by the Soviet Union was a significant motivator and every *body* counted. Decreased economic productivity due to lost lives therefore was of particular concern to U.S. policy makers and was considered a national security issue. The federal government had an incentive to protect the lives of its citizenry and in so doing, protect the economic footing of the nation.

In the case of software, the National Institute of Standards and Technology (NIST) estimated in 2002 the cost of inadequate software testing cost the United States roughly $60 billion (the number quoted at the beginning of the chapter), which is just under 1 percent of GDP. This cost does not account for other social costs associated with software usage such as cyber crime and related identity theft, however. A 2007 report by the Government Account Office (GAO) estimated cyber crime costs the U.S. economy approximately $117 billion a year.[37] David Powner, Director of IT Management at GAO, believes this number is low. "Whatever is reported by organizations," said Mr. Powner, "most of that will likely be underreported because of disincentives to report losses."[38] In real terms, the number might be significantly higher.

According to the GAO report, cybercrime has become a threat to the nation's economic and security interests.[39] Yet software manufacturers, who contribute to this epidemic in part, remain largely unregulated by an NHTSA-equivalent with the exception of a few attempts on the part of the United States Federal Drug Administration (FDA) to regulate software embedded in medical devices (desktops and databases are exempt).[40] Perhaps the best that can be said of this situation is that some software manufacturers are so sclerotic, so ingrained in their manner of doing business, so insulated by contract disclaimers, that a shock—any shock—is needed.

> *Perhaps the best that can be said of this situation is that some software manufacturers are so sclerotic, so ingrained in their manner of doing business, so insulated by contract disclaimers, that a shock—any shock— is needed.*

There might be other important lessons of crash test dummies; these are but a few. That being said, the lessons of crash test dummies presented here can be helpful in putting the story of software and the impact of software on our lives into proper context. Automobiles offer unmistakable benefits to modern civilization, just as software offers unmistakable benefits. Software manufacturers are not out to "get you" any more than auto manufacturers were out to injure or kill people in the 1960s. Nonetheless the realities of business and the realities of the market can make even the most beneficial technologies exceedingly expensive in social terms. As such, it is important to understand the incentives of market participants and how rational activities can have less than rational effects.

Private Benefits, Social Costs

Economics makes an important assumption about market participants: Individuals try to make themselves as well off as possible and *will not intentionally do things that make themselves worse off*. This seems both a reasonable assumption and an accurate observation. It is also critical to a functioning economy in that an individual's desire to make life better for themselves is the engine of commerce. As such, self-interest is a powerful market force. Individuals will seek out products, use services, or engage in certain activities that make them better off than if they refrained. Self-interest is not synonymous with selfishness, however.

Making one's self better off is what economists call "maximizing one's utility." Utility is simply a measure of relative happiness or gratification gained for doing something. Maximizing one's utility is a way of saying individuals try to get the most out of limited time and resources. Utility and "happiness" are not necessarily interchangeable terms in economics, considering that for an economist utility has much broader meaning. For instance, an individual can derive utility from brushing his teeth because good oral hygiene has been shown to prevent heart attacks and strokes.[41] Brushing one's teeth can hardly be said to elicit feelings of happiness, but it does make that person better off. An individual could also derive utility by giving thousands of dollars to charity every year. This makes the charitable person feel better by making others better off, whatever the underlying reasons might be. Charitable activity is certainly self-interested, but not necessarily selfish. In the end, utility is a concept that helps economists figure out why people do things. Economists do not particularly care what we derive utility from, only that we do.

Just because self-interest is not necessarily selfish does not mean that self-interested actions cannot be negative. In fact, self-interest can have both negative and positive consequences for those around us. Economists call these consequences *externalities*. An externality is simply a cost or a benefit imposed on someone with whom we might not have a direct relationship. In fact, it is more than this. An externality is when an individual's private costs of engaging in a particular behavior are different from the social costs. When an individual's self-interested actions result in benefits for others, it is called a *positive externality*. When actions impose a cost on others, it is called a *negative externality*.

For instance, maintaining a beautiful front yard is important to some homeowners. There is certainly a private cost borne by the homeowner for creating and maintaining a beautiful front yard, but the homeowner's behavior results in a positive benefit to neighbors, which they enjoy at no cost and for which the homeowner does not seek compensation. In other words, the homeowner's private cost of maintaining a beautiful front yard, which might be high, is different from the social costs of the neighbors, which are low. The homeowner cannot realistically go around to his neighbors and demand payment to offset his private costs, so the community enjoys the homeowner's horticultural handiwork but does not need to pay him for it. This scenario is known as a *positive externality*; the community is impacted positively by the self-interested actions of an individual.

In contrast, a homeowner might decide to raise and sell pigs in his front yard. The profits from this venture could offset the owners' private costs, ultimately reducing the cost of that activity. If the owner makes a hefty profit, the private cost might even become trivial compared to profit. However, the owner's private benefit would most certainly impose a cost on neighbors in terms of smell, traffic, and noise for which they may not be properly compensated. In this situation, the homeowner's private costs of maintaining a pig sty, which are low, are different from the social costs of the neighbors, which are high. The neighbors might complain loudly, but realistically they could not demand payment to offset the resultant social costs. Actually, they could demand payment, but the homeowner is under no obligation to pay them. This scenario is known as a *negative externality*; the community is negatively impacted by the self-interested actions of an individual.

Externalities are at the center of many public policy issues. For instance, when a city council decides to offer subsidies to real estate developers in order to revitalize a neighborhood park or an aging business district, the city is hoping to attract further development by creating a positive externality. Investing in education is another example of a positive externality because higher levels of education correspond to lower levels of unemployment and poverty, fewer numbers of smokers, lower rates of imprisonment, and higher levels of civic participation including volunteer work.[42]

But in the case of negative externalities, individuals have an incentive to engage in a particular behavior that makes them better off individually but imposes significant costs on others. For example, in the 1950s and 1960s the self-interested actions of auto manufacturers—maximizing profit by omitting useful safety features—imposed a significant social cost through increased auto-related fatalities and subsequent lost worker productivity. Global warming is another example of low private costs of individuals imposing high social costs on everyone and everything else. The private cost of driving a car or burning coal to create electricity is too low compared to the social cost of persistent droughts, rising sea levels, intensified weather, and so on.

When situations like this arise, the market is said to "fail" because participants cannot easily correct themselves. Any self-correction, such as increasing vehicle production costs by adding new safety features or forgoing recreational mobility by driving less, works directly against a market participant's self-interest and the related desire to make themselves better off. To self-correct would mean they would have to *intentionally* make themselves worse off, which according to economists is exactly what a rational person would *not* do (or at least would not do as a general behavioral trait). In the end, people who might not even be involved in a particular market are forced to pay in financial, health, or environmental terms so that another person can enjoy a private benefit.

Without an external stimulus such as taxation, legal action, or government regulation that raises the private costs of a certain behavior, market participants will not reduce or forgo their activities. For instance, heavily taxing gasoline (as is the case in the United Kingdom which has the highest fuel tax in Europe) increases the private cost of driving and therefore acts as an incentive to reduce unnecessary trips to the store. Introducing regulations requiring the inclusion of seat belts in vehicles acts as an incentive to avoid government injunctions. Being subject to strict product liability acts as an incentive to practice due care to avoid litigation.

> *Without an external stimulus such as taxation, legal action, or government regulation that raises the private costs of a certain behavior, market participants will not reduce or forgo their activities.*

When it comes to addressing negative externalities, incentives are important to changing behavior. In fact, for humans incentives are important. Period. We work harder when we're paid more, we borrow more when interest rates are low, we buy more when retail prices are discounted, and we exercise more when health care plans pay for gym memberships (and we have an admiring audience to display our six pack abs). All sorts of human activities are driven by incentives. Incentives are directly related to our self-interest and how we strive to make ourselves better off by maximizing our utility. It also illuminates, in the absence of incentives, why self-correction rarely happens spontaneously and why market failure occurs.

Consider these situations: Why would a company want to purposely decrease profits for an aspect of a product consumers do not demand and government does not require? Why would users consciously choose safer, but less status-worthy and more expensive vehicles? Self-interest often wins over self-correction no matter how sublime or frivolous self-interest might be. In the story of software, then, the relationship between self-interest, incentives, and market failure is significant.

Why would so many software users opt-in, knowingly or not, to become crash test dummies?

The answer: Self-interest. The utility derived from using software acts as a strong incentive to adopt newer, but potentially more buggy applications, which replace older, less functional applications.

Why would the software industry not create more reliable and secure software?

The answer: Self-interest. Just as with auto manufacturers, the profits derived from selling a product without these aspects act as a strong incentive to produce software absent such aspects.

Why would government not regulate software manufacturers?

The answer: Self-interest. The economic benefits derived from uninhibited entrepreneurial ventures (taxes, employment, and so on) act as a strong incentive to avoid government intervention.

Of course, the argument is more nuanced than plain self-interest, but self-interest is a splendid place to start.

Market Failure Martini, Straight Up

Market failure occurs when perfectly rational people acting in a perfectly rational manner create a perfectly unacceptable situation. To be exact, in the instance where a negative externality is large, individual incentives are aligned in such a way that people cannot easily self-correct without great expense to themselves. Left to itself, the market will do nothing to correct the problem and therefore is said to fail. In the choice between "me and thee," "me" almost always wins. As a result, society is worse off.

The pernicious aspect of market failure is that it does not necessarily feel like failure *per se* to a majority of participants.

Ask any individual participant if he or she feels like something is "failing," and the answer would probably be "No." This makes sense. Each participant is enjoying private benefits at low private cost. People drive cars despite global warming, they smoke despite the dangers to themselves and others, and they play loud music despite grimacing neighbors. So the very members that are contributing to market failure are not motivated to alter their behavior. It is important to note that all markets fail to some extent. The outstanding questions are the degree of failure and whether action is required to alleviate the problems market failure brings about.

In the 1950s and 1960s both auto manufacturers and auto buyers were pursuing their self-interests. Auto manufacturers wanted to minimize cost and maximize profit, whereas buyers wanted to minimize cost and maximize pleasure, so to speak, by purchasing aesthetically pleasing cars. There was nothing intrinsically wrong with any of this, and that was, ironically, what was wrong with it. Neither manufactures nor buyers felt they were making a mistake or doing something wrong even though car-related injuries and fatalities were reaching epidemic proportions. The market was failing significantly but not solely in monetary terms.

The real cost of something is not always measured in money. The real cost of something is what you have to give up in order to get it. In the story of automobiles, the real cost of cars could not be measured just in the showroom sticker price, but the price in what people were giving up on the bloodied roadways— their lives and their livelihoods. Contract disclaimers insulated auto manufacturers from legal actions, eliminating any incentive to respond to consumer safety concerns. From this perspective, market failure was significant, so significant that government regulation as well as product liability needed to be introduced to correct the market.

The same might be said in the story of software. The real cost of insecure software is not in the price we pay to manufacturers, but what we give up in order to use software. The costs of cyber crime, insufficient testing, lost productivity, economic losses due to down time, reduction in consumer confidence, and sometimes even death are the private and social costs we pay on a daily basis. It is becoming more and more apparent to the GAO, to

NIST, and a growing number of organizations that the real cost of insecure software lies in what we are giving up—national and economic security. The outstanding question, then, is not so much the degree of failure in the software market, but what actions are required to alleviate the problems market failure brings about.

To impose an external stimulus requires identification of the incentives currently in place and what new incentives might be needed to counteract current incentives that are causing harm. In light of this, identifying the ingredients that comprise the cocktail of incentives driving the software market to the point of failure is important.

> *The outstanding question, then, is not so much the degree of failure in the software market, but what actions are required to alleviate the problems market failure brings about.*

The incentives of participants in the software market are similar to the incentives in the automotive market discussed previously. Software manufacturers want to minimize cost and maximize profit, whereas software buyers want to minimize cost and maximize pleasure, so to speak, by purchasing aesthetically pleasing software with slick user interfaces and lots of features. There is nothing intrinsically wrong with any of this, and that is, ironically, what is wrong with it. Neither manufactures nor buyers feel they are making a mistake or doing anything wrong even though software-related costs are reaching gargantuan proportions. Sound familiar? But the nature of software, the nature of software production, and the nature of the networks software manifests, distort these similarities and magnify their potential consequences.

Specifically, software manufacturers must innovate relentlessly to differentiate themselves from other software manufacturers and must get their product to market as quickly as possible in order to reap the benefits of innovation, which is often substantial profits. To get a product to market more quickly than a competitor often means that at least some elements of production must be reduced if not entirely eliminated.

For instance, designs might not be thoroughly evaluated or validated for correctness, and testing of the design and implementation, which can be difficult and expensive, might be paid only cursory attention. This might be true of other industries to some extent also, but this is of particular concern with software manufacturers.

Historically, the technology industry's philosophy in general and software manufacturer's philosophy in particular has been, "Ship, then test." In other words, do not try to make the product perfect; get it out in the marketplace and then fix the problems consumers tell you about; let the consumer bear the cost of testing. Guy Kawasaki, a noted Silicon Valley venture capitalist, said it best, "Don't worry, be crappy. Just get your product out there."[43] The reliability numbers seem to support this philosophy.

On the whole, the high-tech industry's reliability record leaves much to be desired. In 2000, roughly 25 percent of computers broke down every year compared against other electronic devices such as clothes dryers and refrigerators at 7 and 8 percent, respectively.[44] A survey of commercial retailers in 2007 found that the XBOX 360, Microsoft's premier gaming console, was defective as high as 33 percent of the time, compelling retailers in some cases to double their prices for service warranties to compensate for repair costs.[45] The *lowest* commercial software failure rate, for which any statistics can be found at all, comes in at 10 percent for AIX, an obscure, almost extinct operating system used primarily for back office operations in enterprise businesses.[46] In contrast, nearly 92 percent of vehicles manufactured by Mazda and Honda, aged between *three and nine years* old, experience no mechanical failure of any type.[47]

A side effect of the "don't worry, be crappy" entrepreneurial spirit is that while innovation is high, the execution on that innovation might be flawed; that is, the quality of the product is frustratingly ambiguous. Sometimes software works as expected, and sometimes it doesn't. The reasons might never be known by the user. Unfortunately, the reason might never be known by the manufacturer either for reasons that are discussed shortly. It could be that low-quality software is tolerated by consumers because they might not have any idea of what high-quality software looks or acts like. This is because low-quality products tend to breed other low-quality products. The reason for this lies in

> It could be that low-quality software is tolerated by consumers because they might not have any idea of what high-quality software looks or acts like.

the brutal reality of competition among software manufacturers.

The stereotype of the software mogul is a hot-shot young entrepreneur driving sleek cars and throwing unbelievably extravagant trade show parties all the while awaiting a big fat check written either by the stock market in the form of an initial public offering (IPO) or a hungry corporate behemoth looking to grow its service/product portfolio. Alas, this is not the entire picture, nor is it entirely accurate.

Getting started in the software business can be quite difficult, and competition is brutal. For a software company to survive the first few years, heck, for any company to survive the first few years, cash flow—the amount of money coming in and the amount of money going out—is what matters most. Not profits. While profits are the ultimate goal, just paying the bills is the highest priority for any start up. So there is a rule that must be observed for a company to survive the first few years: *Cash flows when product starts shipping.* It's just that simple. Profits are not needed for survival. Cash is. And cash is what pays the bills. This means many start-up software companies focus on short sales cycles, short payment terms, quick engineering, and little else. In other words, if the product does not ship, cash does not flow. "Don't worry, be crappy. Just get your product out there."

As far as low production costs go, software is king. In fact, software is not only king, it is the whole royal court. While software has a high fixed production cost, the marginal cost is nearly zero. In plain English, this means the cost of making a software application for the first time (the fixed production cost) can be very expensive. Significant amounts of personal time, energy, and money must be invested to create the product. Once the first version is completed however, the cost of producing another copy of the version (the marginal cost) is trivial. For example, if it cost a manufacturer \$1,000 to produce 100 widgets, but \$1,005 to produce 101 widgets, the marginal cost for the 101st widget—the cost of producing just one more widget—is \$5. If widgets have a market price of \$10, it makes sense to make the 101st widget because the cost of producing one more widget is less than the market price. If the market price of a widget is $4, then it does not make sense to produce the 101st widget because the marginal cost ($5) is greater than the market price ($4). Producing software is the same as this simplistic model, only better. Much better.

If it costs a software company $100 to produce the first version of a product, the marginal cost of making just one more copy is, well, barely more than the few calories burned by the developer copying the software to another Compact Disc. How difficult is it to copy a software program? Not very. Hence, the marginal cost is nearly zero even if including packaging and shipping, and other minimal costs. This means that once a software company introduces a product, each subsequent sale becomes more and more profitable. So the stereotype of a software mogul might be true at some point but certainly not at first.

But while high profit might sound glorious and be the desired outcome for any software company, for most software companies the less noble and reality-based self-interest is this: *mere survival.*

Cash flow is critical, as was mentioned before. So selling product is key to survival. The brutal fact is competitors are vying for the same if not greater success. This is true of just about every other industry and is therefore not an insightful observation per se. However, every other manufacturing industry is subject to product liability laws holding them liable should they send defective products into the global stream of commerce. This is not true for software manufacturers, so there are few compelling incentives to design correctly and test thoroughly, just enough to get the product out the door in some semblance of working order. Besides, thorough testing is inefficient from a software manufacturer's point of view.

By releasing an inadequately tested application into the stream of commerce, the software manufacturer allows users to test the applications for them, saving the cost to the manufacturer of evaluating their own code and discovering possible defects. More importantly, from an efficiency standpoint, users will complain only about the aspects of the software application they care about or use frequently. The manufacturer can simply await user feedback to target specific problems as opposed to reviewing the entire software application for defects. In other words, the software manufacturer focuses its limited resources on only those portions of the software application users actually complain about; that is, by shipping without thoroughly testing, the software company will discover what customers truly want fixed and hesitate or will completely forgo fixing other items consumers fail to notice or fail to complain about.[48] Buyers are literally paying to be crash test dummies.

This brutal efficiency is driven by the need to get product out the door as quickly as possible. A new email client, contact manager, or enterprise database might be enticing to the consumer, but if your software company is late to the market, you're an imitator, not an innovator. Worse, by being late to the market, a company threatens its chances at becoming *the* standard by which all others will be measured. Being first to market confers tremendous advantage in the marketplace, but especially in the software market. Speed matters greatly.

The Need for Speed

Market dominance is an incredibly powerful incentive for software companies, is where massive profits come from, and is what almost every software manufacturer strives for, in one context or another. When a software application, whether a desktop application, search engine, or operating system, is widely accepted, so too are the software's implicit ways of doing things such as saving files to disk, how information is indexed for searching, talking to other computers or software applications, placement and order of menus or tool bars, and so on. The greater popularity a software application enjoys, the greater likelihood that an application's "implicit ways of doing things" will become the standard by which users start to evaluate other products. These standards, if proprietary, act as both binding and barrier; that is, the standard *binds* users to a particular way of doing things as well as acts as a *barrier* to potential competitors who cannot copy the standard because of trade secret, copyright, or patent protections. This solidifies the company's hold on the market and promises profits of extraordinary size and scale.

When software is widely accepted, users are not just buying an application, users are "buying in to" a network of other users employing the standard. For instance, documents created by a word processor such as Microsoft Word cannot be opened by another word processor application such as Adobe Acrobat. This means a user can easily share his or her documents with other users of Microsoft Word, but not Adobe Acrobat. This is the "network effect" crooned about by so many technology luminaries. The more popular a software application, the more value the application has to the software's adopters because it eases the difficulty of communicating and sharing information. Positive externalities are generated in that adopters find it easier to inter-communicate, share files, or transfer skills from job to job or company to company.

Microsoft explicitly highlighted such positive externalities in their 2006 "People Ready" marketing campaign.[49] In one People Ready commercial, a lone American computer consultant travels to a distant foreign country, Russia as it happened to be, presumably to help a client with an IT problem. While sitting in the taxi traveling to the client site, the consultant fumbles through a Russian dictionary, trying to learn the word for "hello" in Russian, which isn't easy. The Russian word for "hello" is *zdravstvuite*. Likewise, the Russian business people awaiting the consultant work on their pronunciation of saying "hello" in English. The consultant finally meets his clients, and both exchange incredibly awkward greetings. Nonetheless, they usher the consultant to sit in front of a welcome and familiar site—the business defacto standard—a PC running Microsoft Windows. The underlying (and implied) message of the commercial, and the People Ready campaign in general, was simple: "Where ever people go, they will be productive because we [Microsoft] have 90 percent market share, and almost everyone at some point has probably worked with our software." From an economics perspective, both employers and employees benefit by using Microsoft. For the user, computer skills learned at one company can be easily transferred to jobs at other companies that are using Microsoft. For employers, this means new hires are easier and less expensive to train because they will most likely arrive with a certain level of computer skills.

In contrast, Apple's 2006 marketing campaign "I'm a PC. I'm a Mac," featuring two off-beat actors pretending to be, well, a Mac and a PC, is similar to Microsoft's campaign but in more subtle ways. Apple's campaign is about interoperability with all sorts of electronic devices and the ease with which users can enjoy the computing experience. Compared to an unfriendly PC, a Mac can communicate with a host of electronic devices as well as make it easier for users to communicate with friends about all sorts of social happenings. While not focused on the business community (Apple has never really focused on corporate organizations), the point is that Apple's solutions are *friendlier* and less prone to problems afflicting PCs (such as viruses). While Microsoft focuses on positive externalities regarding work skills, Apple focuses on positive externalities with sharing information. Both are important.

These two examples highlight the power of joining a "network." By joining the Microsoft "network," employees can transfer job skills more easily, and by joining the Apple "network," it is easier to communicate with friends and family. However, when users become dependent on a network, or when more users join a network, it is more difficult for them to leave the network. In other words, trying to leave a network imposes a high cost of switching on the user. For instance, if a user should become so frustrated with Microsoft they forswear its use, the user must learn how to do again on a different operating system what he or she was once accustomed to with Microsoft. Likewise, if a user should become so frustrated with Apple as to forswear its use, the user must make the same difficult transition to a different way of doing things than what he or she was once accustomed to. This switch might be easy, but oftentimes it is not.

> *In other words, even if a better, more attractive, more secure, or "easier" standard is introduced, switching requires users to go through a difficult transition period in which they attempt to overcome familiarity with the previous standard and their own psychological inertia (let alone angst over all the money they spent on the old software).*

In other words, even if a better, more attractive, more secure, or "easier" standard is introduced, switching requires users to go through a difficult transition period in which they attempt to overcome familiarity with the previous standard and their own psychological inertia (let alone angst over all the money they spent on the old software). This switch can prove too difficult for many, firmly binding them to the old standard no matter how good the new standard might be.

Until the introduction of the iPod, Apple's *Switch* commercials, in which users espoused how wonderful (and simpler) it was to use a Mac compared to Windows, were decidedly unsuccessful. No matter how unsatisfied people might have been with Microsoft Windows, the high cost of switching to a Mac—which could range from something as simple as learning how to change time on the system clock to something more nerve racking like migrating data files and purchasing a new laptop—was largely unacceptable. Apple still provides a "Switch 101" guide to help PC users figure out how to work their Macs, which states

---

Whether you want to learn how to get around and access everything on your Mac; find out how to move your old PC files to the Mac OS environment; figure out how to connect your printer, iPod, digital camera, or other device; learn how to do those tasks you did on a PC on a Mac; learn how to use the software that came with your Mac; or even find out what to do when things don't go as planned; we have the answers.[50]

The high cost of switching is not lost on users. Apple's market share for desktops before the halo effect of iPod remained abysmally small, somewhere around 4 percent, well below the 6.22 percent market share Apple enjoyed in January 2007.[51] Microsoft in comparison has 90 percent of the desktop market and 40 percent of the server market (Apple weighs in at 1.2 percent of the server market).

The high cost of switching for users is not lost on software manufacturers either. In the end, the high cost of switching insulates software vendors not only from competitors but from coordinated retaliation by disgruntled users. For example, Apple's iTunes service, which allows users to download music from the iTunes store, is tremendously popular. However, the file format for downloaded music from the Apple iTunes store is proprietary to Apple, binding users to only those software packages and devices that support Apple's standard.[52]

When it was discovered that early iPod's *unreplaceable* battery lasted only 18 months, two brothers, Casey and Van Neistat, trekked around New York City stenciling "iPod's unreplaceable battery only lasts 18 months" on every iPod poster they could find.[53] To have an unreplaceable battery (or one that was expensive to replace) for a proprietary and limited-lifetime device, which was the *only* device capable of playing Apple's media standard, was incorrigible to the brothers (at least that is what can be inferred by their actions).

In fact, it is possible to "replace" an iPod battery (technically, Apple actually replaces the whole iPod with an equivalent new model or factory-refurbished model in a new enclosure; if the iPod was previously engraved by Apple, it will be engraved again).[54] At the time of the brother's protest, replacement costs were $225, which is what precipitated the protest in the first place. Now, of course, Apple has an official battery replacement program for $59. Of course, to leave the Apple "network" and give up their iPods would create an incredibly high cost of switching not only for the renouncing of the iPod itself, which is easily $200 or more, but for all the music previously purchased via iTunes, which could easily reach into the thousands of dollars for some users.

The brothers' protest was only the beginning. In June 2006, the Free Software Foundation organized a nation-wide protest of iTunes in the United States.[55] Sweden, along with France, Denmark, and Norway have all taken Apple to task, sometimes through statutory or legal action, for binding users to Apple's media standard.[56]

Despite the popularity of the Neistat brothers' protest, wider protests by disgruntled users, and legal action on the part of nation states, critical mass of consumer retaliation was never achieved, and sales of iPods as well as music, TV shows, and movies from the iTunes store—each in their own Apple-proprietary format—have increased ever since. Such is the power of standards. The high cost of switching is a powerful disincentive for users and potentially cripples coordinated attempts at consumer action.

So the incentive of market dominance is really the incentive of becoming the cornerstone upon which all others align, willingly or not. The successor's position conveys enormous advantage to the standard holder given that interoperability with other applications can be tightly constrained by copyright, patent law, and/or Byzantine licensing agreements. If the application, such as Apple iTunes, and the application's embedded standards, such as Apple's proprietary music format, is successful enough, the standard becomes the *de facto* standard with which everyone—namely competitors—must comply, attempt to interoperate, or develop a competing standard. Microsoft spent a fortune marketing Zune, a competitor to the iPod, and it is all but an obscure punch line against Apple's success.[57] Unseating the market leader is difficult indeed.

Microsoft has learned this lesson from Google in developing its own search engine capability and from Apple in the downloadable music arena. Apple has learned this lesson from Microsoft in the desktop marketplace. Users become acquainted and familiar with a software application's behavior. Even lousy software applications can enjoy a dedicated following because adopters have come to expect certain behavior and enjoy the positive externalities of the embedded standards. Unless competitors can trigger a new standards competition by offering a more attractive collection of features wrapping a different, but more useful way of doing things, the widely adopted application has little chance of being displaced, further barring competitors from the marketplace. The drive for simple survival, then, is heightened by the promise of market domination and all the privileges it confers, especially financial profit.

But speed-to-market has dark consequences over and above those of binding and barrier. Thorough testing is a financial burden. Thorough testing delays shipping. Thorough testing hurts cash flow. Thorough testing delays a software product's release giving competitors a possible market advantage. Thorough testing is also inefficient given that fixing defects users do not even complain about in the first place is a waste of effort from the manufacturer's perspective. But all these reasons pale in comparison to what failing to thoroughly design and test truly allows....

The Perversity of Patching

The problem with testing software is that it is unlike testing automobiles, bridges, or any other physical item. Unlike physical structures like bridges, which can be tested in a straight forward manner for maximum load bearing capacity, each instruction within software must be tested *individually*. This is a tedious and complex process as prone to error as creating the software itself. For example, if a bridge can support 200 tons, then it can be rightly assumed by the design engineer the bridge can support all weight less than 200 tons. If a bridge can support 300 fully loaded trucks and the bridge is covered in two feet of ice, it is safe to say the bridge can support a person riding a bike on a sunny day. In contrast, software *must be tested for each and every potential value*. A software engineer cannot extrapolate between test cases as a civil engineer would be able to do for a physical structure. If one series of instructions within a software application works correctly (for the sake of argument, it can "support" 10lbs), this says nothing about the ability of a similar series of instructions to handle 8lbs, 7lbs, or even 9.9lbs. In the software engineer's world, each test is separate and distinct, unrelated to and independent from all other tests. This means for even a moderately complex application, billions upon billions of tests must be conducted.

At most, software companies spend about 35 percent of their production time debugging and correcting errors in their products.[58] Unfortunately, due to the immense complexity of testing software, many software errors—particularly damaging defects—remain latent and do not become apparent until a much later time; that is, not until the software application has become popular. By then, it is too late.

As a case in point, Microsoft's Internet Explorer has a long history of vulnerabilities, making it the poster child of "what not to do" from a security perspective when designing and building a web browser. In response to this unsatisfactory performance on the part of Microsoft to improve its web browser's security, multiple news columnists and individuals within the Information Security community in 2004 encouraged computer users to forgo using Internet Explorer and use a free, much more "secure" alternative for a web browser called Firefox.[59] Outside of a few thousand early adopters, however, Firefox was certainly a promising new web browser but hardly what anyone would call a *popular* browser at the time. The call-to-arms changed that, however, and thousands upon thousands of people started downloading Firefox. As friends told friends, Firefox steadily became increasingly popular and increasingly more exposed.

Within months of the call-to-arms, similar vulnerabilities that critics complained about in Internet Explorer were being discovered uncomfortably often in Firefox.[60] Not only were they being discovered, but the vulnerabilities in Firefox were being actively exploited by hackers, thus placing computer users in the same dangerous position they were in with Internet Explorer. What happened?

The Firefox story highlights two important aspects about software testing and ultimately about market competition. First, attackers are drawn to whatever software application is *popular*, whether the application is a browser, word processor, operating system, or music player (Apple iTunes is plagued by security vulnerabilities also). Second, because popularity of an application correlates to the amount of attention paid to it by attackers, latent defects will not be discovered until the application has become popular, at which point it is too late. Everyone has already adopted a security defect-ridden application.

The first aspect is attackers are attracted to popular applications and pay less attention to less popular applications. This is simple economics. Attackers, like everyone else, have limited time and resources. Attackers will attempt to maximize their efforts by looking for vulnerabilities in increasingly popular applications because the more popular an application, the more potential victims exist, and the greater the return on their investment of time and effort. Thus, an application that appears "more secure" than a popular, rival software application might only appear more secure because of its relative obscurity. This happened with Firefox, as well as with Apple and Google. For instance, many a fan of Apple's Mac boasted their operating system was "more secure" than Microsoft's Windows operating system. But this was more a testament of Apple's abysmal popularity in the desktop market (peak 6 percent market share compared to Microsoft's 90 percent) rather than the quality and robustness of its software. Since January 2005, Apple released 262 security patches compared to Microsoft's 157; a growth rate that tracks squarely with Apple's growing popularity due to iPod and the amount of attention paid by hackers because of it.[61] Even vaunted Google has come under attack as hackers see the popularity of its web-based applications rise.[62]

The second aspect of the Firefox story is that software security, or lack thereof, is only considered in any significant way once a software application becomes popular, *not during the popularity contest*. But by then it is too late. It is like trying to install a crumple zone after the car has been built. In other words, because latent defects remain hidden until the software achieves a certain level of popularity, such defects play no role in the software manufacturer's competition to become popular. Therefore, thorough testing and security can be easily ignored or left incomplete by the manufacturer until after the application has become popular, given that only then do defects start being discovered more frequently. At this point, though, there are a large number of potential victims to exploit who have already adopted the application and must now directly bear the burden for the manufacturer's inadequate production practices.

Surprisingly, users of software bear further financial burden for latent defects by purchasing, implementing, and constructing a process around software patching solutions. The irony of a software patching solution is that it is yet another software application that automates the process of fixing the unreliable software purchased in the first place.

> *Even if thoroughly testing software were possible, software companies ultimately have a perverse incentive not to make better software.*

Patching is necessary if users want to protect their software systems from internal errors or exploitation from malicious attacks. Even if the patching solution is provided for free, the *process* of patching is not. Home users experience little upset if the patching solution automatically downloads and installs patches. But even moderately sized organizations can experience painful expenditures keeping up with patches, patch status, auditing, and validation—all necessary for the patching process because of statutory regulations. A 2004 Yankee Group study found that patching could cost an organization an average of $254 per computer.[63]

But patching raises a point that is rather perverse, literally. Even if thoroughly testing software were possible, software companies ultimately have a perverse incentive *not to make better software*.[64] First, because patching is more expense for the software buyer than for the manufacturer. Second, because upgrades create new revenue streams that would otherwise not materialize, and third, because new licensing terms can be negotiated *at will* by the manufacturer.

First, the marginal cost of releasing a patch tracks with the marginal cost of the original software product; that is, while fixing a software defect can be expensive, the marginal cost of releasing a patch is nearly zero. This means the expense related to patching is born almost entirely by software users since it is the user's responsibility to patch their systems. The larger the number of computer systems the software buyer must patch, the greater the expense for the software buyer, as the Yankee Group study shows. For a moderately sized company, this could be nearly a $1 million per year expense. But the software manufacturer has only the fixed production cost of the patch itself. All copies of the patch are produced at essentially zero marginal cost; therefore, the larger the number of computer systems the software buyer must patch, the expense to the manufacturer stays the same. For instance, if a patch costs a software manufacturer $200,000 to release to the public, the manufacturer's cost does not increase with the number of systems that must be patched by software buyers. While estimates place the cost to software vendors for creating an after-market patch at 100 times the cost of fixing the error while in production, this has proven an empty motivator simply because the economics still favor *not* fixing the defect in production. This is where the story of software can get rather more disturbing.

Achieving market dominance often means the dominant software company must compete against itself at some point. There are no other competitors to drive out (or no remaining manufacturers pose a serious threat), so the only applications to compete with are the previous versions of the manufacturer's own product. In other words, earlier versions of successful applications inhibit the acceptance of newer versions of the same application. For instance, the largest competitor to Microsoft Office 2007 is Microsoft Office 2003. This poses a problem for Microsoft, or any software manufacturer in a similar position, considering that once a particular market has been saturated, new revenue can only come from upgrades.

Failure to sufficiently motivate users to upgrade from an earlier version detrimentally affects short and long term revenue of newer versions for the manufacturer. When a company is competing largely against itself, this means the manufacturer can literally put itself out of business unless it can compel buyers to upgrade to the newer version. As such, upgrades are marketed on the basis of new and improved features that software buyers presumably cannot live without. Ironically, the process of adding more and more features to compel users to upgrade increases the number of latent defects in the applications, resulting in a constant stream of new vulnerabilities as well as a constant stream of patches.

Nonetheless, upgrades do work, most of the time. Some users upgrade easily; some do not. But what can be said with a reasonable amount of confidence is that a majority of users will upgrade to the newest version *eventually*. From a marketing and revenue perspective, *eventually* is not sufficient because performance metrics are due (such as profits) to shareholders and the market every fiscal quarter. However, a certain portion of users will remain stridently resistant to upgrades and will forgo newer, better, faster, in favor of familiar and more stable. So these laggards will never upgrade, unless an incentive is applied by the manufacturer.

These holdouts, or laggards, depending on your point of view, are frustrating for software manufacturers. One option for software vendors is to simply refuse to provide patches for earlier versions of a software application. Without a source of patches, users are left exposed to an endless stream of uncertainty:

- Will another defect be discovered that will affect uptime?
- Will an attacker find a weakness that can only be properly mitigated with a patch?
- Will I be able to communicate and share files with others using newer versions?

These rudimentary questions and the implied vulnerabilities usually create sufficient pressure to force upgrades on an unwilling population. But the upgrades might not necessarily be needed because new functionality is compelling, but primarily because manufacturers, having achieved a certain level of market dominance, must force users to upgrade or risk going out of business.

The third and final aspect of the perverse incentives against thorough testing is the ability to offer new licensing terms with the patch or upgrade on a take-it-or-leave-it basis. For instance, to install an upgrade or apply a patch, software buyers must often agree to a software licensing agreement before the patch or upgrade can be installed. By *not* agreeing to the license terms, the user will not be able to fix or upgrade their systems, so they must in many respects accept the new licensing terms, or they are betting against themselves.

However, this creates the perverse incentive for software manufacturers to use upgrades and patches as vehicles for "renegotiating" licensing terms on an ad-hoc basis.[65] This means if the law governing aspects of software contracts should change for any reason, or the vendor wishes to change their contract terms for any arbitrary reason whatsoever, the new, updated language can be included by the manufacturer in a subsequent patch or upgrade. Microsoft has been especially notorious for this behavior with its "hopelessly confusing, practic-ally Byzantine Windows licensing structure," but the same is true for thousands of other software manufacturers.[66]

> *This creates the perverse incentive for software manufacturers to use upgrades and patches as vehicles for "renegotiating" licensing terms on an ad-hoc basis.*

In the end, failing to sufficiently test software not only provides an avenue to force buyers to upgrade, but *also provides an avenue for software vendors to renegotiate licensing agreements for those who do.* Given the constant stream of defects any given software vendor produces and given the tendency of users to accept dreadfully biased licensing agreements that favor only the manufacturer, there is no incentive for software manufacturers to forgo a proven method for collecting continued revenue and a dependable mechanism for re-establishing optimal market and legal protection.

It gets worse.

Irrationally New

As mentioned previously, the primary attraction for software applications in general and upgrades in particular is the addition of newer and better features, features that themselves are likely to introduce more latent defects, thus requiring more patches and upgrades. This is ironic given that fixing latent defects, which is what everyone rushes to accomplish in order to protect themselves from exploitation, might not necessarily make software more reliable or more secure in general. On the contrary, new more serious problems can arise. For example, in 1991, after changing three lines of code in a signaling program that contains millions of lines of code, the local telephone systems in California and along the Eastern seaboard collapsed. Code that might already be brittle in production can be made even more fragile by trying to fix the code after it is deployed widely. As one industry observer stated,

---

When a program grows in power by an evolution of partially understood patches and fixes, the programmer begins to lose track of internal details, loses his ability to predict what will happen, begins to hope instead of to know, and watches the results as though the program were an individual whose range of behavior is uncertain.[67]

The result is programs that seem to work but then fail unexpectedly. Nonetheless, features and fixes are the unrelenting, compelling messages targeting the consumer to convince them to do away with the old and acquire the new. Whether the feature is a new menu bar, better collaboration capabilities, cooler sounds and graphics, or just better interoperability with printer/fax/copier machines, features are what get consumer's attention and make them feel like they are getting more, more, more. In fact, the buyer is getting more than he bargained for.

Features add flexibility to software applications. This much is understood and appreciated by almost every buyer of software. More features, more flexibility—and more ability to do varying types of work (hopefully) more efficiently.

Flexibility comes at the cost of added complexity, however. Greater flexibility means more software must be added to enable the newer and better features. Unfortunately, complexity is the enemy of security. As complexity increases in a given software application, so too does the likelihood the software application is weak, vulnerable, and prone to exploitation. While features are the compelling message to consumers, features are also the primary means by which software vendors screw up.

But features—read "innovations" or whatever marketing parlance you would like to put here—are often the only thing that differentiates one software application from another. More features in one application compared to the other offers the consumer an easy calculus to determine which application, or version of an application, is "better." This is why many a packaging box on the shelves at CompUSA or Staples contains voluminous tables listing which features are included and which features are missing from lesser versions or missing from competitor's versions. In the end, a software vendor's livelihood relies on additional features, not reliability or security.

According to Gary Chapman, director of the 21st Century Project at the University of Texas, "Repeated experiences with software glitches tend to narrow one's use of computers to the familiar and routine. Studies have shown that most users rely on less than 10 percent of the features of common programs."[68] Unreliability actually inclines users to *avoid* using newly added features in a software application because it requires users to have a moderately high level of toleration for frustration and malfunction to explore beyond a given comfort level.

We have all seen this situation before in the dreaded blinking 12:00 on our grandparents' VCR. If a consumer is habituated to the notion that electronics do not work and have a tendency to not work consistently, consumers will tend *not* to explore even the simplest additional features. So despite the notion that elderly folk cannot seem to interact with even simple user interfaces for setting a VCR's clock, it is perhaps more accurate to state elderly folk have a lower tolerance of unreliability. Elderly folks aside, studies show as we just mentioned, that users use only a fraction of features available to them, even well-seasoned users.[69] Given that 77 percent of users do not trust their software, a high level of toleration for frustration and malfunction is not very likely among software buyers.

In practice, this means new features in software make little difference to the actual user experience, yet software companies rely on additional features as a market differentiator. Indeed, users look at and deeply consider feature lists on marketing materials for a software application. Yet, in practice, users are inclined *not to use* the very features that compelled them to purchase the software because of their ingrained and justified skepticism of software reliability. The irony is if consumers were less skeptical of software, they would be more likely to use features that seemed so important in the purchasing decision.

So why, then, would software vendors provide an increasing and ever more fantastic array of features in applications when it is clear that users do not use newer features, and additional features tend to promote the very unreliability that keeps users from employing new features in the first place?

Compared to sufficient testing and proper security development practices, features are *much less expensive* to implement and provide an *easier* method for users to differentiate products *even if* newer features are not employed in practice. From a business perspective, even if features are irrelevant to a purchaser from a functionality perspective, features are not irrelevant to the software vendor where it counts most: the point of sale.

For the copious time and effort consumers spend comparing one list of features against another, the software vendor understands that the *number* of features matters far more than anything of true consequence, whether quality, reliability, and/or security. The software market is a brutal market, and vendors are loathe to invest in anything that consumers cannot easily comprehend and do not value consistently. Herein lies part of the issue with the software crisis: Purchasers of software do not value security consistently; therefore, vendors have no compelling reason to include security as part of their market competition.

How people value security is similar to how people value personal health. Where one individual smokes, drinks, and refuses to exercise, other people will become vegan tri-athletes. Each individual has a notion of how much they value their health and well-being. While some people seem uncomfortably self-destructive, others might seem rather uncomfortably high strung. But even these singular valuations are not consistent across the continuum of a person's life. In college, one might stay up late, drink, smoke, and exist on ramen noodles, while the same individual later in life might have an awakening after a frightening visit to the cardiologist or oncologist. Suddenly, the previous daily regimen consisting of beer and bagels becomes the new daily regimen of egg whites and exercise.

The same phenomenon observed in health is largely true for an individual's valuation of security. Where some people place bars on their windows and carry hand guns to the grocery store, others leave their doors unlocked at night, leave their keys in their cars while running into the convenience mart, and explore interesting but questionable sections of rowdy border towns (Tijuana comes to mind for some reason). All people have their personal notions about how much they value their safety and where they are located on the risk-tolerance spectrum. Some people are more risk-averse than others.

In each case of health or safety, the calculation by which people arrive at their personal risk threshold is unclear and uncertain to outside observers, except through guesswork and anecdote. There are a wide range of disparate companies that all rely on and target differing personal valuations of health of safety *throughout* a person's life. This means GNC, the largest health retailer in the United States, can exist side by side with Phillip Morris USA and Smith and Wesson. Each company might enjoy demographic similarities in age and education, but how a person values his health and safety at a given point in life is different.

In the story of software, inconsistent valuation of security is far more problematic and its identification much less distinct. As stated previously, software cuts across the entire spectrum of societal, economic, and governmental activities. Whereas non-software companies can lay in wait and specifically target individuals as they progress through their life experiences and differing personal valuations, software is the foundation upon which a greater portion of our lives are lived. Instead of living through our "health-nut phase" or "smoking phase," software is present no matter what phase in life we may be in.

This makes a consistent valuation of security much harder to come by in the software world. In fact, the valuation of security tends to be diluted as larger sections of the population begin to use software. Vendors are unable to accurately target an individual's risk valuation and therefore tend toward the lowest common denominator—a trend that is exactly opposite to what is needed for a robust foundation of civilization.

In the end, innovation is valued much more consistently than security. This is understandable, but this also makes innovation the single most important differentiator in a market suffocating in its own unreliability (discovered weaknesses in software has increased approximately 64 percent per year).[70] Left with no other distinguishing or inexpensive avenues, the tendency in the software market is to treat innovation as an end in itself and to justify the ever increasing and ever more fantastic array of features. But this only makes the situation worse.

The fanatical focus on innovation leads to a kind of irrational innovation in which software products become obsolete even before demand is satisfied or, worse, gluts the market from the start due to the expectation of another superseding innovation, which itself is not employed in practice by the very users the innovation was intended for.

Market Failure Martini, with a Twist of Lemon

Irrational innovation exacerbates the lack of security in the software marketplace. When a product is distinguished by fewer and fewer aspects, imbalances arise particularly regarding the amount of information available to buyers compared to sellers. If the imbalance is great enough, the market breaks down. In the case of software, we've seen that features tend to be the single most important aspect to buyers. Features, in other words, are the *sine qua non* of value. Without features, one software application is all but indistinguishable from another.

But this leads to an imbalance of information. Purchasers focus on features because features are the primary aspect by which software applications can be distinguished. As discussed previously, however, the *count* of features is what is apparently most important in buying decisions even though a majority of features go unused after purchase. Other information about reliability, security, and interoperability might be considered by the buyer during the purchasing process, but not nearly to the same extent as feature count. In essence, the buyer is told more through marketing and sales information about features (which are obvious) and little about everything else.

A similar information imbalance was identified by George Akerlof's paper titled, "The Market For Lemons," for which he won a Nobel Prize in 1970. His essay identified shortfalls in the used car market where sellers know more about the quality of a used car than buyers. Where this information imbalance exists, price becomes the distinguishing element in purchasing decisions and eventually overshadows all other considerations.

What Akerlof noted was buyers, uncertain of the used car's quality, tend to demand a lower price. This makes intuitive sense. If a buyer is unsure of the product's quality, the buyer will most likely not make a fair offer for the product given that the value of the purchase is questionable at best. As a result, sellers, who are offered discounted prices for their products, tend to withhold high-quality vehicles from the market because a competitive, or even a fair price, is not likely. This also makes intuitive sense, considering that if I own and wish to sell a pristine condition Chevy Nova, I would probably think twice about selling my car if I knew I could not get what I believe is a fair asking price. I will withhold my higher value (and higher quality) vehicle from the market.

The actions of both buyer and seller coincide with the assumption noted earlier: Users will follow their self-interest and will not do anything that makes them worse off. The buyer will offer a discounted price regardless of whether the quality of the used car is acceptable because to offer more might affect him negatively—that is, spending more money when it might result in purchasing a vehicle that breaks down before he arrives home. Likewise, the seller will forgo putting a high-quality used car into the market because to do so would mean having to contend with discounted prices, which do not reflect the fair value of the car. This vicious cycle repeats itself, constantly lowering the price as well as constantly lowering the quality of cars sellers are willing to put on the market. As a consequence, higher quality used cars are forced out of the market entirely, leaving low quality cars ("lemons") to dominate.

The important aspect in this vicious cycle is that sellers always know more about the quality of a car than buyers and are in the powerful position of determining whether a car should be put on the market. It is the buyers in the market who are disadvantaged by lack of information, not sellers. Buyers, then, who obviously are ignorant of the car's quality, must make the assumption that quality is low—why else would the seller be selling the car? Buyers cannot help but offer discounted prices. The information imbalance leads to inaccurate and incomplete information sharing, which eventually detrimentally affects all participants in the market.

Unfortunately, the software world is not that much different than the world of used cars, at least from a legal perspective. Software, like a used car, is sold "as is" with no warranty guarantees. In the software market, the quality of a software application is truly unknown by the buyer. Yet, whereas *price* is the dominant consideration in the used car market, *features* are the dominant consideration in the software market and as such tend to overshadow all other considerations (at least until it is too late to do anything about them).

> *Unfortunately, the software world is not that much different than the world of used cars, at least from a legal perspective. Software, like a used car, is sold "as is" with no warranty guarantees.*

Buyers of software, just like buyers of used cars, cannot help but employ anecdotal evidence to judge the likely quality of a given software application. Having heard about and personally experienced multiple latent defects and "glitches" in software (and 77 percent of the population have experience said glitchiness), buyers tend to only focus on those elements that provide a discount for their inconvenience. As it turns out, because buyers cannot discount the price of software, they accept the software and demand another form of discount: features.

In effect, features are the discount that software buyers expect, and software vendors willingly provide, to offset the egregious lack of quality, reliability, and security in software applications. The greater the number of features in an application, the more likely a buyer is willing to tolerate other missing aspects to a certain extent.

As discussed previously, the number of features in a software application can be clearly demonstrated to buyers via tables or comparison charts on software packaging and marketing materials. In comparison, quantifying the stability or security of an application is much more difficult; remember there is no five-star rating system for software or any meaningful standard rating system at all. Therefore, information about quality and security of a software application might be known only to the seller. The imbalance of information favors the seller because buyers are incapable of discovering less obvious aspects of the product. Features, then, are much more visible and apparent to the market, whereas security and reliability are less so—that is, until the product reaches its tipping point in popularity, at which point security becomes a substantial concern. By then, as mentioned before, it is too late: The market is flooded with defect-ridden software, hackers are more than happy to exploit.

Once again, when one aspect of a product tends to dominate the buying decision in the minds of buyers, it becomes much easier for the seller to obfuscate other aspects such as quality or security. The buyer's inability to easily distinguish between high and low -quality products makes it increasingly difficult for high-quality products to compete in the marketplace. As a consequence, high-quality software is driven from the market, leaving low-quality and feature-rich software to dominate. But here is where the story is at its darkest. In reality, *neither party* in the software market has clear understanding of software quality. Sellers actually have no more knowledge than buyers.

Sellers, with no compelling incentive to conduct thorough testing and with little willingness to implement thorough testing in the first place due to market pressures, realistically have no idea about the stability or security *of their own product*. Documentation, which explains how the application is intended to operate, goes unwritten, not merely out of laziness, but in actuality because decent documentation would mean the software vendor has an idea how to articulate their understanding of application functions in the first place. This is not always the case. Oftentimes, documentation goes unwritten because knowledge of the application's real functions was lost days after the code was first developed. Once that knowledge is lost, it is like trying to write about your earliest recollections of childhood in a university creative writing class. Sure, parts of the story are true, but mostly it's fantasy.

In more than a few instances, a software developer, even after just a few days have elapsed might have forgotten, (or worse yet, never truly knew) how his code accomplishes what it does. The software might have efficient code. It might be elegant code, and it might even abide by the software company's coding standards, but these judgments are highly subjective and without any reliable or relevant meaning to the seller, the buyer, or the market place. It compiles! Ship it!

There are huge swaths of code embedded into the fabric of our society for which no one has any memory of how it works or what it actually does. Nor might anyone make a meaningful statement as to the code's quality or reliability. It might work, but no one knows how or why for certain. This state of affairs is as far from the notion of discipline in engineering as a profession can get. The foundation of a civilization deserves more.

Wrap Up: The Martini Hangover

In a market economy, self-interest is not a bad thing. It is the engine that makes people want to make better lives. People will spend accordingly to make their lives better, happier, and more enjoyable; subsequently, people will not partake in activities that make their lives worse off. But when a market fails—when the public cost far outstrips the private gain and individuals cannot self-correct except with an external stimulus—self-interest can lead to significant consequences.

If software were merely like new and used automobiles, its failure would be tragic, certainly. But the tragedy would be limited in scope to individual computers or small groups of computers, much like the effect of car accidents are localized to small sections of roadways. A multi-car accident in Los Angeles does not affect the flow of traffic in Detroit. The global interconnection of software, however, combined with software's uncertain quality and the lack of incentives to improve quality, make for an incomprehensively potent and volatile cocktail. The destructive range is global.

As you've seen in this chapter, the automobile in general, and crash test dummies in particular, offer many insights into the plight of the software industry. Manufacturers will produce low-quality products as long as the market allows them, and software buyers will remain crash test dummies in the interim. Poorly informed consumers will decouple feature and consequence, choosing the digital equivalent of tailfins and chrome accoutrements while neglecting the question of whether their software can withstand the demands of the cyber environment. Government can be involved but only when oversight can improve the situation.

Policy makers erroneously assume the software market will self-correct. In their fairy-tale world, software vendors will be self-motivated to greatly improve software quality and security, and buyers will coordinate to punish software vendors that do not. In the real world, this has not happened and will not happen.

The software market has substantial incentives directly opposed to trustworthiness and security and will continue to rebuff self-correction until the incentives change or private costs dramatically increase.

The software industry has known how to construct high-quality, secure software since the 1960s. Since the 1980s Watts Humphrey has given the software world a clear path to better software. However, software manufacturers have chosen time and time again to ignore what is technically viable for what is relatively easy and inexpensive: adding new software features.

Listening to the counterarguments of the software industry, however, software vendors would have us believe that they are simply satisfying market demand because software buyers present un-ending streams of requests for newer, better, and more dazzling features. Yet software buyers are demanding said features because features are the discount that is demanded for having to settle for historically low-quality software. In this case, both buyers and sellers tend to drive out higher-quality software from the market because vendors selling high-quality software with fewer features cannot compete in a market where the primary emblem of value for the buyer is feature count.

A significant disincentive for high-quality software lies in all the advantages conferred by low-quality software—namely, the perverse incentive of being able to force users to purchase upgrades who would otherwise refuse to do so. Lower-quality software allows software vendors to periodically renegotiate software licenses. The irony is that buyers have little to no rights when agreeing to software licenses, allowing software sellers to "renegotiate" agreements which buyers could not negotiate in the first place. Not only are buyers crash test dummies, but buyers do not have any rights as one either.

The disincentive for buyers to coordinate retaliation against a software vendor is tied directly to the network effect of software. Sharing music, pictures, and files is made possible not

> *Lower-quality software allows software vendors to periodically renegotiate software licenses. The irony is that buyers have little to no rights when agreeing to software licenses in the first place, allowing software vendors to renegotiate an agreement for which the software vendor is the only party capable of changing any of the terms.*

only through common file formats, but through a learned process of workflow. To retaliate against a given software vendor—that is, "vote with their dollars" and choose not to purchase or not use the old software vendor's application—there must be a suitable and acceptable alternative. In effect, the user must leave a common network of usability and share-ability and bring all their friends and family with them as quickly as possible. If only one or two users leave, then it is difficult for them to enjoy the same scale of interactivity they enjoyed while in the previous network. The network effect works both ways. Not only does it promote users to join the network in order to enjoy positive externalities of collaboration and sharing, but it also inhibits those who would wish to leave.

Secondly, if new workflow must be learned, as PC users are required when switching to Apple, users must be willing to overcome their own inertia and resistance to learning new methods of accomplishing tasks that were once easy and intuitive. In this sense, the neural pathways in the user's brain, which fire automatically when he or she right-clicked on a file to bring up a context menu, must now realign as the user gets acquainted with the single button on an Apple mouse. This can be ungodly frustrating. The tearing down and realignment of a user's neural pathways is a significant barrier to switching and, therefore, a significant barrier to retaliation.

In the end, buyers must literally make themselves worse off to punish a given software vendor. Knowing what we now know about the assumptions made by economists, this behavior is not likely. People will not knowingly make themselves worse off. Some individuals might have chosen this path; majorities have not. As with any tipping point, if there are an insufficient number of users converting, revolution will not occur. Neither does this address the issue of feature count. Users, even if they switch, bring along the same demands and the same expectations to the alternative product, thereby polluting the alternative application and driving quality downward.

But here again lies the problem. Because vendors are competing to offer an alternative, they abide by the unwritten rules common in the software market. In the end, competing alternatives overlook security and quality because to reap the benefits of the network effect, the competing vendor must win the popularity contest first and worry about everything else later. "Don't worry, be crappy. Just get your product out there." Cash flows when product ships.

There is more to learn from crash test dummies, as I have hinted in this chapter, and I will address this in Chapter 4, "Myopic Oversight." But there are other helpful analogies that illuminate more the real cost of insecure software. What can we learn from broken windows?

CHAPTER 3

The Power of Weaknesses:
Broken Windows and National Security

Let me be clear about the threat to our federal systems: I believe the infiltration by foreign nationals of federal government networks is one of the most critical issues confronting our nation. The acquisition of our government's information by outsiders undermines our strength as a nation. If sensitive information is stolen and absorbed by our enemies, we are strategically harmed...We don't know the scope of our networks. We don't know who's inside our networks. We don't know what information has been stolen. We need to get serious about this threat to our national security.

—*The Honorable James R. Langevin, April 19, 2007*

Approximately 5 percent of cyber criminals are caught.[1] It is surprising, then, that more people do not consider becoming a professional hacker. The tools are simple, substantial technical expertise is not required, weaknesses in software that can be exploited to gain access to computer systems abound, and with a 95 percent chance of avoiding arrest, who wouldn't?

The problem with this statistic, as with many of the statistics about hacking and cyber crime, is the fuzziness of the empirical data from which it is derived. A 5 percent prosecution rate seems shocking, almost embarrassing, until weighed against the fact that we really do not know how many attackers are actually breaking into computer systems and getting away with it. We know *someone* is undertaking these attacks, we know the numbers of cyber criminals are increasing, and we know from multiple credible estimates that financial losses due to cyber crime range well into hundreds of billions of dollars, but we cannot regularly or confidently point a finger at individual perpetrators.[2] Although a 5 percent prosecution rate might be too low most troubling is it may be far too high.[3]

One thing we do know is that, as of 2001, the actual number of computer crime prosecutions in the United States was little more than 100 per year and that this rate of prosecution has not demonstrated pronounced growth since then.[4] News coverage given to high-profile cyber crime defendants belies the hidden truth: Cyber crime prosecutions make headlines because they are the exception, not the rule.

Law enforcement's paltry number of prosecutions and the vast amount of money and international coordination required to obtain them are not wasted on members of organized crime. With potentially huge financial gain to be made (ranging oftentimes into millions of dollars for a single "heist"), an abundance of computer systems loaded with insecure software connected to the Internet, and little chance of being apprehended (let alone prosecuted), the incentives for cyber criminals are compelling indeed. You have a greater likelihood of getting a traffic ticket than getting caught breaking into a computer system. As one talented hacker stated in a 2003 discussion, "If you get caught, you're an idiot. It's just too damn easy to get away with shit."

Once upon a time, the biggest scourge of the Internet was a lonely, 14-year-old white male from the United States with a penchant for free pornography and defacing websites. "Hacking" was for loners and geeks, a subculture that was odd, even freakish, and easily minimized by society. Times have changed. Breaking into computer systems is an international activity from the Ukraine to Indonesia, the Middle East to Brazil; it is turning into big business and a weapon of nations.

This chapter argues that weaknesses in software combined with clear economic incentives and sociological aspects observed in areas of traditional crime explain, at least in part, the current dire situation in which we find ourselves. But this is not a chapter about cyber crime, per se. National and economic security is increasingly an issue of software quality rather than law enforcement's effectiveness or the efficacy of firewall, anti-virus, and fill-in-the-blank security solutions. These aspects are certainly of interest but are not the complete story. The story is about understanding how software weaknesses act as incentives, enticing people to commit acts of crime, espionage, and engage in an aspect of warfare made more accessible by massive interconnection of computer systems: information warfare.

This chapter begins with a discussion of the explosive growth of cyber crime and espionage incidents and then turns to a theory that helps explain this growth and the burgeoning underground market for software vulnerabilities. Next, the emergence of highly sophisticated, professional attackers is discussed; the chapter concludes with what is perhaps the most disconcerting element of this discussion, the contamination of modern civilization's foundation by malicious embedded software.

Only the Stupid Are Caught

Hacker culture began a perceptible evolution in the early 1990s. Hacking transformed itself from an "art" practiced by a limited number of persons who possessed sufficient curiosity, patience, and technical talent to an activity undertaken by a dazzling panoply of novices and joy riders. The tone of hacking also changed from an adventurous mindset of "Let's make this system work," to one of "Let's break this system." Where one approach was centered on creation, the other was focused on destruction.

There were a number of reasons for this transformation. First, technical barriers for breaking into computer systems began to fall as easy-to-use software applications known as "tools" or "utilities" were made widely available by more experienced hackers willing to share their knowledge with others. No longer did aspiring hackers need to learn intricacies of a particular computer system, the nuances of how computers talked to each other over the network, or even how to write code themselves. Tools gave "point and shoot" capability to the curious but inexperienced. Second, online tutorials appeared, and mentorship relationships developed, transforming neophytes from simply *acting* like hackers to *thinking* like them also. Mix in the

> *No longer did aspiring hackers need to learn intricacies of a particular computer system, the nuances of how computers talked to each other over the network, or even how to write code themselves. Tools gave "point and shoot" capability to the curious but inexperienced.*

third element, which was the "coolness factor" of breaking into a computer system (and showing your friends you could do it), and the ranks of hackerdom began to swell. But mainly, there was no real consequence for destroying or breaking into a computer system.

Certainly, the U.S. Computer Crime and Abuse Act cited civil and criminal penalties for breaking into computer systems, but the hacker had to be caught first for the law to have any impact. This proved especially difficult given that a hacker, in an attempt to conceal his real location, would tunnel attacks through multiple computer systems he had previously exploited in different countries around the globe. So an attacker sitting in Florida might "own" or have under his control a computer in a Chinese company, a computer in a German university, a computer in a Dutch oil company, and a computer in a Mexican automobile factory. By setting up connections through each one of those computers, the attacker might launch his attack against a company located in Florida, but as far as the victim is concerned, the attack would appear to be coming out of the network owned by the Dutch oil company or German university. This simple obfuscation technique makes it nearly impossible to trace back where the attacker might actually be. As a case in point, in 2004 nearly 40 percent of computers identified as the source of attacks were owned by Fortune 100 companies.[5] This is because, most likely, it is as far as the attacks could be traced. All these factors, and arguably more, changed hacking into something decidedly more pernicious. A pivotal event in the late 1990s illustrated to U.S. law enforcement just how much the situation had changed.

The event, referred to as Solar Sunrise, was actually a series of events perpetrated by a group of teenage hackers under the tutelage of an 18-year-old Israeli mentor named Ehud Tenebaum. The group gained access to numerous government computers, including those at 11 U.S. Air Force and Naval bases. In all, the group had access to more than 400 military computer systems, approximately 1,000 commercial computer systems, and over 120,000 user accounts. Solar Sunrise served as a warning that considerable hacking capabilities were well within reach of relatively inexperienced people.[6] The lesson was not wasted on law enforcement, and as everyone was to eventually find out, this lesson was not wasted on the criminal community either.

Fast-forward two years.

During the spring of 2000, United States banks and credit card businesses were attacked by Russian hackers who broke into protected electronic files, extracted credit card numbers as well as merchant identification numbers (which demonstrated that the attackers were quite sophisticated regarding financial transactions), and then in some cases, used this information to extort money from victims in exchange for "security consulting services."[7] The attacker's activities resulted in substantial financial damages to the victims. The persistence of the attackers was also notable. As one victim stated, "It was like somebody drove a demolition truck through our front door. This guy was relentless, and we didn't get sleep for many weeks. Every time we'd knock him off the system, he'd come right back."[8] Five years later, the situation is ever more dire.

By the first quarter of 2005, reported bank losses due to cyber crime increased 450 percent over the previous year.[9] While this increase was significant, it was not necessarily surprising; it was quite clear there was money to be made by exploiting lucrative targets connected to the Internet. In 2003, John Shaughnessy, Senior Vice President of Fraud Management for Visa USA, stated that "U.S. Banks are experiencing horrific attacks."[10] Mr. Shaughnessy did not say "serious" attacks or even "alarming" attacks, but *"horrific"* attacks.

Mr. Shaughnessy's statement is further supported by analysis from the World Bank, which commented in 2002 that "law enforcement agencies have documented that Eastern European organized hacker groups have penetrated hundreds of banks worldwide...[and] that many banks are paying off extortion demands for fear of risking their reputations and losing their customer bases to competitors."[11] Even if banks choose to pay the extortion fees, they might still be subject to a thieves' honor. In one instance, hackers penetrated a database containing 10,000 credit card numbers and then demanded a significant sum of money or the credit card numbers would be publicly posted in online chat rooms. Despite assurances to the contrary, each one of the credit cards was charged $12 by the hackers regardless, making the hackers a tidy profit of $120,000 just for lying.[12]

What factors contributed to the explosive growth in attacks? First, speed is both blessing and bane. Not only does software increase the speed at which people and business can get things done, but it also facilitates quicker and more efficient methods of committing old crimes, such as fraud and theft, but in entirely new ways. Historically, stealing 100,000 credit card numbers might have taken highly organized criminals months, even years, to accomplish. Today, one individual using tools freely available from the Internet can hack into a merchant website and steal the same number of cards (along with other identity information of customers) in a few seconds.

The second factor derives from the first. If software makes it easier and quicker to commit old crimes, the amount of money that would historically take one month to earn, now takes only a few seconds. This means the second factor is the simple financial incentive of getting more money for less effort. But it's not just about more money for less work; it's really about more money, period. In other words, the magnitude of illicit gains is also increasing, not just the speed at which the illicit gains are made. In 2001, nearly $2 trillion in transactions per day were transmitted by electronic funds transfer. An enormous amount of money exists primarily in electronic form, making the systems that transmit that money (or the information like credit card numbers that allows that money to be used) lucrative targets to say the least. A criminal that robs a bank can only carry so much cash and jewelry, limiting the total "take" of the heist. But when money is electronic, it doesn't weigh anything at all, allowing attackers to abscond with millions at a time without ever breaking a sweat.

The third factor in the explosive growth of attacks is the sheer volume of reported vulnerabilities in software. These vulnerabilities give attackers a plethora of avenues for exploiting systems of all types and flavors, ranging from enterprise applications such as Oracle and PeopleSoft, to home computers such as Apple OS X and Windows, to gaming systems and smart phones. Since 2000, the number of reported vulnerabilities increased 10-fold, with the U.S. Computer Emergency Response Team (CERT) noting more than 8,000 new vulnerabilities reported in 2006 alone.[13] With so much software in such disarray, it is hard to imagine, as I mentioned before, that more people are not involved in cyber crime.

The fourth factor is that security solutions intended to protect this software from cyber attacks are notoriously difficult to configure correctly (and to be kept configured correctly) or require significant amount of "care and feeding" to assure their efficacy. Regardless, oftentimes these solutions share the same software development and engineering shortcomings as the software they were designed to protect. Take, for instance, the most common security device, the firewall.

Firewalls are viewed as the low-water mark by cyber security professionals for just about any network connection; that is, if you need anything to protect yourself on the Internet, it's a firewall. A firewall is analogous to the front door of a house. Left closed and locked, the front door prevents outsiders from casually entering the home. However, for the house to be useful, the door must be opened on occasion; otherwise, people who want to get into the house can't, and people who want to leave are trapped inside. This means firewalls need to let connections through at some point, otherwise, people can't get anything done. Front doors are very good at stopping opportunistic thieves; they are less helpful in cases of more concerted attempts. If an attacker really wants to break in, the thief might take a sledge hammer or crow bar to the door itself. In other words, weaknesses in the door's construction can be taken advantage of; the same is true of firewalls. Because firewalls also rely on software to accomplish their function, they can share the same "structural deficiencies" as the software the firewall is attempting to protect in the first place.

> *Regardless, oftentimes these solutions share the same software development and engineering shortcomings as the software they were designed to protect. Take, for instance, the most common security device, the firewall.*

Of course, a firewall is far more complex than a simple front door. It can be very specific and detailed regarding who and/or what is allowed in and out of the "house," so to speak. For instance, a possible "front door policy" could be as follows: *Bobby can leave but only if he's going to Sarah's house and he's wearing a blue jacket. Sarah can't come in unless Bobby invites her*. These rules are indicative of what firewall rules do for network traffic. So the equivalent firewall rule set would be the following: *Bobby can go to Amazon.com but only if he uses HTTP to do so. Communication with Amazon.com will be allowed but only if Bobby makes contact with them first.* Simple, right? But as the number of rules increases, however, and the variations in individuals' behavior is accommodated to let people "get things done," the more difficult it is to keep track of who is allowed to do what, when. For even moderately sized organizations, firewalls can have hundreds of rules, each of which might be complementary or conflicting.

The front door analogy is rather fragile when discussing the true function and capabilities of a firewall, so it's helpful not to overextend the example. Sufficed to say, the complexity of firewalls makes them notoriously misconfigured and misused. They are arguably more burden than benefit for many and in the end give a false sense of security. If that weren't enough, firewalls could just simply be circumvented through vulnerabilities in other security products purchased by the organization to protect itself. An excerpt from the *@Risk* newsletter, published by the SANS Institute in October 2006, clarifies

---

This is a week for security flaws in security vendors' software: McAfee, Symantec, Computer Associates, and TrendMicro. If you thought you were seeing an increasing number of flaws in security vendors' products, you are correct. The flaws may have always been there, but the attacker community has targeted these products because they...are so often trusted and so rarely updated. They provide fertile territory for circumventing firewalls.

This is like buying a home security system like ADT only to have it randomly open windows without your knowledge or simply crumble when touched by a thief. And, to make matters worse, the firewall itself might be engineered in such a manner as to be a tool of a foreign government, providing privileged backdoor access to a competing nation's networks and the sensitive information or intellectual property contained therein. More on this scenario is provided later in the chapter.

All in all, whatever defenses might be available to protect users connected to the Internet do not serve as sufficient deterrent or a sufficient disincentive for would-be attackers. Now, this is not to say that firewalls, or even all the other possible security solutions one might use, are not good ideas. When used properly they can, to a certain extent, help reduce the risk of being connected to the Internet. But when 98 percent of companies use firewalls, 97 percent use anti-virus, and the number of organizations suffering from viruses, break-ins, and cyber attacks continues to increase year after year (in some cases more than a 65 percent increase from previous years),[14] the idea of using software-of-uncertain-quality in security products to protect software-of-uncertain-quality in everything else seems nonsensical at best.

The fifth and final potential contributing factor to the explosive growth in cyber attacks is the lack of cross-border coordination of law enforcement across disparate jurisdictional boundaries. In other words, unless there is already an agreement between two nations, and both nations share similar cyber crime laws (such as the U.S. Computer Fraud and Abuse Act), law enforcement agencies of one nation (such as the FBI) will have a difficult time coordinating with law enforcement agencies of another to prosecute cyber crime suspects. This is, in fact, the current "state of the art" in cyber law enforcement. As a consequence, the likelihood of being prosecuted under the U.S. Computer Fraud and Abuse Act (CFAA) is so remote for foreign cyber crime suspects that the law simply does not function as a sufficient deterrent to those participating in cyber crime activities.[15]

> *The likelihood of being prosecuted under the U.S. Computer Fraud and Abuse Act (CFAA) is so remote for foreign cyber crime suspects that the law simply does not function as a sufficient deterrent to those participating in cyber crime activities.*

There have been few successful prosecutions of foreign nationals that have broken into U.S. systems. The few prosecutions that have been achieved were brought about by tricking the suspects, who were stupid enough to visit the United States under pretense of collecting their extortion money, and arresting them upon arrival.[16] The level of coordination and resources required to track down and prosecute a foreign computer criminal in their country of origin, unless some sort of prior law enforcement agreement is established, makes it doubtful international cyber-prosecution will ever become commonplace. This makes computer crime laws least likely to influence those for whom the law was in part enacted. In fact, nations with the strictest cyber crime legislation, the U.S., Britain, Malaysia, and Singapore, have all experienced burgeoning cyber crime rates since 2001.

The lack of international coordination of law enforcement to combat cyber crime is being addressed to some extent by the European Convention on Cybercrime. The Convention requires participating nations to "establish laws against cybercrime, to ensure that their law enforcement officials have the necessary procedural authorities to investigate and prosecute cybercrime offenses effectively, and to provide international cooperation to other parties in the fight against computer-related crime."[17] The U.S. Congress ratified the Convention in 2006. This much is good. By ratifying the Convention, it shows the United States is willing to reach out and cooperate with other nations on the issues of cyber crime. However, of the thirty-four nations present at the ceremonial signing of the Convention in Budapest, Hungary, in 2001, only six have ratified the Convention. No major European country has yet agreed to be bound by the Convention's terms.[18]

The consequence of all these factors is that the number of people engaged in cyber crime as a full-time "profession" in Eastern Europe and Asia is skyrocketing. The anonymity and global connectivity afforded by the Internet, combined with weaknesses in software, lets cyber criminals engage in traditional crimes on a previously impossible scale in previously unthinkably short timeframes, and they can do so from across national borders or even from different continents entirely from the victims. No longer required to be physically present to commit a crime, the risk of capture and prosecution is minimal, if it exists at all. In short, only the stupid or the very unlucky are caught.

While increased effectiveness of law enforcement is certainly important to the issue at hand, the root cause of much cyber crime is negligently designed and implemented software that enables cyber criminals to exploit computer systems in the first place. Address the software quality and security issue, and cyber criminals and cyber attackers face a far more effective obstacle than unenforceable laws. Until that happens, the increasing involvement of organized crime only lends a more ominous tone to the situation and promises to worsen with time.

David Thomas, Chief of the FBI Computer Intrusion Section, stated in 2005, "We haven't seen a big move with the traditional Mafia groups to the Internet...not like we have with the Eastern European hacking groups. But as the money becomes more and more widely publicized, they probably will." And it is no wonder. Breaking into computer systems is now big business that has attracted plenty of predators to the feeding frenzy.

Weakness is an incentive to predators of all types, from the opportunistic to the ruthless. But if weakness gives power to those least responsible and most corrupt, as is the argument in this chapter, the advantage belongs to those with knowledge of software vulnerabilities. It seems reasonable, then, that a market should develop that trades in such advantages.

An Underground Market

There were villains, locked away for 12 years for robbing a bank of ten grand, doing time with drippy hippies who were doing 12 months for smuggling two million quid's worth of puff [marijuana]. I mean, work it out, mate. We're in the wrong f—king game. Drugs. Changed. Everything.

So goes the opening narrative of the movie *Layer Cake*, a story about a savvy business man whose commodity just happens to be cocaine. Some time during the 1970s, criminals realized there was far more money to be made at far less risk to themselves in trafficking drugs than in other forms of crime. Why risk 12 years of hard time for a paltry $10,000 stolen from a bank when millions could be made selling a simple weed? This type of math is not difficult to calculate or understand. Criminals were in the wrong game, and they knew it.

At some point in time during the 1990s, criminals came to the same realization regarding exploitation of software weaknesses as they did about the early days of drug trafficking: There is far more money to be made breaking into computer systems at far less risk than other forms of crime. Instead of learning from "drippy hippies" however, criminals learned from news stories covering teenage hackers who, with relative ease, broke into financial, government, and commercial networks. If the perpetrators were apprehended—and apprehension appeared to be a very big *if*—the criminal penalties were far less severe. Once again, criminals realized they were in the wrong game.

Software. Changed. Everything.

A case in point is the Phonemasters, a group of hackers who broke into the networks of MCI, Sprint, AT&T, and Equifax (a credit reporting agency), causing $1.85 million in losses. Members of the group also broke into the FBI's national crime database, had knowledge of which phones the FBI and the U.S. Drug Enforcement Agency were tapping, and forwarded an FBI phone line to a sex-chat number (incurring $200,000 in costs to the FBI). The mastermind of the Phonemasters, Corey Lindsly, was eventually apprehended and prosecuted simply because the Phonemasters got sloppy. Lindsly was sentenced to 41 months in prison.[19]

While 41 months is not necessarily insignificant as far as criminal penalties go, it is certainly much less than Lindsly would have served had he physically broken into each victim organization and certainly less had he caused millions of dollars in losses in some other situation. Secondly, if you were a criminal and you knew only 5 percent of cyber criminals are ever apprehended, how much would you be willing to risk for the kind of access Lindsly had to the FBI's and DEA's networks? Or any other network containing valuable information for that matter?

Weakness is an incentive for predators of all types, from the opportunistic to the ruthless. And weaknesses in software give predators wide latitude. Indeed, software vulnerabilities are the raw materials of cyber intrusions.[20] Exploiting the weaknesses of software to gain access to private and financial information is the new drug trade and as such has spawned its own market for services, product, and talent. Certainly there are savvy businessmen out there whose commodity is no longer cocaine, but software vulnerabilities. But how much to sell a newly discovered vulnerability for? This is difficult to answer.

In 2001, a small commercial company by the name of iDefense started buying software vulnerabilities from hackers for a few hundred dollars apiece with the intention of using the information to protect their clients from being exploited as well as informing software manufacturers of the weakness in their products. The hope was that by a legitimate company offering money for vulnerabilities, iDefense would bring to light software vulnerabilities that would otherwise stay undiscovered, or worse, discovered but remain a secret known and used by only a few. Over the years, iDefense has offered as much as $24,000 for specific vulnerabilities.[21]

In 2005, another security company, TippingPoint, started its Zero Day Initiative, which also paid "security researchers" for newly discovered vulnerabilities. At the time of this writing, Tipping Point offers approximately $1,500 per reported vulnerability, although the actual amount might be high as $10,000 for some vulnerabilities. In some ways, the practice of offering monetary reward by these companies is good. However, in many other ways, this practice is bad.

First, these actions are beneficial because they encourage hackers to share knowledge of discovered vulnerabilities with the general community so that vulnerabilities do not stay hidden. A software manufacturer cannot produce a patch for a vulnerability it does not know about. This practice is bad, because it can be easily copied by others with less noble intentions and far greater sums of money. Knowledge of a vulnerability could potentially provide millions of dollars in return for cyber criminals should they choose to exploit it as well as provide special and continued access to a computer system of choice. This means cyber criminals, like the drug cartels before them, are flush with cash, willing to pay significantly higher prices than legitimate companies or governments could possibly be willing to pay. Indeed, this appears to be the case.

The black market in vulnerabilities is thriving. Estimates based on U.S. government sources state that some vulnerabilities have been purchased for as high as $250,000 with the U.S.

government itself paying $50,000 for a vulnerability in an open-source software application.[22] The first evidence of this market was documented in 1994. Vladimir Levin, a Russian mathematician, purchased an exploit for $100 from a group of Russian hackers and proceeded to steal $10 million from Citibank. Levin was eventually caught and sentenced to 36 months in jail, far less time than had he physically broken into a bank's vault and walked away with the same amount. For the most part, Levin's actions were the first time anyone had heard of purchasing an exploit. It seemed interesting but not necessarily foretelling.

Another instance of a developing underground market for vulnerabilities occurred with the Windows Metafile (WMF) vulnerability in late 2005. The vulnerability allowed attackers to hijack vulnerable computers without the victim's knowledge simply by tricking the victim into viewing an image or picture file. A (still) anonymous researcher-turned-seller sold an exploit for the WMF vulnerability for $4,000 and is believed to have sold the exploit to multiple buyers.[23] The buyers' potential profit from purchasing this exploit is really only limited by their imagination. Installing spyware and adware without consent of the computer's owner is one possible avenue for leveraging this vulnerability. (Attackers can earn up to 10 cents per installation, resulting in $10,000 for just 100,000 installations.) Just as compelling, the vulnerability can also be used for conducting espionage against a specific company or government by surreptitiously installing specially designed software on vulnerable computers that captures information users type, view, send, and store. At the time of sale, the exploit was not known to anyone except the buyers and sellers. This kind of knowledge provides extraordinarily privileged access to systems around the world. Not bad for a $4,000 "entry" fee.

But the Windows Metafile vulnerability was only the tip of the iceberg. In December 2006, zero-day vulnerabilities for Microsoft's newest operating system, Windows Vista, were being sold at underground hacker sites for as much as $50,000.[24] According to a research paper released by Michael Sutton at iDefense Labs

---

We are seeing more signs of the underground's profit motive. Spam, spyware, adware and phishing attacks, while largely illegal, are fueled by the money they can generate. It is clear

that such attacks are no longer simply the work of misguided individuals, they are now well orchestrated attacks funded by organized crime. Given the profit potential in the underground, we can expect this market to grow.[25]

Knowledge of a victim's weakness gives power to those who would take advantage of that weakness. In short, weakness gives power. And a world-wide computer network full of weaknesses gives power to those least responsible and most corrupt. The power, then, belongs not to those with the weakness, but to those who exploit the weakness. And some people will pay handsomely to wield power over others, to get privileged access to millions of systems, and make considerable sums of money while doing so. How much would you pay to have unlimited access to your colleague's computer, your boss's computer, or to a competitor's network?

To be clear, iDefense and TippingPoint are not at fault for creating or even exacerbating the growth of the underground market for software vulnerabilities. They are incidental to the pricing process required for such markets to function. The underground market is responding as markets do; raw materials are being traded just as in any other market. What is disturbing is that there is little to control this market and the more money offered by illicit players, the more likely vulnerabilities that should be made known publicly simply will not.

Numbers Don't Always Measure

There is an interesting consequence to the growth of the underground vulnerability market, and it relates to how we measure security. For the longest time, the information security community has been focused on the *quantity* of vulnerabilities. The general model follows that more reported vulnerabilities means less security. Conversely, fewer reported vulnerabilities likely means greater security.

This focus was in part to bring attention to the lack of security in the information technology industry, and, yes, an undeniable ancillary incentive to sell more security products. The idea, of course, is to let the listener infer fear, uncertainty and doubt: "Look at how dangerous it is out there. Look at how many vulnerabilities there are! You really need our product/service/training." Whether it is Symantec, Checkpoint, or Cisco selling the message, the existence and growing number of software vulnerabilities is as much a fact as it is a not-so-implicit selling point for services, products, or training.

The information security community uses the quantity of vulnerabilities as a metric, and I am plainly guilty considering that I've referenced vulnerability statistics many times in this book. But the deeper question is why do we focus on them in the first place? The short answer is because it is all we have. Unlike scientists studying global warming, who may have a myriad of data points to consider and debate, the information security community uses the rather blunt and ultimately inaccurate measure of counting vulnerabilities as a means of gauging the severity of security problems. The problem with this measuring stick is that it doesn't really tell us anything empirically meaningful.

For the longest time, Apple could sit smugly and jeer at the enormous number of vulnerabilities discovered in its larger rival's software. Apple even based its 2006 marketing campaign partially on this derision. The inference was, of course, that Apple was "more secure" because the actual count of vulnerabilities in its software was less than Microsoft's. This was short-sighted. As Apple came to discover, it had plenty to worry about. In 2006, the same year as its famous marketing campaign of, "Hi, I'm a PC. Hi, I'm a Mac," we talked about in Chapter 2, "Six Billion Crash Test Dummies," Apple exceeded Microsoft in number of reported vulnerabilities (to refresh your memory, Microsoft had 157, Apple had 262). But do these numbers really matter? Yes and no. As it turns out, vulnerability statistics are also highly susceptible to the underground vulnerabilities market and not just to the popularity of a given software application or vendor, as discussed in Chapter 2.

Given the likely growth of the underground vulnerabilities market (no one knows for certain how big it actually is), one would expect, in time, the number of *reported* software vulnerabilities to *decrease*. Yes, *decrease*. That is, in the coming years, we should see a decrease in the number of weaknesses in software. Does that mean our systems are more secure? Not necessarily.

The decrease will most likely be due to the incentives attackers have in *withholding* knowledge about vulnerabilities from the market. By withholding information, attackers can potentially collect substantial profits by selectively selling vulnerabilities to multiple, but limited, buyers. This practice makes the underground software vulnerabilities market similar to the illegal arms trade because of what is being sold: the ability to wield power over others.

So the number of publicly reported vulnerabilities for a particular software application cannot be reliably used as a measure of security, risk, or anything else that sounds remotely objective. Apple is no better and no worse than Microsoft; Microsoft no better and no worse than Linux. Whichever has more or less vulnerabilities is a specious argument. If attackers keep knowledge of vulnerabilities to themselves, what good is the number of reported vulnerabilities? Secondly, patches are only made available for weaknesses that are *known*. By keeping knowledge of software weaknesses to themselves, attackers retain all the privileges and capabilities those weaknesses confer with a window of opportunity that is profoundly advantageous. Until someone is lucky enough—and ethical enough—to discover and report the exact same vulnerability discovered by the attacker, it could be years before a patch is distributed, finally stopping the attacker's access to vulnerable, but as of yet, unexploited computer systems.

Now, of course, there are plenty of problems with an underground economic model. One, it is based mainly on exclusivity. As with the WMF exploit, if someone deploys the exploit poorly, that is, should they blunder onto networks without properly cloaking themselves, the security community or the vendor might become aware of the vulnerability. In such cases, while the deployed exploit could still be relatively successful, knowledge of the vulnerability is no longer limited. Thus patches will likely be made available, and security solutions will be updated. Also the investment other buyers have made in the vulnerability might be lost depending on how quick they are to deploy their "solution" to the outside world—which brings up the second problem.

Vulnerabilities have limited lifetimes.

If the vulnerability is publicly known, it is, for the most part, not as valuable as when the vulnerability was secret. The return on investment is lower than expected. For certain, there are still plenty of systems that will remain unpatched for long periods of time; this has historically been the case. But even if the vulnerability is a secret, other un-related patches could *accidentally* alter the target systems in such a way as to minimize or entirely mitigate the undisclosed vulnerability. Such is the sloppiness of software. Even patches sometimes require patches. It is incumbent upon the buyer of the vulnerability, then, in order to make the greatest possible profit, to create the most efficient, timely, and well-crafted delivery vehicle by which to exploit the target system's weakness.

The counter to this market problem is to sell vulnerabilities to the smallest number of buyers at the greatest possible price, or better yet, auction the vulnerability off to the highest bidder. But auctions carry another set of problems.

First, the seller has no idea how talented the buyers may be. Second, buyers could have paltry knowledge of other sellers' talents. This means the seller could relinquish the vulnerability to a rank amateur, one with no ability to craft world-class exploits. Second, once knowledge of a vulnerability is shared with potential buyers, the sale price is instantly discounted because knowledge of the vulnerability is what buyers are paying for. In this instance, buyers must purchase on trust that "it's a really good vulnerability."

In effect, vulnerability buyers are purchasing within a situation of asymmetric information (the seller knows more than the buyer), which tends to suppress the asking price in the first place. It also makes auctions all but impossible given that while more buyers tend to raise the price, more buyers also bring the risk of the seller unintentionally disclosing too much information about the actual vulnerability. This could allow potential buyers to infer critical details regarding the vulnerability and thus exploit the vulnerability without paying the seller.

Of course, outside of auctions, the difficulty with selling vulnerabilities reliably in an underground market is potentially a self-correcting problem. As with the illegal drug and arms trade, hardened criminals do not take kindly to being cheated and will spend considerable resources to find the cheater and punish them accordingly. In other words, if the vulnerability is not as good as advertised, heads roll.

Regardless, the underground market for vulnerabilities is promising to all but the victims. As with any illicit market, it is uncontrolled, and law enforcement, while occasionally lucky, cannot successfully combat a robust collection of economic incentives. So long as software quality remains opaque and its quality non-standardized, and substantial profits can be realized, the underground market for vulnerabilities will thrive to the detriment of us all.

Fraud and Terror

The weaknesses in software and the money that can be attained by exploiting it are becoming more and more apparent, even to those who are relatively new to the game. Imam Samudra, the Al Qaeda chief in Indonesia, known as the "Bali Bomber," attempted to finance his bombing attacks through "traditional" forms of crime such as robbing retail jewelry stores. In one such instance, Samudra reportedly netted five pounds of gold and five hundred dollars. All told, the estimated gain from that single heist might have been somewhere around $17,000, although the actual amount is unknown.[26] Whatever the actual amount, Indonesian law enforcement officials surmised that Samudra was sufficiently dissatisfied with the results to look for more lucrative targets on the Internet to fund his activities.[27] Apparently much more satisfied with the results of hacking, Samudra wrote the following in his 2004 jailhouse autobiography under the chapter titled "Hacking, Why Not?":

If hacking is successful, get ready to gain windfall income for just 3 to 6 hours of work, greater than the income a policeman earns in 6 months of work. But, please do not do that for alone! I want to motivate the youth and Moslem men who are granted perfect mind by Allah; I want America and its cronies to be crushed in all aspects.[28]

Samudra's explanations in this chapter are not so much a "hacking how-to" as they are a course of study for aspiring hackers. It lists which websites to visit to learn how to hack, where to find mentors in online chat rooms, and how to conduct online credit card fraud and money laundering. According to Evan Kohlmann, an international terrorism consultant who analyzed Samudra's chapter, "This [chapter] is hacking for dummies. But in this day and age, you don't have to be an expert hacker to have a tremendous impact."[29] To make matters worse, Kohlmann, as well as other cyber-terrorism experts, believe the activities promoted by Samudra would become increasingly attractive for other terrorist cells in several regions around the globe. This belief proved rather accurate.

In 2007, the first case outside Indonesia to definitely establish a link between terrorism and cyber crime was brought to trial in Britain. Three men in their early twenties pleaded guilty to using the Internet to incite murder. On laptops seized by law enforcement officers, investigators found 37,000 credit card numbers along with the credit card holders' addresses, dates of birth, credit balances, and credit limits.[30] The suspects had acquired the credit card numbers by using a combination of phishing attacks and Trojan horse programs. A phishing attack takes the form of a fake email message that looks as if it were sent from a legitimate company such as eBay, PayPal, or Bank of America. The message might ask the user to "update your profile" and direct the user to visit a website that looks exactly like the legitimate company's website but is in fact owned by the attackers. In so visiting, the user is duped into providing sensitive information such as account information or account passwords. Attackers then use this information to access the victim's accounts.

A phishing attack might also direct the user to visit a bogus website made to look like the legitimate site in question, but instead of a form to fill out, the website contains software specifically designed to exploit weaknesses in the user's software on his home computer. If the user's computer does not have the latest software patches, it is infected with a Trojan horse (just one of the many kinds of malware) just by visiting the site. The user is none the wiser what happened. Once a computer is infected, the Trojan gives complete control over the machine to the scammers. Hackers can view what sites the victim is visiting, capture what the user is typing, and even potentially turn on webcams attached to the user's computer, viewing the user while they type or are engaged in various personal activities. After the computer is infected, it truly is no longer the user's computer, but the equivalent to a listening device for everything the user does on, near, and around the computer.

The British suspects were quite successful, making more than $3.5 million in fraudulent charges. The money was laundered through more than a dozen online gambling casinos. The laundered money was then used to pay for hosting jihadist websites (more than 180 domain names at 95 different web hosting companies), buy equipment such as global positioning receivers and hundreds of pre-paid mobile phones, and purchase more than 250 airline tickets.[31] Said one U.S. victim of credit card fraud, "I'm just mortified to think that my stolen information had any type of connection with terrorism." Sadly, it did.

This story illustrates that weaknesses in software, in addition to public ignorance regarding the severity of the situation, provide a lucrative avenue for terrorists to fund their activities. This situation is made that much more tragic because, unlike the illicit drug trade that finances itself from personal transgressions, terrorists can finance their agenda from the bank accounts of innocents.

> *This situation is made that much more tragic because, unlike the illicit drug trade that finances itself from personal transgressions, terrorists can finance their agenda from the bank accounts of innocents.*

This also illustrates that, contrary to popular belief, terrorists will most likely not opt to unleash a "holy digital war" focused on the destruction or disruption of commercial and national infrastructure because the effect would simply not be comparable to surreptitiously-placed explosive devices. The sad irony is a "cyber-terrorist attack" would be largely indistinguishable from routine software failure. Was it Al Qaeda or another hiccup in the software we are using? Such ambiguity is simply not a terrorist weapon. *Terror* is the objective of terrorists, not *fretfulness*. It is becoming clearer to anti-terrorist analysts and to computer security experts alike that terrorists' growing interest with hacking is based on nothing more than the acquisition of funds in addition to the complementary aims of collecting information about intended victims.[32]

While criminal and terrorist involvement in hacking is certainly cause for grave concern, perhaps more unsettling is the entry of nation states into the realm of hacking. If hacking no longer necessarily requires a technically competent person to assault an information system, it means, as Kohlmann stated earlier, that non-experts can be quite successful and have tremendous impact by breaking into websites and computer systems despite lack of technical knowledge (and even talent). But imagine what a truly technically competent person or a group of people could accomplish if they were trained, funded, equipped, and sanctioned by a government that desired to exploit weaknesses in an adversary's software. What if the incentive of software exploitation were not solely monetary gain, but market and national supremacy? What might be the impact then?

Information's War

The growth of state-sponsored cyber espionage and cyber warfare is perhaps even more disturbing than the growth in cyber crime. In large part, organized criminals and terrorist cells are rogue entities operating outside the defined laws and morals of civilization. Very few sanction or support the actions of these groups. In contrast, state-sponsored cyber espionage and cyber warfare can be undertaken with the blessing, support, and legal foundation provided by a nation state.

To date, more than 30 countries are believed to have Information Warfare programs, including India, China, Taiwan, Iran, Israel, France, Russia, Brazil, and the United States.[33] Information Warfare is a term used to describe activities involved in conducting cyber warfare and cyber espionage, such as stealing sensitive or secret information from a competing nation's computer systems; stealing intellectual property from commercial organizations; or potentially crippling a competing nation's information infrastructure, financial and banking systems, or national defense systems. Specifically, Information Warfare is defined as the "actions intended to protect, exploit, corrupt, deny, or destroy information or information resources in order to achieve a significant advantage, objective, or victory over an adversary."

In reality, Information Warfare is a murky term made all the murkier by its actions, actions that would otherwise be considered illegal by a nation state if perpetrated by any entity other than itself. This is what makes the growth of Information Warfare so disturbing—nations sanctioning activities its own laws clearly criminalize.

But the incentives for nation states to conduct these murky operations are perhaps just as compelling as the incentives for cyber criminals and terrorists, if not more. Global competition is the reality of the twenty-first century and "globalization" the word on every corporate executive's lips. Since the end of the Cold War, the power of a nation is judged more by the strength of its economy than by its military power.[34] As such, national security is, as former U.S. Secretary of State Christopher Warren stated, "inseparable from economic security."[35] In a globalized marketplace, therefore, nation states have a vested interest in the success of their companies, entrepreneurs, and enterprises.

> *Global competition is the reality of the twenty-first century and "globalization" the word on every corporate executive's lips. Since the end of the Cold War, the power of a nation is judged more by the strength of its economy than by its military power.*

While protectionist tariffs on imports are one manner by which countries attempt to (erroneously) protect their national businesses from competition, actively stealing intellectual property and trade secret information from foreign competitors is one method by which nations seek to gain a distinct marketplace advantage. Stealing intellectual property and trade secrets is far less expensive than deriving the information oneself, thereby saving the time and enormous cost of research and development. Also once that stolen information has been passed along to the foreign nation's companies and translated into manufactured products (which are typically exact replicas of the originals), the products can be sold at far lower prices than the original company's product given that the cost to the counterfeiter of "research and development" was never incurred in the first place.

As a result of globalization and increased competition in a globalized marketplace, trade secrets and intellectual property are more valuable than ever. And the United States, which has 10 times the amount of intellectual property as the rest of the industrialized world combined, is the principal target.[36] With so many competitors' computer systems connected to the Internet, so much intellectual property and trade secrets residing on those systems, and so many weaknesses in software making access to that information possible from a continent away, it is no wonder state-sponsored cyber-espionage is part and parcel of nations' competitive strategies.

Globalization is critical to expanding economic prosperity, yet the vast interconnection of networks using software rife with vulnerabilities introduces unprecedented risks to national and economic security. In 2001, former Defense Secretary William Cohen remarked

---

What is a code word that constantly is invoked if you're trying to streamline, get more efficient and downsize?
You outsource. We did a good deal of this in the Pentagon itself, but there has been an increasing acceleration on the part of businesses to outsource anything that's not regarded as a core competency in activities that were done in-house from the back office functions to logistics and production, and a company will often give its supplier privileged access to facilities and increasingly to its network so they can become an effective member of the team. But the suppliers are also electronically networked in ways that you have never even thought of. They themselves face pressures of outsourcing some of their non-core competencies. And so you have a series of a chain of trust being delegated to relationships upon relationships until you finally have complete strangers who are interconnected to your innermost working databases....

As this chain of connectivity grows exponentially, the number of weak links is going to grow even faster, and no one—I will say no one—is properly prepared to protect themselves in this emerging, embedded, networked environment. And so there are quite a few people who are working very hard to exploit your vulnerability.

Of the 30 countries with information warfare programs, China, Russia, and France are most brazen. After the fall of the Berlin Wall in 1985, the head of the KGB, Vladimir Kryuchkov, announced that his agents would be busier than ever with an enhanced focus on industrial and economic espionage.[37] This came after decades of proven successes in conducting espionage against the United States. As a case in point, the Soviets were so historically adept at espionage that Soviet military intelligence stole America's plans for an atomic weapon even before President Truman knew of the bomb's existence. More on the Soviets later in the chapter.

The former director of the French Intelligence directorate, Pierre Marion, stated quite publicly that he directed French intelligence forces to secretly collect and pass on to French companies information stolen from competitors in the United States and elsewhere.[38] "This espionage activity," stated *Messr.* Marion, "is an essential way for France to keep abreast of international commerce and technology. Of course, it was directed against the United States as well as others. You must remember that while we are allies in defense matters, we are also economic competitors in the world."[39]

But of the three, the People's Liberation Army (PLA) of China is most notorious for its information warfare efforts.[40] Starting (or at least becoming noticeable) in the summer of 2005, coordinated cyber attacks emanating from Guangdong province on the southernmost coast of China exploited weaknesses in software on U.S. government systems and has since expanded its attacks to other nations around the world. U.S. investigators assigned a code name to China's systematic and world-wide exploitation of computer systems: Titan Rain.

At first, cyber attacks emanating from Guangdong province could not be attributed to any group in particular. Such is the problem with identifying cyber attackers on digital networks. Attacks could be originating from one or more unrelated hackers in Guangdong province, or attackers could be sitting anywhere else in the world and simply leveraging hacked computers (of which there are many) within Guangdong as a pass-through—as is typical of hackers trying to hide their true locations. Frankly, it could be any number of possible scenarios, not just these two. The fact the attacks could be traced back to China revealed little about the true source.

The actual perpetrators of the attacks remained speculative until Shawn Carpenter, a security analyst at Sandia National Laboratories, did what official government entities were not permitted to do openly; he broke into the originating systems, thus giving investigators an idea of who the attackers might be.[41] Based on Mr. Carpenter's analysis, as well as contributions by other security analysts, the size, scope, discipline, and sophistication of the attacks pointed to one probable perpetrator—the PLA.

When confronted with this information, a spokesman for the Chinese government stated, "If there are such allegations then it is subject to further investigation."[42] In the vernacular of international politics, this statement is equivalent to the school yard retort, "Oh, yeah? Prove it."

Which we can't—not conclusively. It is hard to fathom that a state-sponsored intelligence activity that demonstrates such discipline and competence in its cyber attacks should be so clumsy as to leave a trail leading directly to its front doorstep. Nonetheless, evidence points strongly in China's direction. In recent years, writings from the People's Liberation Army call for the use of all means necessary to support or advance their nation's interest, including information warfare.[43] In particular, a book titled *Unrestricted Warfare*, authored in 1999 by two colonels in the PLA, argues that the spread of information technology and wide spread connection to the Internet has removed traditional boundaries to conducting war and expanded the arena of war beyond warfighters. "The new principles of war," states the authors, "are no longer using armed force to compel the enemy to submit to one's will, but rather using all means, including armed forces or non-armed force, military and non-military, and lethal and non-lethal means to compel the enemy to accept one's interests."

In essence, the philosophy of *Unrestricted Warfare* expands the traditional targets of warfare such as soldiers, tanks, and ships to include private citizens and commercial infrastructures.[44] More importantly, Chinese institutions are known to employ thousands of researchers and IT engineers drawn from universities and corporations to investigate methods to "exploit weak spots in technologically superior foes using computer attacks, electronic interference and other information warfare techniques."[45]

The strongest empirical evidence comes from Major General William Lord, Director of Information, Services and Integration in the Air Force's Office of Warfighting Integration and Chief Information Officer. Based on estimates from General Lord's office, approximately 10 to 20 terabytes of data have been downloaded solely from non-classified DoD networks to locations within China. To put this in context, 20 terabytes is roughly the same amount of printed material stored in the Library of Congress.[46]

In keeping with the philosophy stated in *Unrestricted Warfare*, attacks emanating from China targeted civilian corporations and infrastructures around the world (not just the United States) in any way related to military defense, including but not limited to automobile and aircraft manufacturers, telecommunications, oil, and food service companies and any company with personal information of employees related to those industries.[47] What are attackers looking for in all that data?

> *Chinese institutions are known to employ thousands of researchers and IT engineers drawn from universities and corporations to investigate methods to "exploit weak spots in technologically superior foes using computer attacks, electronic interference and other information warfare techniques."*

The attackers are looking within those terabytes of captured data for information to help them target specific individuals and then use weaknesses in computer systems and software applications to gain access to victims' computers. Typical avenues of attack take the form of unsolicited bulk email—otherwise known as spam—containing malicious content specially customized for the intended victim. In some cases, only a handful of employees at a company out of thousands of employees receive such emails demonstrating the focused and deliberate intent of the attacks. The content of the email message infects user's computer with professional grade spyware or Trojans (as mentioned earlier, Trojan Horses are software applications that act like "normal" software but that give remote access and other privileges to the attacker).

But spam is only one method of attack. Attacks can also take the form of exploitation of software weaknesses in specific network resources such as routers, web servers, and the databases connected to those web servers. While the attackers have appeared quite focused, they have also demonstrated themselves at times to be opportunistic and indiscriminate. In short, any computer system connected to the Internet and containing intellectual property worth protecting is a potential target. Even companies that believe they have nothing to fear or have nothing of value sophisticated attackers might want, could, if weaknesses in their software are exploited, become platforms by which attackers launch assaults against other computer systems.

Until recently, the successfulness of nation-state operations (let alone the success of cyber criminals) was under-appreciated. The actual level of success remains unclear however. The quote from Congressman Langevin at the beginning of this chapter highlights a new-found appreciation by U.S. policy makers for the significance of these activities as well as frustration with the lack of information regarding the extent and success of these attacks. It is no wonder. Estimates claim the U.S. Department of Defense detects only 4 percent of successful *friendly* intrusions; that is, when DoD systems undergo infiltration testing by qualified U.S. government contractors or employees to look for weaknesses, a large majority of the attacks go undetected.[48] But this isn't just the problem of the Department of Defense. In studies evaluating commercial and other government systems, the number of successfully detected intrusions is estimated at a *maximum* of 10 percent.[49] Even these numbers are difficult to substantiate because it is hard to tell how many intrusions go undetected. While a healthy amount of skepticism should be applied to these numbers, the situation brought about by systemic software weaknesses is clearly far from acceptable.

The Internet increasingly connects everything to everything else. This makes software increasingly connected and increasingly at risk irrespective of where it is located and who owns it. The intermixture of computer systems and the infrastructure it both supports and creates means the front lines of cyber warfare are in our homes, our hospitals, our companies, and our governments. Software weaknesses are the world's problem, not just the problem of the United States.

In the long view, countries should fret less about (but not entirely ignore) who may be perpetrating cyber crimes, cyber espionage, and cyber warfare and focus greater attention to the basic issue of software security: who creates this software and what effort goes into its manufacture. The grossly inadequate software that creates the Information Superhighway and the global digital neighborhood connected to it allows anyone to land on your front doorstep and break into your "residence" relatively easily. Unreliable and insecure software gives opportunity a whole new meaning. The empirical evidence of the last 20 years shows that stricter laws, both relating to cyber crime and intellectual property, have not provided adequate deterrent to attackers. In many cases, potential civil or criminal penalties are so rarely enforced that they are accepted simply as the cost of doing business for hackers, and a minimal cost at that. Those attackers protected and sanctioned by nation states to conduct cyber attacks will forever remain out of reach of these laws regardless. Indeed, we are too busy mopping the floor of cyber attacks to demonstrate sufficient initiative to turn off the faucet of insecure software.

So how did it get this way? How did we shift from talented but mischievous hobbyists hacking computers to make them "better" to full-fledged criminal exploitation and state-sponsored cyber espionage and warfare targeting national and economic infrastructures?

A simple theory might help.

> *Indeed, we are too busy mopping the floor of cyber attacks to demonstrate sufficient initiative to turn off the faucet of insecure software.*

The Theory of Broken Windows

In the 1990s, violent crime declined across the United States, but the decline was most significant in New York City. This was odd. There were a number of factors that contributed to the overall decline of violent crime in the United States (more jobs, less inflation, aging population, and so on), but New York City was the most difficult to explain. Despite a general drop in crime across the entire United States, New York City's drastic decline in violent crime occurred while the City's economy remained relatively unimproved, and drug dealing, while reduced, was still significant. Why, when all things being equal and distributed across the population, should the decline in New York City's violent crime rates be so pronounced? Did a large portion of New Yorkers suddenly find Jesus?

No. Part of the decline might be attributed to a controversial theory put forward in 2001 by Steven Levitt and John Donohue. The theory contended that legalization of abortion in the 1973 Supreme Court decision *Roe* v. *Wade* led to fewer low-income and disadvantaged women bearing children. Because social statistics demonstrate low-income and single-parent homes are among the strongest predictors that a child might have a criminal future, it seems reasonable that as greater numbers of low-income, teenage mothers opted for abortion, the incidence of crime would decline proportionally. To put it bluntly, fewer "disadvantaged" births mean fewer potential criminals. This makes sense, even if to some the theory is repulsive.

A decline in criminal activity would not happen immediately, of course. The effects would be delayed by 15 to 25 years after abortion's legalization. Decline would become noticeable only when the first group of children (minus those aborted) reached their late teen years—the years children are most likely to become involved in criminal activity.

In fact, this is what the numbers from Levitt and Donohue's analysis appear to demonstrate. Starting in 1988, those states that legalized abortion as early as 1970—such as New York, California, and Hawaii—experienced a 13 percent decline in violent crime compared to other states that had not legalized abortion prior to *Roe* v. *Wade*. By 1994 the decline in violent crime between early-legalizing states and late-legalizing states had expanded to 23 percent. This meant that those states that legalized abortion prior to *Roe* v. *Wade*—like New York—experienced a noticeable and persistent drop in violent crime ahead of those states that delayed legalization.

But while the number of *potential* criminals might have been falling across the nation and within New York City itself, the number of *actual* criminals committing violent acts was still a problem for New York City. The assertion by Levitt and

Donohue that the potential pool of criminals might be declining due to more abortions did not change the fact that plenty of violent crime was occurring in New York City in particular. In other words, despite the plausibility of Levitt and Donohue's findings, it did not account for the fact that New York City had plenty of people acting badly during the 1980s and 1990s who hadn't been aborted. New York City needed to do something about the problem of crime among the living.

New York City addressed this need by focusing on two apparently insignificant and irrelevant issues relating to violent crime: subway vandalism and fare-beating (avoiding payment of subway fares by jumping turnstiles). David Gunn, President of the New York Transit Authority from 1984 to 1990, and William Bratton, Chief of Transit Police from 1990 to 1992, were at first highly criticized for focusing on such seemingly trivial matters.

Anyone who can remember the New York subway system in the early 1980s recalls an appalling environment. Not only were subway cars filthy and in disrepair, the subway system itself was a dangerous place rife with hoodlums, thugs, and criminals. Robbery, rape, and murder found rich soil in which to take root within the New York City subway system. Just commuting to work was a dangerous proposition, let alone using the subway to enjoy some of the City's late night cultural events. Conventional wisdom of the day dictated addressing more serious crimes first like rape and murder, not vandalism and fare-beating. It would be tantamount to painting your home or organizing your closet while an invading army amassed outside your city.

> *At base, the Theory of Broken Windows states that smaller elements of disorder are invitations to more serious crime.*

Both Gunn and Bratton were inclined toward a theory known as the *Theory of Broken Windows*. The Theory of Broken Windows was formulated by two criminologists, George Kelling and James Wilson in the early 1980s.[50] At base, the Theory of Broken Windows states that smaller elements of disorder are invitations to more serious crime:

We used the image of broken windows to explain how neighborhoods might decay into disorder and even crime if no one attends faithfully to their maintenance. If a factory or office window is broken, passersby observing it will conclude that no one cares or no one is in charge. In time, a few will be throwing rocks to break more windows. Soon all the windows will be broken, and now a passerby will think that, not only is no one in charge of the building, no one is in charge of the street on which it faces. Only the young, the criminal, or the foolhardy have any business on an unprotected avenue, and so more and more citizens will abandon the street to those they assume prowl it. Small disorders lead to larger and larger ones, and perhaps even to crime.[51]

To Gunn and Bratton, then, combating graffiti and fare-beating was far from trivial in their plan for reclaiming the subways for the residents of New York City. To combat smaller elements of disorder, Gunn promoted a zero tolerance policy regarding vandalism and graffiti in 1984 called the *Clean Car Program*, while in 1990 Bratton streamlined the process of arresting fare beaters.

Gunn took the position that once a car was cleaned, repaired, or graffiti removed, the car should never be allowed to be vandalized again. This seemingly hard line stance abided by the Broken Windows theory. Graffiti and disrepair told citizens the subways were out of control. By removing graffiti and combating disrepair, the implicit environmental message broadcast to both passengers and ne'er-do-wells alike would be significantly different.

The *Clean Car Program* was a daily religious endeavor requiring cars to be cleaned during changeover (typically a small window of time of no more than two hours). To put this task in perspective and to understand the magnitude of this endeavor, the New York City subway system had more than 5,000 subway cars in use during peak hours at the time.[52] If a car could not be cleaned in that window of time, the car was removed from service until cleaning was complete. As a result, no matter how extensive graffiti or disrepair might be on any given subway car, graffitists would never see their "tags" on clean trains again, and vandals would see their handiwork consistently reversed.[53]

Gunn's program succeeded where previous attempts failed. Gunn attacked the basic motives—the incentives—of graffitists: They desired to be recognized. Take away the canvas (or more accurately relentlessly paint over it after a graffitist completed their work), and recognition, along with the feelings that go with it, disappear. But Gunn's program was based on more than just removing incentives. According to Kelling's account

---

Officials knew they were winning when graffitists who managed to penetrate yards tagged graffiti-covered cars rather than clean ones. Graffitists were learning the rules, rules which I believe had some moral force over and above the "Incentive" effect of never letting the graffitists show their work. A clean train is a clear sign that the rules forbid graffiti and the rules are being enforced.[54]

So again, the environment sends the message. Not only were incentives of graffitists taken away, but so too was the feeling of lawlessness—that no one was in control. But simply combating graffiti, though important, was not enough. Other elements of disorder remained.

Complementing Gunn's work, William Bratton took to combating the lawlessness of the subways in 1990 by focusing on reducing fare-beating, disorder, and robberies. Bratton's persistent theme to the public was that fare-beating, disorder, and robbery were linked together conceptually and sequentially. "You deal with one, you deal with all," was Bratton's message. By the time Bratton came into his position in 1990, fare-beating was out of control. According to Kelling

---

Farebeating created an additional sense of lawlessness. Popular scams included jumping over or backcocking (placing backward pressure on turnstiles and then slipping through them without paying); coin sucking (blocking the token receptacle with some foreign object and sucking out a

> *deposited coin); and most outrageously, disabling all token*
> *receptacles, holding open gates, and collecting fares from*
> *persons entering the system. During rush hours, this latter*
> *maneuver resulted in bedlam, with confused passengers being*
> *channeled to one gate and confronted by intimidating youths*
> *who extorted fares from them...Youths emboldened by the*
> *apparent anarchy attacked token receptacles...[and when]*
> *token receptacles were hardened with vaults, predators*
> *turned on tolltakers collecting tokens from the vaults,*
> *assaulting and robbing them.*[55]

The financial loss to New York City was estimated at $60 to $120 million per year. Kelling pointed out later in his analysis this cost did not account for the social costs of indignation, demoralization, and fear felt by city dwellers, paying passengers, and transit staff alike. Worse, these small elements of disorder led to a dramatic increase of more significant felonies in 1987. To some extent, this increase in felonies contradicts the expected decline in crime put forward by Levitt and Dohonue's abortion-crime theory. New York legalized abortions in 1970. By 1985, and especially by 1987 (17 years after legalization), there should have been an appreciable decline in felonies due to smaller numbers of criminally-inclined teenagers, not a steep increase. While an overall decrease in crime might have been true for New York State in general, it remains unclear to what extent the abortion-crime connection applied to New York City in particular. What was obvious was that crime was on the rise, and the culprit appeared to be an environment of disorder.

William Bratton combated fare-beating by stationing plain-clothes police near turnstiles at stations where fare-beating was worst. Groups of fare-beaters and scammers were handcuffed together for all to see and were quickly booked and processed in a mobile police station (a retrofitted city bus known as the "booking bus," complete with fax and fingerprinting capabilities). Again, critics thought this irrelevant to the task at hand. Catching "turnstile hoppers" is a far cry from the serious and imperative need for prosecuting rapists, muggers, and murders.

But what the police discovered in combating fare-beating was both unexpected and remarkable: nearly one in ten fare-beaters had outstanding warrants for their arrest on felony charges or was carrying weapons or drugs.[56] While a majority of fare-beaters were just ordinary citizens going along with the disorderly message of the environment, a small, but not insignificant percentage (10 percent) of fare-beaters were established felons or on their way to become felons. As fare-beating declined due to Bratton's simple but direct program, so too did serious offenses. In fact, analysis of that time period showed felonies declined by 75 percent and robberies by 64 percent.[57] The message Gunn and Bratton were sending was clear: Someone was in control again.

Like Levitt and Donohue's abortion-crime theory, Kelling and Wilson's theory was and is controversial. Debates still rage over how accurate these theories might be and what the statistics (and how the data was collected to derive the statistics) might actually be telling us. That being said, strong empirical support for the validity of the Theory of Broken Windows was provided by Northwestern University Political Science Professor Wesley Skogan in 1990. Merging more than 13,000 records collected from Houston, Newark, Chicago, and Atlanta, Skogan established causal links between disorder and serious crime and published his findings in *Disorder and Decline: Crime and the Spiral of Decay in American Neighborhoods.*[58] According to Skogan

> *Analysis of that time period showed felonies declined by 75 percent and robberies by 64 percent.*[57] *The message Gunn and Bratton were sending was clear: Someone was in control again.*

The evidence suggests that poverty, instability, and the racial composition of neighborhoods are strongly linked to area crime, but a substantial portion of that linkage is through disorder: their link to area crime virtually disappears when disorder is brought into the picture. Our data on urban neighborhoods is consistent...[and] can be tested. The statistical findings...are based on 30 areas in which

> *consistent questions about robbery victimization were*
> *included. In those areas, the effects of poverty, instability,*
> *and neighborhood racial composition were all about the*
> *same.... There were no significant paths between those*
> *social and economic variables and neighborhood crime,*
> *except through disorder.[59]*

Skogan concluded from his research that investigating neighborhood crime also required an investigation into the neighborhood's level of disorder given that disorder "both directly and through crime...plays an important role in neighborhood decline."[60] "Broken Windows," stated Skogan, "do need to be repaired quickly."

Based on Skogan's findings, the conventional wisdom of going after "real" crime and serious criminals rather than lesser offenses like graffiti and fare-beating would most likely have led Gunn and Bratton down a historically failure-ridden path. So can the decline of crime in New York City be attributed primarily to their use of the Broken Windows theory? Yes and no. While Levitt and Donohue's theory remains plausible and cannot be entirely discounted, their theory does not completely account for a decline in criminal activities among the "already living." Surely a lower total number of individuals inclined toward crime may mean fewer total crimes, but reducing criminal activities among those actively participating in crime is a different aspect of the situation entirely. Regarding this, the Theory of Broken Windows seems compelling.

Broken Upon Receipt

A broken window, as Kelling pointed out, serves merely as an analogy for disorder. A "broken window" could be literal, of course, but a broken window can refer to any form of disorder a community takes issue with, such as loud music, loitering, pan-handling, graffiti, vandalism, or, in cyberspace, defacing websites. And therein lies a possible connection between the theory of Broken Windows, the dramatic growth in cyber attacks, and our problems with software.

When hackers deface websites, they break into them by exploiting known vulnerabilities in websites' software and replace the sites' current text (along with any graphics such as pictures) with something far less wholesome than the original. Profanity and pornographic images are two favorite replacements, although more apparently innocuous forms of defacement are not uncommon. The message, "Hackers loooooooooove noodles," was a particularly funny defacement immortalized on thousands of hacked websites in 2001.

Sometimes websites are hacked for fun. Hackers leaving their "tags" behind is much like graffitists leaving their tags on a subway train or brick wall. In many cases though, websites are defaced to spread a political message among the public or to protest certain events such as when Palestinian and Israeli peace talks broke down in 2000 and hackers on both sides defaced each other's government websites—or when U.S. hackers defaced Afghan and Pakistani websites after September 11th.

Like graffiti and vandalism, website defacements can range from the funny to the hateful. In any event, whatever the intent of the attacker, the victim is almost always embarrassed, and the implicit environmental message is always the same: No one is in control.

In essence, the disorderly environment of the New York City subway system in the early 1980s sent a message to the general population that no one was in control. As the level of disorder increased, the level and frequency of crime escalated proportionately as more serious criminals were *attracted to* and *created by* the environment.

But if the message to New Yorkers in the early 1990s was a proclamation of a return to order, the opposite message continues to be sent through an endless stream of software defects to the global neighborhood of the Internet. *Weaknesses in software are broken windows, manifesting and communicating disorder into the environment.* Whether through website defacements, viruses, worms, spyware, cyber intrusions, or the specific events of Solar Sunrise or Titan Rain, each event sends a message to the general population that no one is in control of software or the networks software makes possible. It is no wonder, then, that

But if the message to New Yorkers in the early 1990s was a proclamation of a return to order, the opposite message continues to be sent through an endless stream of software defects to the global neighborhood of the Internet. Weaknesses in software are broken windows, manifesting and communicating disorder into the environment.

the number of people engaged in cyber crime as a full-time profession in Eastern Europe and in Asia is skyrocketing or that a terrorist like Sumudra strongly encourages hacking among his followers. Similar to New York subways in the 1980s, the level and frequency of disorder in the software world escalates as more serious criminals are *attracted to* and *created by* the environment.

Skogan's admonition that "broken windows should be repaired quickly" is irksome when viewed in the context of the software crisis, however. A natural inference from Skogan's statement is that to combat broken windows in software, software users should more aggressively patch their software. But this recommendation is misplaced and would only exacerbate the market imbalances noted in Chapter 2 which were that patches in part serve as a perverse incentive to software manufacturers. So as a recommendation, more aggressive patching is a less than satisfactory answer and distracts from the issue at hand.

To address this issue, we must look more closely at a fundamental assumption of the Theory of Broken Windows, which is that a house, building, or neighborhood is well-cared for at some point in time *and then falls into disrepair*. Neighborhoods decline because order is *lost* compared to an earlier more orderly time in the past. Unfortunately, the same assumption cannot be made regarding software. In the software world, the "structure"—whether an enterprise application, desktop word processor, website, operating system, or firewall—*is already in disrepair upon purchase*. The windows are already broken, and therefore the "neighborhood" was never orderly to begin with.

Whoever software consumers happen to be—a corporation, a government, or an individual—they expect that when they install new software, they are purchasing the equivalent of a state-of-the-art building. In reality, software consumers are purchasing software that is often the equivalent of a fixer-upper where the total number of broken windows is not known to either themselves or the seller. And there is no warranty on the structure that gives the buyer recourse should the structure not only fail, but completely collapse. In other words, consumers are *buying into disorder* and then must absorb the additional financial burden of preventing cyber crime and any subsequent losses stemming from their failure to do so.

> *In reality, software consumers are purchasing software that is often the equivalent of a fixer-upper where the total number of broken windows is not known to either themselves or the seller.*

This situation leads to a rather dysfunctional and misplaced attempt to solve the problem of software quality through frenetic software patching or acquiring elaborate defensive architectures comprised of firewalls, anti-virus, intrusion detection systems, and so on. While patching and security software arguably help mitigate problems with insecure software to a certain extent if religiously and relentlessly employed, empirically they have proven to be far too difficult to employ consistently even by large, wealthy corporations. Recall that nearly 40 percent of attacks originate from the networks of Fortune 100 companies, even though 98 percent have firewalls and 97 percent have anti-virus protection. As a result, the responses to disorder have proven inadequate at instilling or promoting the appearance of order in the cyber environment. And so the neighborhood declines more. Worse, these responses act as veneers over a systemic software engineering problem and do nothing to change the incentives or production practices of software manufacturers.

Nonetheless, more responsible software consumers, left with few apparent options, attempt to act much like David Gunn in his pursuit of reclaiming subway cars from vandalism by applying software patches as quickly as possible. Consumers believe they are fighting disorder. In fact, market participants are perpetuating it. Like Gunn, software buyers try to impose a zero tolerance policy and "paint over" software defects as quickly as possible. Today, many compliance regimes, such as the Payment Card Industry's Data Security Standard that imposes minimum security standards on businesses handling credit card information, require software patches to be applied to all affected systems within 30 days after the patch has been made available by the software manufacturer. At first glance, this practice makes sense because patching software is arguably still pragmatically better than not patching—until we look even deeper into the issue.

Blind Risk

While the theory of Broken Windows provides us with a bit more understanding of disorder and criminal incentivization, it is important to realize that there are major differences between the physical environment of New York City and the cyber environment created by software. The first major difference is this: Gunn could win the race against graffiti and vandalism. He and his fellow New Yorkers could *visibly see* which cars were and were not cleaned and repaired. *Disrepair was obvious.* Gunn could take away the motive of graffitists by removing their public displays.

In the software world, software consumers *can never win the vandalism race* because no one, not even the software vendor, has knowledge of how many items are broken within a given software application or how severe the application's "brokenness" may be. As a result broken windows, that is, software vulnerabilities, always threaten to appear unexpectedly, such as in 2004 when the Sasser worm, which exploited a vulnerability in the Microsoft Windows operating system, suddenly infected 500,000 computers in three days. Some of those infected machines belonged to the Sydney, Australia transit system. As a result, more than 300,000 commuters were left stranded because the trains, which depended on Microsoft Windows for their scheduling and operations, could not run on time. Events such as these only increase the sense of disorder and uncertainty in the environment. The fact that a software patch was available for the vulnerability is distracting to the issue at hand. The vulnerability, as well as the 6,000 other vulnerabilities discovered that year in thousands of software products, should not have been there in the first place.

While patching might *feel* responsible, while deploying anti-virus, firewalls, and intrusion detection systems might *feel* conscientious, these solutions *do not impede the message of disorder from being communicated and therefore cannot sufficiently mitigate more serious forms of crime.* Indeed, many security solutions are so complex, so inelegantly architected, or require such meticulous gymnastics to maintain their efficacy, it leaves consumers looking like The Keystone Cops tripping over their own feet. This hardly sends a countervailing message of order and discipline.

A lingering question might be how do broken windows get discovered and fixed in the software industry in the first place? In some cases, software vendors are lucky enough to discover the problems themselves, allowing them to save face by releasing patches or "uprades."

> *While patching might feel responsible, while deploying anti-virus, firewalls, and intrusion detection systems might feel conscientious, these solutions do not impede the message of disorder from being communicated and therefore cannot sufficiently mitigate more serious forms of crime.*

In all other cases, a group of hackers, security professionals, security researchers, or just some lucky guy happens to discover a problem within a given software application. The problem could be something as simple as "this thingy doesn't update properly" to "when I do this, I get privileged access to do really bad things." If the world is lucky, the discoverer will *only* inform the software vendor, and a patch will hopefully be issued quickly. If the world is not so lucky, the discoverer informs the vendor as well as simultaneously releases publicly available proof-of-concept code, which for all intents and purposes tells other "researchers" how to exploit the vulnerability. While the intent might be to shame software vendors into fixing the problem more quickly, this practice too perpetuates the message of disorder. Until a patch is released, every system with the discovered weakness is potentially at risk.

If the world is simply unlucky, the discoverer might choose to retain knowledge of the vulnerability and *not* inform the vendor. In this case, the vendor cannot produce a patch because it is unaware of the problem. The discoverer is free to exploit the vulnerability at his leisure. And finally, if the world's luck is absolutely abysmal, the discoverer sells the vulnerability on an underground black market where other talented attackers can build an arsenal of software exploits for which there is no known defense because there is no patch available. These attackers can enter most computer systems at will.

In any case, Gunn would be hard pressed to fix the New York City subway problem if vandals had more knowledge, more information, and greater access to the subway cars than his team did. The advantage in this battle belongs to those with knowledge of the weaknesses. Weakness gives power.

Remember, patches are released when the software vendor *knows* about a problem. If the software vendor does not know about a weakness, a patch cannot be generated. Gunn could repaint a subway car when graffiti was *observed*, and with every repaint, the environmental signals would inhibit further delinquency. In the software world, even with religious software patching, the network environment and the signals it sends to attackers *do not change*. The message is always the same: No one is in control of software—not consumers, not manufacturers, and certainly not law enforcement.

The second major difference between the physical environment of New York and the cyber environment created by software stems from the first. Requoting Kelling and Wilson,

---

Only the young, the criminal, or the foolhardy have any business on an unprotected avenue, and so more and more citizens *will abandon the street to those they assume prowl it*. [my italics]

In the physical world, abandonment of a declining neighborhood is demonstrated frequently, often in the context of "urban flight." The New York City subways were not only losing money from fare-beating, but from the tens of thousands of

New Yorkers who were financially capable of choosing other forms of transportation and chose to avoid the subway altogether, precipitating further decline. Disorder was obvious, and some New Yorkers voted with their dollars to avoid it.

But in the software world, people have no way of measuring or detecting the apparent safety of a digital neighborhood. The populace has no idea how many windows are actually broken, how many cars are truly vandalized, how much graffiti is on the walls, or how many hoodlums await more victims. Thus, the populace is robbed of the ability to accurately assess risk. Without visual cues, the populace is blinded to those things in the online world that would be obvious in the real world. Instead of refusing to go online, more and more people rush to connect to the Internet and hand their personal information over to companies with online services, thus creating ever more targets—and ever more incentives—for attackers. In the software world the population does not run away from danger as they would in the real world. The population runs headlong into danger and repeatedly bumps up against it like a drunk in the dark. An unaware population, combined with hobbled law enforcement, substandard software, and irrelevant or insufficient protective mechanisms, is a compelling incentive for cyber criminals.

Another major difference between the physical and cyber worlds is the ineffectiveness of law enforcement in the cyber world. This is not necessarily their fault. The environment puts law enforcement at a disadvantage. William Bratton had a number of advantages that current law enforcement officers prosecuting cyber crime do not enjoy. For one, Bratton had locality and detectability on his side and a long legal history of criminal prosecutions that provided precedent. Most of these advantages are absent in the realm of cyber enforcement. Attackers can sit a continent away, tunneling their activities through numerous servers, which practically guarantees their anonymity. Since cyber criminals do not need to be physically present at the scene of the crime, nor are they easily detectable, law enforcement is hard pressed to track down perpetrators of cyber crime. Whatever the case, a 5 percent conviction rate does not lend itself to meaningful deterrence. The outstanding question government policy makers must contemplate is how and to what extent law enforcement can best be used and whether a high conviction rate is meaningful whatsoever when the flood of software vulnerabilities continues to rise.

The final major difference, and perhaps most important, pertains to the depth of Gunn's battle against disorder. Gunn was not trying to fix fundamental engineering flaws in subway cars that could lead to the car's endangerment of human life; Gunn was addressing far more superficial issues. Subsequently, neither he nor his staff required deep technical knowledge of the subway car's undercarriage, steel frame, or electrical or braking systems. Gunn was attempting to stop vandalism, which is a problem at the surface, not at the structural core, of subway cars.

Imagine what might have happened if Gunn, instead of religiously painting over tags to stop graffitists, had to re-weld the steel frame of subway cars and "patch" intricate portions of the electrical system for which there was only shoddy or incomplete documentation available at best. Gunn did not need to deploy and coordinate complex "anti-graffiti architectures and event correlation engines" operated by a horde of eager third-party vendors as is so often the case among corporate software buyers in general. No, paint and patience represent all that Gunn required to support and ultimately win his battle.

In contrast, the elements of disorder in the software world are much deeper than simple graffiti and cannot be resolved with the equivalent of earnest re-painting or patching. The engineering shortcomings of subway cars did not promote graffiti or even crime. However, in the software world, engineering shortcomings are a clear and compelling invitation to further and increased disorder. The shortcomings of software manufacturing are what proliferate disorder and in so doing, proliferate crime. To change the message of disorder, then, systemic software manufacturing problems must be excused less by the market—and demands for improvement pursued more forcefully.

> The shortcomings of software manufacturing are what proliferate disorder and in so doing, proliferate crime.

The Theory of Broken Windows provides a powerful, if

imperfect, way of gaining insight into the software crisis. We used the analogy of Broken Windows to tie the concept and causes of disorder to the growing trend in cyber crime. We also used the analogy to illuminate the depth of brokenness in our software and to clarify that software patching and using firewalls (among other solutions) are insufficient to alter the implicit environmental message of disorder. Attackers are created by and attracted to disorderly environments; thus, it was only a matter of time before more serious criminals, and eventually organized crime, would be attracted to perhaps the most expansive and disorderly neighborhood in human history, cyberspace. The feeding frenzy made possible by insecure software has attracted predators of all types in the criminal food chain. And, as with any food chain, there is always a top predator.

Enter the Dragons

If cyber criminals, cyber terrorists, and cyber warfare did not augur ill enough for civilization's newest foundation, there is one final member to the cast of the story that must be illuminated. Dragons.

Dragons keep me up at night, not because they exploit Instant Messaging clients of teenagers or send infectious emails to unsuspecting victims, or give shout-outs on numerous defaced websites to popular hackers with names like Rain Forrest Puppy or Mudge. No. Dragons do not act like idiots. Dragons are consummate professionals and probably do not know they are called dragons at all. Typically dragons are from the former Eastern Bloc countries (though less true now), and they are usually highly-trained, former intelligence operatives or out-of-work mathematicians or software programmers living in a country with a defunct economy, a corrupt government, or both. They might even by backed by a legitimate government seeking plausible deniability in conducting cyber activities.

Dragons do not post on public newsgroups, do not release proof-of-concept code, do not write security tools for the cyber security community, and certainly do not bring attention to themselves. They do not inform vendors about discovered weaknesses in software, and they do not waste their time with commodity malware like worms, viruses, adware, or spyware.

Neither does a person aspire to be called a dragon. It is antithetical to what a dragon is. A hacker is, by the nature of his actions, a dragon.

Dragons are top predators, and there is little anyone can do to stop them. They retain their own arsenal of exploits, are well disciplined, patient, and focused. They might work for themselves, sell their services, or be employed by well-financed overseers.

Now, an immediate question that comes to mind is, do dragons actually exist, or are they a figment of imagination? They sound superhuman. Are they just another example of the relentless stream of fear, uncertainty, and doubt spread liberally by the risk-averse, paranoid members of the technology community? Probably not.

It is difficult to get an unambiguous picture about the reality of dragons for a number of reasons, not least of which is the historical unwillingness of organizations to report cyber intrusions and the well-documented inability of a majority of software users to reliably detect even the most clumsy cyber intrusions. Because of their professionalism, dragons leave few clues as to their activities or whereabouts even for the most experienced cyber investigators. What we know is largely by inference—except when we get lucky.

In 2003, a Ukrainian dragon was caught in Cypress after transferring approximately $15,000 from his Swiss account for vacation.[61] Alerted by the funds transfer, Interpol was at his hotel door roughly one hour later. Vladimir[62] happened to be running a website selling hundreds of thousands of stolen credit card numbers. The website and his more blatant selling activities are what tipped law enforcement as to his existence. Even dragons make mistakes sometimes.

After a forensic analysis of his computer systems, it was discovered Vladimir had more than 100 zero day exploits. A *zero day exploit* is an exploit for a software weakness for which there is no known patch or defense because the vendor has not been told about the vulnerability and security products have no reliable way of detecting and therefore protecting against the exploit.

To put the number of exploits Vladimir had in context, a talented hacker (for instance, a curious and gifted computer science graduate) discovers perhaps five to ten significant or critical software weaknesses during their peak years. Extraordinarily talented hackers like George Guninski and David Lichtfield, who use their talents to help software users defend themselves from malicious hackers, have each found upwards of 30 or more vulnerabilities...but their individual success is the exception. With more than 100 zero day exploits, Vladimir could have walked into just about any network of his choice. But he didn't. That is why he is considered a dragon.

Vladimir was part of a discussion by a number of security professionals during a Visa USA conference in 2003. Vladimir was caught because he was openly dealing in stolen credit card information on the Internet. However, dragons are thought to deal more frequently in intellectual property and trade secret theft and are hired specifically for acquiring that information. Without a public outlet to sell their contraband or connection to an illicit market (such as stolen credit cards), dragons remain frustratingly hidden.

So short of being human and subject to the foibles of humanity (greed, avarice, and so on), dragons represent a significant problem for the manufacturers and buyers of software. Weaknesses give power, and weaknesses in software give those who would wield that power global reach.

The only saving grace from dragons is they appear extremely selective with regard to victims. As mentioned previously, current security controls like anti-virus, anti-spyware, and yes, even firewalls, are like the doors and windows on your house. They might hinder casual attackers. However, if a professional burglar cases your house for weeks and knows the patterns of your opening and closing the windows and doors, or knows the very walls themselves contain manufacturing defects that allow undetectable entry, any potential deterrents become irrelevant. The professional burglar easily makes his way in. If a dragon comes to your "house," you probably won't even know it.

To be fair, the existence of dragons is still hotly debated. I asked multiple colleagues if they have ever heard of dragons. Many said no, so what I describe here can be rightly questioned and debated. To some, even mentioning dragons raises the hysteria index disproportionately and clouds the issue. *Risk mitigation* is the mantra of the information security community and the presence of super human hackers undermines the rational message of management and control of what we can manage and control. "We can't have people worrying about stuff that might never happen to them," is often the counterargument. I agree, but only to a point. Dragons are a very important aspect of the software crisis and force us to look more intently at root causes. Software will only spread more and in so doing, expand the disorder and weakness that attracts the full spectrum of predators. The Theory of Broken Windows teaches us this. If global interconnection allows hackers possessing even minimal skill to delve deeply into our networks, dragons are top predators whose appetite is limited only by self-restraint.

> *If global interconnection allows hackers possessing even minimal skill to delve deeply into our networks, dragons are top predators whose appetite is limited only by self-restraint.*

So putting the dragon debate aside, there is an even greater, more realistic, and foremost concern of national security advisors regarding the software crisis. The concern is this: It is difficult enough to detect when a well-intentioned software developer makes an honest mistake in software. *It is even harder to detect when an ill-intentioned software developer purposely does something evil.*

Evil Inside

In the first release of Microsoft Excel 2000, a special piece of code was embedded in the application unbeknownst to Microsoft program managers or executives. Microsoft failed to detect this piece of code before releasing Excel 2000 to the public. The special piece of code was not a bug, nor was it a little quirk, or even a special version of one of those annoying animated helpers like Clippy, the infamous dancing paper clip in Microsoft Office. It was an entire video game called Spy Hunter, a popular arcade game that consisted of driving an armored sports car and destroying as many enemy vehicles as possible all while enjoying the *Peter Gunn* theme. To launch Spy Hunter in Excel 2000, the user would need to follow a rather convoluted sequence:

1. Open Excel.
2. Highlight row 2000 and press TAB on column WC.
3. Hold the CTRL, ALT, SHIFT keys and select the Office icon with the mouse.
4. Spy Hunter starts up.
5. Arrow keys drive the car. Space bar shoots, "O" for oil slick, and so on.

This is perhaps the coolest Easter Egg ever. Well, except for FlightSimulator being embedded in Excel 97, Pinball in Word 97, "Elvis is not dead" in Lotus Notes 4.0, Tetris within the Mac OS X terminal, or yet another flight simulator embedded in Google Earth in 2007.

Easter Eggs are innocuous pieces of code hidden within a larger software application. Often Easter Eggs are simply hidden messages from the development team, a special sound or graphic effect, or a display of the program's creators with some type of animation (like scrolling credits). Other times, Easter Eggs are full-fledged applications within applications, as in the case of Spy Hunter within Excel 2000.

Easter Eggs touch directly on the greater issues of who is in control of software. Technically, an Easter Egg—like a software vulnerability—is a broken window. It sends a message of disorder about the structure and ultimately about the neighborhood in which the software resides. Who is in control? What is being written in software that goes undiscovered?

Both Microsoft and Apple have forbidden the inclusion of Easter Eggs by its software developers. But Easter Eggs keep showing up in software applications, although now, because of greater scrutiny, Easter Eggs are less full-fledged applications and much more obscure, looking more like software bugs than anything else—which itself is still not comforting. That code can be embedded into a larger software application without knowledge of others in the software

> *Technically, an Easter Egg—like a software vulnerability—is a broken window. It sends a message of disorder about the structure and ultimately about the neighborhood in which the software resides.*

manufacturing process is distressing and hints at another type of embedded software that is not so innocuous: a logic bomb.

The difference between an Easter Egg and a logic bomb is the intent of the software developer. A logic bomb is a specially crafted piece of software intentionally injected into an application during manufacturing that executes malicious actions at some later time on a victim computer when a set of one or more predetermined conditions are satisfied. In the case of Spy Hunter, the user needed to go to a predetermined row and column, hold down three specific keys, and click on a particular icon. Multiple conditions needed to be satisfied to trigger the game. As an Easter Egg, the embedded Spy Hunter game did nothing intentionally malicious to the user's system. In contrast, a logic bomb might work something like the following.

From the 1960s onward, the Soviet Union was stealing as much technology from the United States and Allied countries as they possibly could. They were very successful. Despite a backward economic model, unworkable economy, corrupt governance, and a notoriously unmotivated workforce, the Soviet Union somehow managed, functioning essentially as a third-world nation, to become one of the largest military powers in direct competition with the United States. For some political analysts on the outside of the Soviet system, the answer seemed to be found in the fact that perhaps socialism and Soviet communism was indeed an acceptable alternative to Western democracy and a free market. The real reason was far less dignified as Soviet intelligence agencies stripped America and NATO arsenals of just about every technical secret locked in a safe.

It was estimated that nearly two-thirds to three-fourths of the Soviet civil and military sectors were dependent on stolen information gathered largely through KBG-sponsored espionage, in particular through a KGB unit called "Line X."[63] The existence of Line X was discovered by the capture of a Soviet colonel, code named "Farewell," who described the unit's actions against Western targets. This program was so successful and Soviet theft of Western secrets so rampant that the White House was greatly perturbed. Something needed to be done. But what?

In 1982, President Reagan approved a CIA plan that would not only stop KGB theft of Western secrets, but ultimately sound the death knell of the Soviet Union itself by disrupting its dysfunctional economy. Instead of deporting many of the agents responsible for espionage against the United States, as was the practice, the U.S. National Security Council made the decision to "help the Soviets with their shopping."[64] In other words, the United States would not try to stop Soviet agents from stealing but allow them to steal the products they desired. Instead of providing normal functioning products for Soviet agents to steal, however, selected products such as computer chips would be specifically designed to pass Soviet quality tests only to fail in operation at some later, non-deterministic time.

Of critical importance to the Soviets in the 1980s was the creation of a trans-Siberian pipeline. The pipeline would provide much needed hard currency for the Soviets given that natural resources were primarily all that the Soviets had to exchange on the world market (Soviet products were so shoddy that economists thought Soviet factories were actually destroying, rather than increasing, the value of raw materials). The United States pressured Western Europe to refrain from importing natural gas from the Soviet Union because this hard currency would have further propped up the dysfunctional Soviet economy. Because Western Europe resisted U.S. pressure and was moving forward with their purchase, the United States needed to take another approach, one in keeping with President Reagan's approved plan.

One technology necessary for the success of the pipeline that the Soviets did not already posses was sophisticated software that controlled the pipeline's pumps, turbines, and valves. When the United States turned down the Soviets' request for the much needed software, the Soviets, true to their practice, sent a covert agent to steal the software from a Canadian oil company. This little feint on the part of the United States was important to keep Soviet suspicions to a minimum; the United States also needed plausible deniability for what was about to occur. The U.S., tipped off by an informer when the agent was going to strike, sent its own agents to embed into the pipeline software "extra software," which, at some later, non-deterministic time would cause the pumps, valves, and turbines in the pipeline to malfunction, causing pressures far beyond acceptable limits of the pipeline's joints and welds.[65]

The Soviet agent did indeed steal the maliciously modified software and sent it home to the Soviet Union. In 1982, the specially crafted embedded software was activated, causing "the most monumental non-nuclear explosion seen from space," vaporizing thousands of acres of Siberian forest.[66] The North American Aerospace Defense command (NORAD) supposedly went on alert because of the massive conflagration (that much heat in a single location is bound to get the attention of temperature-sensing satellites). Logic bombs can be very, very nasty.

At that point, the world was a very different place for the Soviets. Not only did the Soviets lose a substantial amount of much needed income, which among other things precipitated their demise, but the Soviets did not know which stolen software, which stolen computer chips, or which stolen products to trust and which to not. All of a sudden, the Soviet leadership needed to ask themselves, "which of the products also had logic bombs in them that would not just fail, but fail in such a manner as to catastrophically disrupt their economy or some other critical piece of infrastructure?" Twenty-five years later, not much has changed for the Russians—or anyone else for that matter.

Embedded malicious software is a global concern. In the age of globalization, software is written all over the world by people of varying loyalties and allegiances in networks with countless and often vaguely understood network connections. There is no telling for sure, what is in our software and what our software actually does in addition to its functions intended by the manufacturer. Now, we need to be careful here. We are about to tread on some very sensitive nationality issues in the next few paragraphs, so let's treat the next couple of moments together very delicately.

First, the qualification. I am a big fan of nation-state interdependence. I believe nations that are interdependent are much less likely to try to kill each other. I like the fact it takes more than 100 countries to collaborate on building my car or the jet engine in the commercial aircraft I fly in around the world. I like that the world works together to achieve economic vibrancy for larger and larger segments of the population. I like that globalization focuses on spreading the wealth around. Wealthy people tend to respect wealth, and the greater the number of wealthy people, the greater the likelihood wealth will be respected as opposed to denigrated. While it may be debatable how "happy" wealthy people are, angst beats abject poverty any day of the week.

That being said, interdependence is not a guarantee of good behavior when competitors are in pursuit of state or commercial interests. As we have seen earlier in the chapter, economic espionage after the fall of the Soviet Union has only become more rampant, not less. Loyalties, allegiances, and prejudices that might be inimical to another nation cannot be entirely ignored in the field of global competition. Competition, especially between nation-states, is vicious. If nations are willing to take something out of a competitor's network to gain a competitive market advantage (such as stealing intellectual property), who is to say they are not willing to put something in? In other words, not only could competitors sanction network-based attacks to steal trade secrets, state secrets, or intellectual property, but it is well within the rationale of competitor's strategies to also embed "extra features" in software that ruins a competitor's automobiles, mobile phones, financial systems, oil refineries, nuclear reactors, or defense systems. Software is everywhere in modern civilization. The choice of target is open.

> *If nations are willing to take something out of a competitor's network to gain a competitive market advantage (such as stealing intellectual property), who is to say they are not willing to put something in?*

The problem of malicious embedded code made by overseas software developers is subject to all sorts of nasty interpretations and innuendos, none of them complimentary to the indicted or the indictor. In short, why should a Pakistani trust a Hindi developer to write code that runs their infrastructure or a critical business process? Why should an American trust a Chinese developer to create code that operates their home computer and a majority of U.S. businesses? Why? Because in one respect interdependence matters greatly to everyone's continued welfare. The benefit of software produced in geographically disparate places and the wealth such production creates might simply outweigh any potential risk. But in another respect, the reality of global competition and the influence each country seeks on the global stage cannot be entirely ignored either. Competitors do not and have not always played fair.

Of course, in the big picture *where* code is developed is irrelevant. Location does not matter much in the digital age. A foreign national working within a U.S. company on U.S. soil could just as easily inject malicious code into a particular application regardless if the software development were off-shored, out-sourced, or in-sourced. For the right price from a foreign intelligence agency or organized crime syndicate, logic bombs could also be embedded by an employee of the same nationality as the software's buyers. The issue here is not necessarily to pick on a nationality or debate whether off-shoring is good or bad from a national security perspective. It is, in fact, a red herring. Our inability to know who is writing precisely what in software is unconscionable. It is not necessarily a nationality problem; it's a software manufacturing problem. No one is in control of software.

> *Our inability to know who is writing precisely what in software is unconscionable.*

And it is not just a proprietary software issue. Open source software, software whose source code is publicly available and can be evaluated by many, many sets of eyes, has been the victim of multiple injections of malicious code ranging from hacking tools, to application servers, to operating systems. (Open source software is discussed in more detail in Chapter 6.) It doesn't really matter how many eyes look at code, a talented developer can often develop software that no else understands and sometimes, as we've seen in the last chapter, generate code he himself cannot comprehend at a later point in time. That's the problem.

Software's complexity and our lack of control over software make it almost impossible to determine when software is *accidentally* defective, let alone *purposely* defective. The United States crafted products and software to pass Soviet quality and validity tests only to fail in operation. What's to stop the Chinese, or the Brazilians, or the Israelis, or any other nationality on earth, from doing the same to software that operates the national and commercial infrastructure of a competitor? What's to stop organized crime from financing college students'

> *Software's complexity and our lack of control over software make it almost impossible to determine when software is accidentally defective, let alone purposely defective.*

educations in order to plant the new graduates within software development companies writing code for financial institutions? How is one to determine if something malicious lives in 30 million lines of code? We find thousands of latent defects in software every year. How many undiscovered "features," how many logic bombs are awaiting activation?

Software gives self-interest a new destructive range.

Fixing Broken Windows

Software is now, by nature of its widespread usage, vast interconnection, and well-documented exploitation, a global dilemma on par with environmental disaster—but with more immediate effects. The ice caps might indeed melt, and the rain forests might disappear, but not for a time. Right now, however, terrorists, nation states, and organized crime are in growing numbers attacking governments, banking systems, commercial infrastructure, and private citizens through weaknesses in software. As highlighted in this chapter, the entry of profit-seeking, professional hackers into the field of play augurs ill for all of us. That attackers are potentially embedding logic bombs that we cannot detect into the systems we rely on for national and economic security is even more disturbing. Why *look* for weaknesses in commercial software applications, when you can just *create* them during manufacturing? Weakness gives power over us to those least concerned for our welfare.

It does not have to be this way.

The Theory of Broken Windows teaches us much about human behavior and how environmental signals affect it. Character is not so much a function of genetic inheritance or moral turpitude, though certainly these elements have something to do with it. Character, at least in the context of criminal research literature, is largely a function of environment. Anyone who has witnessed the behavior of a mob or the situation in the New York City subways can attest. Perfectly moral people can act immorally, and perfectly ethical people can act unethically if the environment says such behavior is permissible either by explicit or implicit messaging. The extraordinary growth of cyber crime as a profession in Eastern Europe and Asia is understandable in this context. Graffiti-ridden subways, vandalized

> *Graffiti-ridden subways, vandalized cars, filthy walkways, and software engineering blunders for which an endless stream of patches is required all send a similar message. Inattention and sloppiness invite disorder. And disorder invites greater disorder, even crime.*

cars, filthy walkways, and software engineering blunders for which an endless stream of patches is required all send a similar message. Inattention and sloppiness invite disorder. And disorder invites greater disorder, even crime.

But whereas the effects of disorder were once isolated to a particular city or neighborhood, the vast interconnection of insecure software gives local aberrations in personal character global consequences. A solitary street mugger in New York City is a problem solely for New York City, not for London or Tokyo. A solitary cyber criminal in Ukraine, however, is simultaneously everyone's problem. Hackers located anywhere in the world can exercise their character flaws in the networks of the United States, or any other country employing insecure software, without ever leaving home and with little fear of being caught.

Unfortunately for all of us, the consequences of poor software engineering send exactly the wrong environmental message at exactly the wrong time. The Internet is not a gleaming Information Superhighway upon which we can reliably support the needs of rapidly globalizing economies. It is a decrepit, vandalized neighborhood attracting more and greater predators. And, as has been argued in this chapter, insecure software has made it this way. As long as we respond to cyber disorder with any technique that ignores the shortfalls in software manufacturing—the very activity that creates broken windows—we will never satisfactorily alter the message of disorder or the malevolent activities deriving from it. As a result, our national and economic security will remain unclear and in the hands of those least responsible and most corrupt.

Weaknesses are always with us. It is part of the human condition. But we can structure our response such that weaknesses become a blemish outside, or at minimum beside, the success and accomplishment of manufacturing software. I believe we can structure our response as to make the potential strengths and innovations of software relevant and lasting instead of ephemeral and dangerous. But this will require incentives, incentives that to date have not yet materialized in the marketplace.

In the next chapter, we turn our attention away from the incentives of attackers and cyber criminals and investigate the first of a series of incentives to change status quo—the incentives created by government and industry regulation of the software market. Given the historic opposition of almost every industry to outside intervention in their activities, and the long record of ineffective oversight by some government agencies, it could turn out that just the mere threat of regulation of software might in fact be an important incentive to changing the message of disorder. It might also be, however, that the threat of regulation is overrated and that legal action against software companies is a far more compelling incentive. Chapter 5, "Absolute Immunity," takes a look at this second incentive.

CHAPTER 4

Myopic Oversight:
Blinded by Speed, Baffled by Churn

In Chapter 1, "The Foundation of Civilization," I stated that networks are simply a manifestation of software, but the power of software is greater than this. Software not only manifests networks; software is the ruler and sole adjudicator of cyberspace.

It is software that allows users to enjoy the Internet, and it is software that imposes a set of default rules on users whether they are aware of these rules or not. Email arrives at your desktop because software says it can. Messages are exchanged through Instant Messaging clients because software allows it. Music files can be played, shared, and copied because software makes such actions possible. The anti-locking brakes on your vehicle ensure a non-sliding stop because software dictates the behavior of the brakes. Nothing happens in cyberspace, and nothing happens on your home computer, mobile phone, or automobile, without the warrant and agreement of software.

In his book *Code and Other Laws of Cyberspace*, Lawrence Lessig solidified the authoritative notion of software. To summarize Lessig, "Code is law." In other words, software defines the very essence and fabric of cyberspace; software embeds certain principles and defines certain behaviors. It also limits—or enables—*people*. Without software, cyberspace and every activity and every "thing" within it would not be possible.

In the physical world, atoms are controlled and influenced by various laws of Nature: electrical, gravitational, quantum, and so forth. Humanity can identify these laws, understand them, and attempt to use them to its own benefit. Humanity cannot create new laws of Nature or alter discovered laws. In the physical world, we are *discoverers* of Nature's laws, not *progenitors* of them.

Cyberspace is a completely different ball game. The "atoms" of cyberspace are bits, and you can do anything to a bit that you'd like as long as you can write software that tells the bits how to structure themselves, what the bits represent, and what the bits should do. There is only one law in cyberspace: software.

If the physical world were like cyberspace, scientists could make a helium atom weigh as much as an elephant or change the gravitational constant of the universe for each individual person so that Jenny Craig, Weight Watchers, the South Beach Diet and every other diet program on the planet were all made irrelevant. Would you like to weigh 120 pounds and be a size four? Or would you like pecs of steel and six-pack abs? Well, let me mix together some software and...viola! There you go.

So far as we can tell, Nature's laws are predictable and unalterable. This is beneficial. Consistency in Nature's laws allows us to construct and test planetary rovers on Earth and have them operate reliably on Mars. Consistency of Nature's laws allows engineers to design bridges, cars, and homes without worrying about the location in which these things will be used. If the laws of Nature changed arbitrarily, it would make the universe a considerably more confusing and unstable place. Yet this is exactly the current state of cyberspace.

Not only do the laws of cyberspace change based on software version, but the laws of cyberspace change based on each software manufacturer's notion of what the law should be. In fact, laws might not only be different, they might directly contradict each other. Worse, as we discussed in Chapter 3, "The Power of Weaknesses," rouge software developers can inject new laws into cyberspace, superseding—and even over-writing—laws already widely adopted. If software is law, however, this makes those who write software *legislators*.

This is a critical realization.

No other laws created by humanity and that govern or impact the breadth of human endeavors are subject to less analysis, oversight, or evaluation than the laws imposed by software. And no other group of people that so widely influence the success of our endeavors are held blameless, undergo less examination of qualifications or so thoroughly evade public scrutiny. Immunity merely breeds irresponsibility.

This chapter investigates the history of software regulation (and lack thereof), expands on the lessons of crash test dummies from Chapter 2, "Six Billion Crash Test Dummies," and broadens our perspective on software manufacturers' legal and regulatory insulation by comparing it with some unexpected markets that enjoy far greater oversight.

The Law of Churn, the Decree of Speed

Ninety percent of security threats exploit known flaws in software, yet software manufacturers remain immune to much, if not all, of the consequences.[1] Imagine if 90 percent of individuals were able to commit felony acts by exploiting known weaknesses in the laws of the state? Or imagine if 90 percent of scientists could arbitrarily change the laws of Nature in their favor and to your detriment? Who would tolerate this situation or the individuals who exploit it?

The quality of "software law" is as critical to the function of cyberspace—and the protection of those who use it—as constitutional laws are to the viability of government or Nature's laws are to the stability of the universe. As long as software manufacturers continue to enjoy immunity from liability, accountability, and oversight, they have few compelling incentives to provide meaningful protection to those that use and buy software.

The best of software manufacturer's intentions—free patches, trustworthiness programs, security evangelism, and so on—distract from the issue at hand. Better software is their responsibility to make, not our responsibility to repair. When these "best intention" programs fail to alter the predominate environment of disorder discussed in Chapter 3, software manufacturers have and continue

> *Better software is their responsibility to make, not our responsibility to repair.*

to shrug their shoulders. The world is writing gargantuan checks to subsidize software manufacturer's insouciance.

The lack of oversight of software manufacturers is understandable but entirely indefensible. The rapid adoption of technology has sheltered software, making it a moving target difficult to pin down, constrain, or control. Any attempt at limiting software's innovations and innovating power has been met with howls of protest. However, history has shown that whenever a technology has come to impact society as a whole, a degree of control has been necessary to limit its more deleterious effects regardless of countervailing arguments. Society has rarely tolerated immunity for long no matter how beneficial the person, group, technology, or industry may prove.

The rapid overturn of technology is known as *churn* and was popularized in part by a 1997 *Wired Magazine* article titled "New Rules for the New Economy."[2] Churn has proven itself a compelling and persistent concept in the technology industry, so much so that *Wired Magazine* codified it as the *Law of Churn*.

The Law of Churn dictates that "churn topples the incumbent and creates a platform ideal for more innovation and birth. It is *compounded rebirth*. And this genesis hovers on the edge of chaos." In short, innovation is a disruption. Constant innovation is perpetual disruption that brings relentless renewal and growth. Churn is not for the fainthearted, weak-willed, risk-averse, or stodgy old-world business people. Churn is vogue. And as it just so happens, it is part of the natural ecology of the planet. *Wired* goes on to say, "As we know from recent ecological studies, no balance exists in nature; rather, as evolution proceeds, there is perpetual disruption as new species displace old, as natural biomes shift in their makeup, and as organisms and environments transform each other."

In 1997 this sounded quite insightful—indeed, compelling. Applying ecological principles of species-replacing-species to the technology environment seemed to qualify and even justify the notion that rapid overturn was the only viable path for the New Economy. The quicker the innovation, the faster the churn. Churn was good, but the *speed* at which churn occurred was even more striking.

In Austin, Texas, it was noted that businesses with the shortest lifespan also had the fastest-growing number of jobs and the highest wages. These facts seemed to hold true for any city or county seeking to partake in the technology revolution, especially in Silicon Valley, the cradle of technology. "The sustained vitality of a complex network," said *Wired*, "requires that the [Internet] keep provoking itself out of balance. If the system settles into harmony and equilibrium, it will eventually stagnate and die."

So there you go. Churn and live. Be fast or die.

But speed, as it turns out, was and continues to be largely an excuse both for creators and buyers of software. Speed certainly has advantages in a highly competitive market, but it offers absolution to the swift, which is rarely deserved. In *Crossing the Unknown Sea, Work as a Pilgrimage of Identity*, David Whyte makes important observations about speed:

Speed in work has compensations. Speed gets noticed. Speed is praised by others. Speed is self-important. Speed absolves us. Speed means we don't really belong to any particular thing or person ...and thus appears to elevate us above the ground of our labors. When it becomes all-consuming, speed is the ultimate defense, the antidote to stopping and really looking. If we really saw what we were doing ...we feel we might not survive the stopping and the accompanying self-appraisal. So we don't stop, and the faster we go, the harder it becomes to stop.

In other words, speed is the excuse for not doing what we should be doing, not saying what we should be saying, not looking for what we should be looking for. By inhibiting the speed of technology, we fear "it"—the profits, goodness, innovation, whatever—just might disappear, that the benefits so loudly espoused by so many, might truly be as ephemeral as the technology itself appears to be. Perhaps it is truly not worth the tremendous efforts required to keep the whole thing going, but we are too scared to slow down to determine if this is true or not. So we don't slow down, and the faster we go, the harder it becomes to rationalize why we should slow down at all.

Speed and technology in the modern era are practically synonymous. But speed has consequences. Not only has speed promoted irrational innovation, but improper oversight. Speed is the ultimate defense used by the software industry to prevent us from really looking at what we are buying; rapid adoption of technology has been our own excuse for tolerating the "shockingly sloppy" software produced year after year. So long as the software industry remains fast and makes newer versions available quickly, we have historically turned a blind eye to their issues and therefore failed to prosecute carelessness we would never tolerate in any other industry.

> *So long as the software industry remains fast and makes newer versions available quickly, we have historically turned a blind eye to their issues and therefore failed to prosecute carelessness we would never tolerate in any other industry.*

David Whyte makes another important observation about speed, "...speed by itself has never been associated with good work by those who have achieved mastery in any given field. Speed does not come from speed. Speed is a result, an outcome, an ecology of combining factors in a person's approach to work; deep attention, well-laid and well-sharpened tools, care, patience...."

And this observation seems to prove rather accurate for software manufacturers seeking to decrease their time to market. Speed in the software industry is a thing in itself, and it is all-consuming. Before the first version of a software application is out the door, the next version is already under development. Yet developing and replacing software at a rapid pace is not a result of professionalism as David Whyte illuminates but a singular rationalization to compete with others who demonstrate an equal disregard for quality, deep attention, and sincere proficiency. But the fault does not rest on software manufacturers alone. Speed has also been an excuse for software buyers to overlook what software actually does *for* us and *to* us. As such, we lack a certain amount of intimacy with a technology that touches us more every day.

Intimacy requires a certain amount of transparency and reflection and the time to employ both. Intimacy requires a period for evaluation, consideration, and an accounting of those who wish to be intimate. If anything, we are not intimate with our software though software's involvement in our private and sensitive information increases and deepens daily. We are not intimate with the very thing that is most intimate with our identities and existence in cyberspace. We cannot touch software, we cannot evaluate it, we cannot even seem to control it. Yet it touches *us*, evaluates *us* in a myriad of different algorithms, and determines what *we* can and cannot do from the simplest mouse movement to trying to print a document. The angst and unease created by this asymmetry of intimacy becomes more and more apparent, yet we feel inexorably pulled forward by the momentum and speed of technology adoption.

As citizens of civilized and law-abiding nations, we demand transparency into how our governments formulate, create, and enact laws because of the special relationship government has in our everyday lives. It is more than reasonable to demand the same transparency from manufacturers that formulate, create, and encode the laws comprising the foundation of our civilizations. Churn and speed are no longer acceptable excuses to do otherwise.

Free Hands Have Consequences

If speed is an "antidote to stopping and really looking at what we are doing," it is understandable then that speed might be used as part of an informal, even unconscious decision-making framework. Speed has that effect. It blurs our vision to anything not moving at the same velocity so we become partially blind and make decisions that are rationalized by that partial blindness. Until 1997, speed and rapid technology adoption was the informal policy of the United States. The Clinton Administration changed this.

Speed—and the implicit absolution that comes with it—became formal policy.

In 1997, the Clinton White House released a document titled "A Framework for Global Electronic Commerce" that states, "For electronic commerce to flourish, the private sector must *continue to lead* [my emphasis]. Innovation, expanded services, broader participation, and lower prices will arise in a market driven arena, not in an environment that operates as a regulated industry."[3]

This is very much a "hands off" policy. Government is rightly concerned that incorrect intervention might hamper a fledgling industry and frankly curb American dominance in the market. The last thing any national leader would want to do is undermine economic competitiveness, especially when your nation already enjoys a substantial and healthy lead. This is understandable.   •

Further liberty was given to the software industry by another statement within the same White House document, "Existing laws and regulations that may hinder electronic commerce should be reviewed and revised *or eliminated* [my emphasis] to reflect the needs of the new electronic age." The message from the White House was clear: "We won't mess with you. In fact, we will help you as much as we can."

This was as responsible a statement as the White House could make at the time. In essence, the White House gave the software industry *carte blanche* to innovate and drive technology as fast and as hard as the entrepreneur spirit would allow. It resulted in an amazing explosion of wonderful and not so wonderful inventions. However, the continued freedom extended to software manufacturers has resulted in the proliferation of software that regularly fails security, stability, reliability, and quality measures. While the White House statement, "We won't mess with you," reflects a pro-innovation stance, the resulting effect has been more in line with Guy Kawasaki's proclamation, "Don't worry, be crappy."

Innovation is certainly desirable, but innovation without accountability—at least at some point in time—is troublesome. Not only would there fail to be any oversight of software in the 1990s, but technology in general would proceed largely unhindered by government involvement. Worse, as technology proliferated, government purchasing power actually diminished as a greater number of companies came to the market seeking software to run their corporate infrastructures. Suddenly, this made government purchasing requirements less effectual in the marketplace.[4] There were plenty of commercial companies out there willing to purchase software that did not consider, recognize or think applicable the same security needs as defined by government stipulations, and there were a growing number of software manufacturers more than willing to sell to them. Given that IT expenditures world-wide is currently estimated at $1 trillion, even the U.S. government's considerable spending power has been substantially diluted by such market demand. As a case in point, in 2007 the U.S. Office of Management and Budget organized all federal buyers to aggregate their federal buying power—$70 billion—to persuade hardware and software vendors to abide by greater security measures.[5] However, this amount compared against the global market for

IT represents roughly 7 percent of total world wide IT expenditures. While not insignificant, it is not compelling either since 93 percent of the market might perceive different or lesser security needs as the United States government.

In retrospect, the White House document was created at a time when the full scope and consequence of software-driven systems was unclear. Churn was the compelling message, not responsibility. Considering the broad readership of *Wired Magazine*, the love affair with the theology of the New Economy, and the cultural zeitgeist at the time, myopia is entirely understandable. Why get in the way of the inevitable progress of technology? What could possibly go wrong? It is hard to imagine that NATO's concern about the software crisis in 1967 was not mirrored by the White House some 30 years later. Nothing in the software industry had improved in the interim.

> It is hard to imagine that NATO's concern about the software crisis in 1967 was not mirrored by the White House some 30 years later. Nothing in the software industry had improved in the interim.

In a January 7, 2000, turn-about, President Clinton declared war on cyber-terrorism, promising $91 million for a program that would "offer college scholarships to students in the field of computer security in exchange for their public service afterward."[6] This program proved to be less than successful. The problem was not that the United States needed more computer security experts to act as guards, but incentives for better software manufacturing practices to address the question of why guards and security products were needed in the first place.

In February 2003, the Bush Administration tried its hand at cyber security policy. President Bush released "The National Strategy to Secure Cyberspace," and while this document at least *mentions* the need to address software vulnerabilities,[7] the software industry remains largely unaffected by accountability, liability, or oversight. The Bush Strategy document goes on to say, "Federal regulation will not become the primary means of securing cyberspace...the market itself is expected to provide the major impetus to improve cyber-security." But as discussed in Chapter 2, the market is not inclined to demand security directly from software manufacturers but seeks security from a bevy of third-party applications meant to counterbalance the failures of software manufacturers. The market is looking in the wrong place. To secure cyberspace requires improving the software that comprises it, not obfuscating it with further technologies that are themselves comprised of software. It is imperative any policy statement should account for this. The Bush strategy document does this to some extent but misses by too wide a margin.

The Bush strategy document states, "The Department of Homeland Security (DHS) will *promulgate* best practices and methodologies that promote integrity, security, and reliability in software code development." DHS will also "*promulgate* processes and procedures that diminish the possibilities of erroneous code, malicious code, or trap doors that could be introduced during development." But neither DHS nor any other government entity is tasked with holding software manufacturers responsible for any of the best practices or methodologies.

It is understandable to offer a friendly hand to software manufacturers to invite them to become better educated about developing more secure products, but the industry is far enough out of its infancy to be a major player in the economy and in national infrastructure. If software is going to play in the big leagues, it can surely play by big league rules. Accountability, and not just information sharing, is certainly well within reason in this context.

> The assumption that government, by involving itself in the software industry, can do nothing except screw up the industry is as irrational as saying the software market will automatically correct itself.

At base, policy makers assume markets will *eventually* provide the right incentive for software manufacturers to produce higher quality and more secure software. Yet since the Clinton and Bush documents were released, software has only gotten worse and the problems of national and economic cyber-security more intertwined and complicated. The assumption that government, by involving itself in the software industry, can do nothing except screw up the industry is as irrational as saying the software market will automatically correct itself.

But let's back up for a moment. So far the discussion has assumed that oversight will improve the situation if only given the chance. We need to be clear whether regulators, and the way regulation is currently undertaken, necessarily solves the kinds of problems introduced by inadequate software engineering practices and what might actually need to be done to change the status quo.

X-Rays Show More Than You Think

One federal institution that has attempted to challenge the insulation of the software industry is the U.S. Food and Drug Administration (FDA). Although the challenge is relatively small, limited primarily to software in medical devices, it is a challenge nonetheless.

Interestingly, it is the 1976 amendment to the 1938 Food, Drug, and Cosmetic Act that allows the FDA to oversee and regulate medical devices. The amendment was passed after thousands of women were injured by the Dalkon shield intrauterine device (IUD). Under the 1976 amendment, a medical device is defined as an "instrument, apparatus, implement, machine, contrivance, implant, in vitro reagent, or related article, including any component, part, or accessory...intended for use in the diagnosis of disease or other conditions, or in the cure, mitigation, treatment, or prevention of disease, or intended to affect the structure or function of the body." This is very broad language.

Medical devices soon lost their simplicity as mere tools when sophisticated software was added to interact with doctors, diagnose diseases, administer treatments, and guide patients. The broad definition of a medical device allowed the FDA to regulate any software used for medical purposes or used to make medical devices unless the FDA saw fit to exempt it. But in the 1980s the FDA's attempt to regulate software was far from successful. In fact, it was abysmal. Software vendors practically snickered behind the FDA's back. It took tragedy to bring about any meaningful change. It also took yet another act of Congress.

The 1990 Safe Medical Device Act was passed due to massive radiation overdoses to cancer patients by the Therac-25, a linear accelerator developed by Atomic Energy of Canada Limited (AECL) to destroy tumors while minimizing damage to surrounding healthy tissue. Six patients died.[8] A detailed account of the incident, summarized in part here, was written by Nancy Leveson from the University of Washington.

The Therac-25 was quite different from its predecessors, the Therac-6 and Therac-20. In terms of efficacy, the Therac-25 could deliver 25 million electron volts (MeV) compared to 6 MeV and 20 MeV, respectively, for previous Therac versions. The higher energy generated by the Therac-25 allowed the system to take advantage of a phenomenon called *depth dose*. As energy increases, so too does the depth at which radiation builds up. In other words, higher energy allows the system to target tumors deep with the human body while sparing damage to tissue above the tumor.

But the critical distinction between the Therac-25 and previous versions was the primary reliance on software to perform critical safety checks. Whereas the Therac-6 and Therac-20 constrained software with independent electrical and mechanical systems, software was the sole ruler and adjudicator in the Therac-25. Fail safe electrical and mechanical systems were not present in the Therac-25. A similar bug, which caused the Therac-25 overdoses, was also found in the Therac-20; however, non-software-related controls in the Therac-20 prevented catastrophic overdoses. Unbelievably, safety analysis by AECL failed to include the Therac-25's software in their evaluation and testing procedures despite the Therac-25's singular reliance on software to provide safety controls.

To read Nancy Leveson's entire description of the Therac-25 incident is to be maddened and appalled. Patients received anywhere from 16,000 to 27,000 rads (radiation absorbed dose) during their treatments. To put these numbers into perspective, Chernobyl exposed the surrounding population to 10 rads, a therapeutic dose of radiation for cancer treatment is somewhere around 200 rads, and the nuclear fallout in Nagasaki exposed its victims to 400 rads.[9] Five hundred rads will cause death in 50 percent of those exposed if medical treatment is not received immediately. Of course, the length of time and area of exposure is also a considerable factor when comparing these numbers. Whereas victims of Chernobyl and Nagasaki experienced whole-body exposure over the course of months and years, cancer patients received radiation over a period of seconds to very specific locations on their bodies. At 16,000 to 27,000 rads, patients were literally scorched by the Therac-25 in addition to experiencing all the pain and suffering that comes with radiological overdose.

A 61-year lady undergoing thyroid treatment near her neck experienced burns to her chest and shoulder. Her oncologist noted matching reddening on the patient's back "as though a burn had gone right through her body." Indeed it had. In an East Texas Cancer Center a male patient that was being treated for the removal of a tumor from his back felt like his "arm was being shocked by electricity and that his hand was leaving his body." To quote Leveson directly

---

Over the weeks following the accident, the patient continued to have pain in his neck and shoulder. He lost the function of his left arm and had periodic bouts of nausea and vomiting. He was eventually hospitalized for radiation-induced myelitis of the cervical cord causing paralysis of his left arm and both legs, left vocal cord paralysis (which left him unable to speak), neurogenic bowel and bladder, and paralysis of the left diaphragm. He also had a lesion on his left lung and recurrent herpes simplex skin infections. He died from complications of the overdose five months after the accident.

AECL, when confronted with hospital reports, refused to believe it was caused by the Therac-25; however, AECL could not confirm, substantiate, or validate its own device, reporting on more than one occasion an inability to determine the problem, or worse, stating the problem was identified and corrected without adequate evidence of actually doing so. Therac-25s that were involved in overdose incidents were often returned to service without proper determination of cause. Given the abysmal software design and implementation errors, it is unlikely even AECL knew what their software was doing. The only thing that could have made the whole scenario worse was if the Therac-25 were connected to a network.

According to Leveson, the FDA responded impressively to the Therac debacle, considering how little experience the FDA had with software-enabled medical devices. However, the Safe Medical Device Act opened the door for more adequate oversight by the FDA in the 1990s. The FDA still had much to learn, however, and was still not quite ready to deal with the software industry's greatest defense: speed.

Don't Slow Us Down, We Have Lives to Save

In 1994, the FDA issued regulations for software that managed blood banks. Due to the threat to public safety posed by HIV/AIDS, the FDA felt it necessary to ensure that faulty software did not taint the blood supply. Besides, a blood-type mismatch can kill a person within 15 minutes. Software that managed blood banks needed oversight, so the FDA laid down more specific rules that came into direct conflict with the speed paradigm.

Two articles, one by *Wired Magazine* and one by *Reason Online*, took particularly defensive positions in favor of the software industry, outlining what appeared to be valid, reasonable arguments. The *Wired Magazine* article was titled "Since When Does the FDA Regulate Software?"[10] *ReasonOnline* simply titled their article "Software Pirates."[11]

Whereas software evolves rapidly and sometimes changes daily according to the user's needs, as the arguments went, the FDA is slow, rigid, and cannot possibly move faster than market-driven technologies. Blood management software manufacturers found they could not submit a new version of their software given that the FDA had not yet approved the earlier version. "Knowing the hoops [software manufacturers] would have to jump through," said *ReasonOnline*, "software manufacturers [were] less inclined to enhance their products in the first place." *ReasonOnline* went on to state, "Better software improves the blood supply; slowing the process down could cost lives."

Rational enough arguments. The message seemed fairly clear: By slowing down software manufacturers and impinging on their innovative natures, the FDA was threatening lives, not protecting lives. In other words, be fast or die, literally. In response, the FDA stated it was not trying to be burdensome, just abiding by their responsibilities. Don McLearn, spokesman for the FDA in 1994 stated, "With safety, there is sometimes a cost, but I think most people would agree that it's a small price for safe blood."

According to *Wired Magazine*, however, "...this better-safe-than-sorry approach doesn't wash with the software manufacturers, who say the FDA clearly needs a better understanding of what software is." In fact, despite the condescension, the FDA might understand perfectly "what software is" and be unwilling to give special dispensation to innovation for innovation's sake. An underlying question might be, then: Are software manufacturers truly so innovative that each new version of blood bank software promises to save hundreds of more lives than the previous version, or is innovation simply a market tool used to compel companies to purchase new products even if they might not need them? In the end, whereas slowing the process down *could* cost lives, faulty software in blood bank applications *does* cost lives.

But *ReasonOnline* went on to state that the FDA "gets bad publicity if something it approves hurts someone but none if someone dies because of regulatory delay." And this is true, going slow is due to the simple legal reality the FDA, and most organizations, are subject to. A defect in a non-existent medical device or procedure is difficult to litigate. While the potential loss of human life due to a product delayed by regulatory activity is certainly saddening, *actual* loss of human life is maddening. The critical lapse in the observation put forward by *ReasonOnline* is that the FDA is not insulated from accountability and public scrutiny; the software industry is. Subsequently, software manufacturers can aggressively promote speed untroubled by consequence; the FDA enjoys no such luxury and therefore must act more responsibly. Immunity breeds irresponsibility.

> While the potential loss of human life due to a product delayed by regulatory activity is certainly saddening, actual loss of human life is maddening.

This little spat illustrates the pervasiveness of the speed paradigm in the software industry and the disbelief, even condescension, directed toward those who do not "buy in" or insist on the rather reasonable desire to slow down. The arguments of churn, speed, and innovation make anyone who wishes to impose oversight feel antediluvian at best and obstructionist at worst.

Discovered Only After the Damage Is Done

Despite this little spat, the FDA has made progress since 1994. In 1996, the FDA released Quality System Regulations (QSRs), which *mentions* software as a regulatory requirement. The QSRs in turn led to the publication of the "Guidance on the General Principles of Software Validation" in 1997. The Guidance document states

---

This guidance recommends an integration of software life cycle management and risk management activities. Based on the intended use and the safety risk associated with the software to be developed, the software developer should determine the specific approach, the combination of techniques to be used, and the level of effort to be applied. While this guidance does not recommend any specific life cycle model or any specific technique or method, it does recommend that software validation and verification activities be conducted throughout the entire software life cycle.[12]

The FDA considers software validation to be "confirmation by examination and provision of objective evidence that software specifications conform to user needs and intended uses, and that the particular requirements implemented through software can be consistently fulfilled." Knowing how much evidence is enough is left to the discretion of software manufacturers, however. The FDA states that "in large measure, software validation is a matter of developing a *level of confidence* that the device meets all requirements and user expectations for the software automated functions and features of the device." So the Guidance document does not necessarily say *how* software validation is conducted by the manufacturer, only that it *should* be conducted.

The FDA stops short of specifying a quality rating system on medical devices similar to the five-star rating on automobiles. In fact, much of the software validation process is left to the good intentions of the device manufacturer with little if any requirement for external objectivity. The entire software validation program appears largely a documentation exercise providing minimal accountability to the FDA should something go wrong. And if something does go wrong, as in the case of Multidata Systems, 10 years and 21 deaths can ensue before the vestiges of accountability appear.

To be fair, since the FDA QSRs have been engaged, medical device recalls due to faulty software increased from six in 1996 to more than 80 recalls in 2004. Twenty-two devices were recalled just in the first four months of 2007. But the fiasco with Multidata Systems represents the anguish that many software buyers experience attempting to hold software manufacturers accountable.

Like AECL, Multidata Systems manufactures medical devices used in treating cancer. And like AECL, faulty software led to radiological overdoses. What complicates the matter with Multidata Systems, however, is that physicians were able to enter instructions into the system, which the x-ray machine did not properly interpret. This was partly the fault of the hospital and physicians. It was also partly the fault of the software, which did not properly constrain how users could enter information. Patients received doses ranging up to double the intended amount—not nearly as astronomical as the Therac-25 overdoses, but lethal nonetheless.

While the physicians were indicted for second-degree murder, patients have been unable to hold Multidata Systems accountable in court.[13] This was despite repeated warnings issued to Multidata Systems by the FDA for continuing to manufacture medical devices that threatened public health. During an inspection of Multidata Systems in approximately 2002, the FDA found that

Multidata failed to establish, maintain and follow procedures to control the design of the radiation treatment planning software to ensure the specifications were met; failed to establish and follow procedures for taking preventive and corrective action; failed to establish and follow procedures for investigating all complaints; and failed to adhere to other standard good manufacturing practices. In addition, the firm failed to identify the root cause of software code problems when brought to its attention.[14]

In 2003, the FDA finally filed an injunction against Multidata Systems forcing it out of the radiation therapy market. To have the injunction lifted, Multidata must improve its design and manufacturing methods; upgrade its record-keeping mechanisms; and retain a medical-device design expert to inspect the company's manufacturing activities, check over its software code, and provide evidence of such back to the FDA.[15]

The AECL and Multidata scenarios highlight the two fundamentally opposed philosophies between the FDA and the software manufacturer's mindset. Imperfection does not sit well with the FDA given that it is often blamed when it approves something that ends up killing or hurting people; imperfection costs lives. In the software industry, however, imperfection is not only expected, but part and parcel of the innovation mechanism. The FDA is unwilling to tolerate unsatisfactory development practices when it even hints at endangering human life. In comparison, some software manufacturers appear much more comfortable with it.

Jim Albertine, a lobbyist for a software manufacturer, stated during the FDA's attempt to regulate blood bank software, "The FDA has to show that there is a real risk involved in using this software, and they haven't." This statement only solidifies the notion that software users are crash test dummies. If it is difficult to rationalize software safety for medical devices in defense of our physical lives, how much more difficult will it be to rationalize protection of our digital selves to other software manufacturers? How many lives did it take before the automotive industry stopped blaming human error? How many lives will it take for software manufacturers? Should our morality be based on simple arithmetic? Some software manufacturers appear more than happy to risk your well-being in the pursuit of innovation for innovation's sake and the profit derived from it. The problem is, these manufacturers are only discovered after the damage is done.

Knobs of Unknown Origin

As much progress as the FDA has made, its challenge to software manufacturers is small with limited collateral effect. The nature of the software industry is making it more and more difficult for the FDA to oversee effectively. First, the number of medical devices employing software increases yearly as does the complexity of the software. The FDA cannot possibly cope. To provide some modicum of control, the FDA allows device manufacturers to shortcut the approval process via "pre-market notification."

Products that are radically different from anything in the market go through the FDA's "pre-market approval" process that requires formal scientific reviews and tests. Pre-market *notification* permits device manufacturers to attest to their development and manufacturing processes without FDA testing or field trials. Pre-market notification is reserved for products that are *not* radically different from devices already in the market. For instance, if x-ray machines were already a recognized category of device by the FDA, other medical device companies could introduce x-ray machines through the pre-market notification process. In fact, Multidata Systems used the pre-market notification process.

Not only are more devices employing software, but each iteration of a device introduces more software that might not be suitably robust. Bob Morton, former head of the FDA unit in charge of radiation-therapy equipment stated in 2004, "...devices [in general] are being released before they're ready."[16] This meant that the software had not been thoroughly tested before being released into the stream of commerce. Mr. Morton declined to name specific companies, but this speaks to the overwhelming lead software manufacturers have in befuddling those who would hold them to task.

The second aspect that makes it difficult for the FDA to oversee software effectively is the growing adoption of general purpose computer hardware (like personal computers) for medical devices. This adoption allows device manufacturers to use off-the-shelf software, that is, software that is ready-made and available for sale, lease, or license to the public.[17] For instance, Microsoft makes a version of Microsoft Windows XP that can be embedded in products like automated teller machines (ATMs). Embedded XP is an example of off-the-shelf software.

The use of off-the-shelf software is compelling. Not only does it reduce overall system development costs but it involves less development time because software can be bought instead of developed from scratch.[18] In a market where speed is all-consuming, employing off-the-shelf software makes sense. Yet there are nuances, if left implicit, that are problematic.

Off-the-shelf software immediately makes the software industry's dysfunction the FDA's headache—not that the FDA can do anything about it. Licensing agreements are a significant source of immunity for software manufacturers (discussed in more depth in Chapter 5, "Absolute Immunity"), that indemnifies the software vendor from just about any accountability whatsoever. This creates a chasm between standards imposed by the FDA and the need to abide by those standards. In essence, while the FDA can attempt to oversee medical device manufacturers, it cannot oversee, control, or realistically restrict manufacturers of off-the-shelf software. In light of this—and in recognition of their limited sphere of influence—the FDA demonstrates a delicate touch when addressing the use of off-the-shelf software in medical devices. In fact, the FDA is incredibly lenient almost to the point of creating a loophole in their own requirements. The FDA document, "Off-The-Shelf Software Use in Medical Devices" states

---

The use of the off-the-shelf software in a medical device allows the manufacturer to concentrate on the application software needed to run device-specific functions. However, off-the-shelf software intended for general purpose computing may not be appropriate for a given specific use in a medical device. The medical device manufacturer using off-the-shelf software generally gives up...control, but it still bears the responsibility for the continued safe and effective performance of the medical device.[19]

In other words, you can use someone else's potential mistake, just rationalize and document it. Given that medical device manufacturers must be prodded into assessing their own software, it is unlikely they will be able to effectively assess the quality of another manufacturer's software, especially if source code (the human readable version of computer instructions) is unavailable or documentation is incomplete or non-existent. While the FDA retains its ability to hold the device manufacturer accountable, the deeper layers of software remain insulated through disclaimers that disclaim all meaningful warranties and therefore are unaffected by FDA requirements. This means that potentially only a small subset of all software running on the device is subject to FDA review, even though defects in any portion of the entire software on the device might endanger the patient through a latent defect.

But the nuances go from the uncomfortable to the disturbing. In another FDA document titled, "Guidance for Content of Premarket Submissions for Software Contained in Medical Devices," the FDA states

---

Some or all of the software contained in a software device may have been obtained by the submitter from a third party. The type and quality of documentation that accompanies this software can vary considerably. Software for which adequate documentation may be difficult to obtain is referred to as Software of Unknown Pedigree or "SOUP."

It may be difficult for you to obtain, generate, or reconstruct appropriate design documentation as described in this guidance for SOUP. Therefore, we recommend that you explain the origin of the software and the circumstances surrounding the software documentation. Additionally, your Hazard Analysis should encompass the risks associated with the SOUP regarding missing or incomplete documentation or lack of documentation of prior testing. Nonetheless, the responsibility for adequate testing of the device and for providing appropriate documentation of software test plans and results remains with you.

SOUP. It doesn't get much more lenient than this. Or does it? Each page of the document is labeled, "Contains Nonbinding Recommendations." It is one thing when an auto manufacturer acquires plastic knobs and buttons from a shady mom-and-pop shop in Brazil, but the nature of software is such that the addition of, or change in even a small piece of code not only may detrimentally affect the entire system, it can cause catastrophic failure. Knobs of "unknown origin" tend not to weaken the viability of the vehicle as a whole. Software of unknown origin, however, adds to the law of the system and therefore either strengthens the total system or undermines it.

What is perhaps most interesting is what is *missing* from the FDA's guidance documents. The FDA leaves much to the discretion of software developers without articulating a standard for the software developers themselves. It is as if there were a standard for medical practice, yet no qualification for becoming a doctor...or even a technician. There is no requirement for licensure or certification to work on medical software, including life-critical medical device software.[20] Self-regulation is acceptable as a least burdensome approach if the "self" that is being regulated is disciplined and competent. Such characteristics are difficult to corroborate in the software industry.

> Self-regulation is acceptable as a least burdensome approach if the "self" that is being regulated is disciplined and competent.

If lobbyists for medical software manufacturers are reticent about oversight, the rest of the software industry is positively repulsed by the idea. In truth, the FDA cannot regulate the whole software industry, nor should it. The discussion so far simply illuminates difficulties facing regulatory bodies in overseeing software production.

To be fair, many medical companies have already taken steps to improve the safety and reliability of their products—partly because some companies see the humanity through the speed and the churn and partly because they know that increased software flaws might prompt greater FDA regulation. In reality, the threat of regulation is only meaningful when the threat of further regulation is possible. This threat is not wasted on others.

We'll Be Compliant, Later

An industry that has been trying to avoid expanded regulation is the already heavily regulated financial industry, in particular, credit card companies such as Visa, MasterCard, American Express, and so on. Cyber crime is big business. Trafficking stolen credit cards is big money, and digitized card numbers stored in software rife with preventable defects is too enticing for attackers of all stripes, nationalities, or political slants to ignore, as discussed in Chapter 3 at length. The problem for the credit card companies is that concerted (and successful) attacks against financial systems elevate the losses experienced by banks. These elevated losses, when high enough, also tend to draw the attention of government because the health and well-being of banks is important for the nation's health and well-being.

In an attempt to reduce losses and avert greater government scrutiny, the credit card companies have tried in earnest to stop the monetary bleeding. In September 2006, Visa, MasterCard, JCB, Discover, and American Express standardized their disparate cyber-security requirements under a single standard known as the Payment Card Industry Data Security Standard (PCI DSS), referred to simply as "the PCI standard," or just PCI.

Under PCI, companies that accept, transmit, or store credit cards must abide by 12 stringent categories requiring such things as installing firewalls, encrypting stored and transmitted card holder information, and documenting system processes.

PCI exists not only to mitigate massive financial losses due to cyber-attacks but to avoid legislation by Congress as the former Chief Information Security Officer of American Express pointed out, "Remember, the reason the PCI standard exists is to avoid legislation from Congress."[21] It is no secret that corporate America considers self-regulation, rather than government involvement, the solution for information security failures, but self-regulation must be effective to preclude government intrusion.[22] But with incidents of massive credit card number theft like TJX[23] in 2006 and CardSystems[24] in 2005—each individually accounting for approximately 40 million stolen credit cards and millions of dollars of fraud—government intrusion may be inevitable. The credit industry released its security standard in 2000, more than half a decade prior. Incidents of this magnitude should not be happening, but is there more to the story?

If any industry could self-regulate, goes the thinking, it is the credit card industry. They have the money, the resources, and the commercial clout. Unlike the FDA where court injunctions are realistically their only meaningful option for punishing non-compliance, credit card companies can simply cut off the ability of chronically non-compliant companies to accept credit cards. This would cripple, if not completely bankrupt, most companies. An equivalent fiasco like Multidata Systems—a company able to keep the FDA at bay for years—should not happen within the credit card industry. But to date, the industry has only cut off one company, Card Systems—a fact not wasted on others and that highlights a limiting aspect of PCI itself. The credit card companies would only hurt themselves financially if they were to cut off too many companies. So the incentive is to wave the big stick but use it selectively.

As significant as the leverage of the card industry might be, however, compliance with PCI hovers around 36 percent. Despite deadlines that have come and gone, $20 million in incentives, the Sword of PCI dangling above merchants' heads, and a host of proposed incentives, 36 percent cannot be considered a ground swell of compliance.

The standard itself might be the cause of low compliance for a number of reasons. One, the standard is painfully ambiguous on some topics. Two, where PCI is not ambiguous, it is rigorous, expensive, or both. Says Avivah Litan, Vice President and Research Director at Gartner, a consultancy and research firm, "[PCI] is a good step. It's good for the card brands to enforce security, but it's impractical to expect 5 million retailers to become security experts." And that is, in fact, what the card industry (among others) expects.

> *"It's good for the card brands to enforce security, but it's impractical to expect 5 million retailers to become security experts."*

Two simple examples of this expectation are requiring two-factor authentication and the use of split-knowledge, dual-control key management for cryptography. Don't know what either of those mean? Neither do most merchants (or apparently some consultants who help companies try to achieve compliance). So in addition to trying to achieve compliance, there is a massive educational requirement that must run concurrently with compliance efforts. But if these requirements are difficult to understand and implement now, it only gets harder in 2008.

The PCI standard to date has restricted its scope to network and architectural cyber-security issues, limiting its specific guidance regarding software security to "make sure your commercial computer systems are patched." In June 2008, the PCI standard adds a significant requirement to specifically protect Internet-facing web applications (like Amazon.com or eBay) that accept credit card information. Other software, such as the operating systems all these applications run on, is excluded from evaluation. These must simply be patched.

Gartner weighed in almost immediately upon this announcement, stating that enterprises that process credit card information should "scan applications for vulnerabilities, using either manual code reviews or application-scanning tools (which are better-equipped and more reliable). This practice should be given priority over the use of web-application firewalls, which should be used in addition to, not instead of, ensuring that applications are secure."[25]

These new "software security" requirements could mean a drop in the percentage of companies that comply with PCI. If companies found previous requirements rigorous, they will find the newest requirement crushing. Not only must companies protect their applications from a range of known web application coding mistakes, they must also implement control and documentation processes of software development similar in intent to the FDA's requirements. Unlike the FDA, PCI does require training of developers[26] but stops short at mandating licensure, certification, or qualification of software developers.

What is interesting about the whole PCI story is, like the FDA, the card industry is surprisingly limited in its sphere of influence. It desperately seeks to avoid government oversight, but for all its influence, not even the card industry could, or even think to, impose requirements on the quality of off-the-shelf software such as commercial operating systems. It is interesting that credit card companies would rather assume the cost, burden, and potential liability of self-regulation than demand, wait for, or pay for, better software. Such is the insulation of software manufacturers that not even financial institutions seek to engage fully in the battle for better software.

> *It is interesting that credit card companies would rather assume the cost, burden, and potential liability of self-regulation than demand, wait for, or pay for, better software.*

The primary reason why PCI was *initiated* was not due to problems in web applications but flaws in software that act as the foundation for the network and the systems that host web applications and databases. Early attacks were exploiting publicly known vulnerabilities in flawed computer systems, not web applications. Firewalls and security architecture are necessary because of weaknesses in the software that governs routers, switches, servers, and desktops. Even the most aggressive software patching campaigns cannot stop an attacker that has knowledge of a software weakness and for which no patch exists. Like the FDA, Visa leaves a majority of software manufacturers unaffected by accountability, liability, or oversight.

Instead of fighting this battle, the card industry expected "5 million retailers to become security experts." To be fair, however, this expectation might be the lesser of two impracticalities. It could be argued that it is easier to struggle against the inertia of 5 million merchants than battle software manufacturers highly insulated from your powers. This is a shame. The root cause does not lay with retailers, but the software employed by retailers, governments, hospitals, and businesses at the most fundamental level of operations.

Speed Blind

The plight of the card industry and the FDA illuminate the problems with oversight. The point here is not that oversight is inefficient or inappropriate—this can certainly be the case—but that we might be overseeing the wrong things. This might be due in large part to our technology-induced myopia. The PCI standard and the FDA's QSRs encompass a rather small subset of software and only apply to how card processors or the FDA interprets the world. There is nothing inherently wrong with this limited vision. In reality, we must all limit the scope of our concerns or risk becoming overwhelmed. But limited vision is made more dangerous by the blurring of our sight due to the speed of our endeavors.

This plight also provides insight into the larger issue of infrastructure protection. The world is in dire need of efficient infrastructure. Software development practices threaten to make this infrastructure inefficient and exceedingly expensive. Worse, it makes our infrastructure a hazard to our national, economic, and personal well-being. If self-regulation falters, it will not be for lack of effort, but for applying effort in the wrong place. The FDA and credit card companies are fighting small battles in a larger conflict, but their efforts like many others are disjointed, limited, and uncoordinated. Private companies, as well as government must work cooperatively toward removing the insulation of the software industry from the real impact of its lack of quality.

> *The FDA and credit card companies are fighting small battles in a larger conflict, but their efforts like many others are disjointed, limited, and uncoordinated.*

Just how pervasive has our speed-exacerbated myopia become?

In April 2007, the Internet Security Alliance (ISAlliance), a large trade group, released a rather baffling document to the public. The ISAlliance called for a "new set of guidelines for fighting cyber-criminals that calls on privately-held companies to do a better job of securing their IT systems, but asks the federal government to lend a hand in that work" in the form of incentives and not regulation.[27]

Ken Silva, Chairman of the Alliance, stated, "The private sector knows a good deal about how to protect this infrastructure; the federal government's role ought to be to provide incentives encouraging corporations to utilize these practices." This much is understandable and sounds perfectly reasonable. The credit card industry would agree.

Among the suggested policies, however, are a series of interesting recommendations:

- For federal agencies to establish a mechanism that will enable companies that adopt standards-based security practices to be qualified to receive incentives.
- For private companies to be able to acquire additional cyber-security insurance to cover losses arising from catastrophic events and limit their liability to third parties.
- For the Department of Homeland Security to create a national program for temporary, short-term reinsurance through which insurers can purchase reinsurance coverage for their exposure to catastrophic losses under these policies.

- For companies with appropriate attack insurance to have litigation-related incentives available, excluding liability for consequential and punitive damages.
- To create privacy reform legislation establishing federal limitation of liability for companies that experience breaches of personal information that occur despite their use of standards-based security best practices.[28]

Insurance, it appears, is the means to incentivize corporations toward better information security even though breaches might occur "despite their use of standards-based security best practices." In essence, the practice of information security is a Sisyphean feat: No matter how good you might be at cyber-security, you still lose. But why do we lose? The core issue is not whether corporations can protect their infrastructure. Standards-based security best practices do not address the core issues of corporate susceptibility to cyber-intrusion when the software not only in their IT infrastructure is flawed, but also in their cyber-security products as well. But this, so the argument goes, is why corporations need insurance. In actuality, corporations need cyber insurance because in the absence of adequate contractual remedies for defective software—for which software manufacturers disclaim completely—corporations must purchase specialized insurance to cover risks that should be borne by software manufacturers themselves.

> In actuality, corporations need cyber insurance because in the absence of adequate contractual remedies for defective software—for which software manufacturers disclaim completely—corporations must purchase specialized insurance to cover risks that should be borne by software manufacturers themselves.

Nowhere in the ISAlliance recommendations is there call for any accountability or pressure on software manufacturers, nor do any of the proposed insurance programs pertain to software companies that might be responsible for releasing defective software. It is simply the responsibility of software buyers to protect their software from exploitation but not the responsibility of software manufacturers to mitigate exploitation in the first place.

The incentives recommended by ISAlliance, in short, apply to everyone except to software manufacturers. In fact, it acts to further insulate the software industry, leaving software buyers to fight amongst themselves over whose insurance will cover the losses actualized by, and through, defective software. This scenario can be likened to a savvy, two-timing letch of a man who snickers when his multiple girlfriends—having discovered each other—come to blows over his infidelities but refuse to leave him or hold him to account.

A plausible counterargument might be that directly addressing software security was not the intended goal of the ISAlliance document. But that is exactly the point. With "security" in the title of the organization, one would hope that core issues of security would be addressed as opposed to making recommendations that appear to benefit members and sponsors of the ISAlliance that have commercial interests in security products and insurance.

Another trade group with the word "security" in their name that exhibits the same myopia is the Cyber Security Industry Alliance (CSIA). In 2004, CSIA released "Talking Points for Cyber Security, Preventing Identity Theft, Protecting Intellectual Property and Critical Infrastructure, Increasing Accountability." In Talking Points, CSIA lists solutions to dealing with cyber insecurity:

- Anti-Virus Software automatically checks new files entering a PC for infection.
- Asset Management used to match inventory against scans for known vulnerabilities; helps pinpoint specific security holes so those holes can be efficiently repaired through patches or other remediation.
- Authentication Digital certificates and secure ID technology verify identities of web sites and authorized users.
- Education Teaches users why and how to practice security-wise behavior.
- Intrusion Detection/Prevention Technologies that monitor content of network traffic for infections and block traffic carrying infected files or programs.
- Encryption Transforms data into password (key)-protected packets that prevent reading by unauthorized users.

- Firewall Blocks unauthorized traffic from entering PCs and servers from the Internet.

- Patch Fixes vulnerability in software by replacing a portion of faulty code.

- Policy Management Enforces security rules and regulations of IT systems.

- Vulnerability Management Processes and tools to identify and remediate cyber vulnerabilities in the 5 major classes, including unsecured accounts, misconfigurations, software defects, unnecessary services, and malware (spyware, backdoors, trojans, etc.)[29]

Again, all reasonable and responsible recommendations heard time and time again. But notice anything missing? About the closest CSIA gets to dealing with weaknesses in software is the classic "patch and scan your systems for vulnerabilities." The list here is not so much a list of solutions as it is a list of responsibilities—two totally different concepts. A solution solves a problem. None of these "solutions" solve the problem of grossly inadequate software engineering practices or the insulation of software manufacturers from accountability.

Again, the counterargument can be made that directly addressing software security was not the intent of CSIA in its Talking Points. And again, that is exactly the point. Who is lighting the fire under software manufacturers if not two of the largest "security alliances?"

To CSIA's credit, in July 2005, CSIA urged the U.S. Congress to elevate cyber security research and development efforts and to follow the recommendations made by the President's Information Technology Advisory Committee (PITAC), which included among its Top 10 R&D priorities, "Secure Software Engineering and Software Assurance." Whew. But there is a marked difference between promoting increased spending for another group's priorities (the PITAC was dissolved, by the way) and bearing down on the real issue at hand.

In 2007, CSIA released its Agenda for U.S. Government Action, which called for a "comprehensive federal law to secure sensitive personal information and notify consumers in case of a breach," for DHS to "quickly establish cyber security and telecommunications priorities that address situational awareness, emergency communications and recovery and reconstitution and ensure that appropriate funding is in place," and to "effectively establish and maintain a comprehensive information security program." Somewhere buried within all this are a few lonesome checklists for specifically addressing software quality and security.[30] Not nearly the visibility a problem of this magnitude needs.

The frustration in all these scenarios is that it does not appear anyone is sufficiently addressing the fundamental issues and reasons why we have increasingly complex and articulated security architectures, incentives programs—as well as growing calls for data breach notification laws—focusing on entities that might share *some* culpability, but not *all* culpability.

But effective oversight of the software industry is not impossible; it is simply too immature. This immaturity is compounded by distortion, as this chapter has argued, due to the unchallenged rationalizations of speed and churn. There are many industries that might not like oversight or are difficult to regulate, but are regulated nonetheless. Software manufacturers should be no different. While regulation is certainly not a panacea, it is not an inevitable disaster as the following section argues.

You Can Learn a Lot From an Interstate Highway System

The expectation of credit card companies that 5 million merchants should become security experts is like the Federal government expecting 200 million drivers to become physicists and engineers in order to reduce vehicular fatalities. Such expectations are not reasonable.

Since when have drivers been required by the Federal government to construct center-lane dividers to ensure their individual safety or configure after-market crumple zones in their cars? Since when have drivers been expected to conduct detailed inspections of an auto's design or to evaluate and report on a vehicle's resilience to head-on collisions?

The answer is never. To be sure, some level of driver education is to be expected and encouraged, but the amount of education demanded for software users to use their software safely is disproportionate and unrealistic. About the most complex engineering tasks a driver needs to undertake is to ensure his seat belt is latched and the car door is closed before leaving the driveway. The most difficult safety evaluation required of buyers is to determine the level of risk they are willing to accept by purchasing a vehicle rated less than five stars. As far as required knowledge of physics, well, the right pedal makes the car speed up; the center pedal makes the car slow down. Every other item of consequence of vehicle and road falls on the shoulders of trained professionals, who construct safety apparatuses according to a defined standard and who themselves are bound to standards of care and knowledge.

> *Where drivers are culpable, there is an expectation and requirement they drive responsibly, maintain their vehicle, don't drink while driving, and have insurance. There is a clean separation between what the driver is responsible for and everything else. When it comes to software, this model is turned on its head.*

Where drivers *are* culpable, there is an expectation and requirement they drive responsibly, maintain their vehicle, don't drink while driving, and have insurance. There is a clean separation between what the driver is responsible for and everything else. When it comes to software, this model is turned on its head.

When a buyer uses software, she is expected to build the roadway, install the center-dividers, paint the lines, bank the turns, ensure proper sight-distance, configure and install the crumple zones, check the brakes, fix the car and patch the roadway, learn to drive (and teach others to drive), and, now, be liable if she fails to do any of these correctly as well as be liable for any manufacturer's defects in the product itself. It is a jumbled mess the software buyer cannot possibly get right. Software is infrastructure, and software is law; it is the foundation of our civilization. It is unreasonable to foist upon the population tasks that they will never be qualified to undertake or make them liable for manufacturing failures not their doing.

In Chapter 2, I introduced the lessons of crash test dummies. Crash test dummies tell only part of the story in human safety on the roadways and how it relates to the nature of security in cyberspace. The lessons are much broader: To enjoy the full benefit of safer cars, one must also have safe highways and skilled drivers.

The United State Interstate highway system is actually a *system of systems*, each system inter-joining with the other, creating a synergistic safety net. A five-star rated car on a dirt road traveling 80 miles per hour at 2:00 a.m. on a rainy Saturday night with an under-aged, unlicensed, inebriated driver simply cannot compare safety-wise to a family driving to church on I-80 in a similar car a few hours later. Crash test dummies certainly help in making safe cars, but they do not necessarily make traveling in cars safe. So the Interstate "system of systems"—in fact, any roadway in the United States—is really a triumvirate consisting of the roadway, the cars, and the people.

The roadway must be designed to handle certain speeds and certain volumes of traffic. The concrete that comprises the roadway must adhere to some 24 different quality tests. The vehicle is required to have a certain bumper height, visibility requirements, safety features, and so on. (Heck, even the placement of controls on the dashboard has specific government-imposed requirements.) The driver is mandated to be licensed, sober, and be physically capable of the tasks required for driving. Each of these systems is subject to separate but complementary engineering standards and government oversight. And rightly so. If any of these systems function sub-optimally or fail completely, the likelihood of death increases dramatically.

To understand the impact of this synergistic safety net, it is helpful to compare two nations, which differ in their handling and involvement of their transportation systems: China and the United States. The United States has spent five decades and $329 billion[31] building and refining its Interstate highway system. China has not, and it shows.

As the wealth of China's population has increased, so too has its appetite for car ownership. In 2003, demand for cars soared 75 percent and is expected to increase 10 to 20 percent annually.[32] These are huge numbers and sweet music to the ears of auto manufacturers. But although Chinese buyers are acquiring the same reliable vehicles the rest of the world enjoys (Mercedes, Ford, Hyundai, and so on), China lacks the other two complementary systems: safe highways and skilled drivers. It also lacks sufficient oversight of both.

China has been plagued by insufficient construction standards and by widespread corruption that makes driving dangerous and obtaining drivers licenses by ill-suited drivers rather easy. As a result, the World Health Organization (WHO) estimated in 2004 that more than 600 people are killed and more than 45,000 injured *per day* on China's roadways.[33] This equates to around 219,000 people killed *every year*. Compare this to the United States vehicular death rate, which has held steady at about 40,000 deaths per year for the past few decades despite massive growth in private car ownership and usage. What makes the tragedy of China's death rate so severe—beyond the actual loss of human life—is the number of private cars in China is only *half* the number of cars in America *at the onset of the Great Depression*.[34] And the miles traveled per year by Chinese drivers cannot even compare to their U.S. counterparts. U.S. drivers travel approximately 1.7 trillion miles annually on highways and 1.2 trillion miles annually on rural roads.[35] China has significantly fewer vehicles, and Chinese drivers travel significantly less, yet daily fatalities are nearly six times that of the United States.

Sadly, if nothing is done to stop the carnage, China's death rate is expected to increase to almost 500,000 per year by 2020, costing China approximately 1.5 percent of its Gross Domestic Product ($12–$20 billion U.S. dollars).[36] Despite the wide availability of high safety-rated vehicles, the absence of safe highways and skilled drivers takes a significant toll on human life as well as economic health.

A strong economy is built upon strong infrastructure. The United States holds considerable comparative advantage over its international competitors due to the Interstate system. The U.S. Interstate system saves lives, preserving labor's productivity and reducing manufacturing and distribution costs in its domestic market. Both in turn make U.S. products more competitive in world markets. While China is known for inexpensive products, their products would be even more competitive if their infrastructure were on par with the United States and their labor pools were not being literally slaughtered.

In short, to compete on the global stage, nations require infrastructure suitable to the task. Even mature economies like the European Union spent an estimated $100 billion adding and upgrading some 12,000 miles of highway infrastructure from

1996 to 2006. The highway is a critical component in the global economic arms race.

To address shortfalls in its highway infrastructure, China passed its first Road Traffic Safety Law in May 2004 and is aggressively pursuing other relevant laws and regulations to promote driver safety.[37] Until now, China's oversight on highway safety has been all but non-existent, which is ironic given its historically intense oversight of everything else. China is also improving its highway system, literally starting from nothing 20 years ago to adding more than 40,000 miles of highways (compared to the U.S. Interstate system, which has approximately 47,000 miles) and improving current roads with "sharp turns, steep grades, sections with poor sight distance and sections with dangerous roadside conditions."[38]

A majority of U.S. drivers, when traveling to the store, perhaps take their driving environment for granted, not recognizing the thousands of regulations, requirements, and standards applied to each system within the transportation triumvirate that makes the trip possible—and safe—in the first place. It also affects the price of the products that are the reason for the trip. Certainly, drivers see some of these requirements—dashed white lines, paved surfaces, stop signs, tail-lights, and so on—but much remains transparent or concealed. Drivers are also not required to design, construct, or repair any of it.

This might be what is so beautiful and elegant about the U.S. Interstate system. Much of what protects our lives and our families on the roadway does not require extensive or conscious thought on the part of drivers (most of the time), nor does it require deep technical understanding. The complexity of safety mechanisms has in large part been abstracted away from drivers, freeing them to enjoy rather than dread the driving experience for the most part. In fact, any idiot in the United States can drive a car, and according to my elderly mother, apparently any idiot does. Despite the inevitable idiot, however (a 2005 study found that 1 in 10 U.S. drivers do not know basic driving rules[39]), vehicular death rates in the United State remain consistently low.

In comparison, the software world foists incredible responsibility upon software users and leaves them to fumble through a dizzying array of after-market "fixes" for which they must pay substantial costs to acquire, pay substantial attention to

> *In comparison, the software world foists incredible responsibility upon software users and leaves them to fumble through a dizzying array of after-market "fixes" for which they must pay substantial costs to acquire, pay substantial attention to configure, and pay dearly should they get any of it wrong.*

configure, and pay dearly should they get any of it wrong. This is unfair. It is also hazardous to national infrastructure.

The U.S. Interstate system was designed with safety *and* throughput in mind *from the beginning*, reducing the amount of risk drivers experience on a daily basis. The Federal-Aid Highway Act of 1956—which brought the Interstate to life—called for the enforcement of uniform geometric and construction standards. According to early statements, "High standards were adopted for the interstate highway system. Access to all interstates was to be fully controlled. There would be no intersections or traffic signals. All traffic and railroad crossings would be grade separated, requiring the construction of more than 55,000 bridges. Interstates were to be divided and have at least four wide traffic lanes (two in each direction) and adequate shoulders. Curves were to be engineered for safe negotiation at high speed, while grades were to be moderated, eliminating blind hills. Rest areas were to be conveniently spaced. Each interstate was to be designed to handle traffic loads expected 20 years after completion."[40]

In contrast, the Internet was cobbled together through experimental protocols that were never sufficiently re-engineered to meet the demands of mission critical functions; nor were software development practices sufficiently advanced to meet the minimum construction needs of infrastructure. It would be as if Joseph Bazalgette, who was discussed in Chapter 1, failed to update his techniques and quality control measures around using a superior, new but unproven type of cement for the London sewer system. Bazalgette realized that his new type of cement called for a new way of employing it; otherwise, he would endanger the success of his project and the benefits it would bring. The same cannot be said for the construction and components of the Internet.

Contrary to Al Gore's statement about the Internet being the "Information Super Highway," the Internet is more like a 1920s two-lane farm road built by local-yokels—and about as safe. When a nation attempts to jam an enterprise-class commerce model down a two-lane farm road, is it any wonder significant tribulations arise?

The realization that a strong economy requires strong infrastructure was in large part why President Eisenhower pushed for an Interstate highway system. The injury rate for interstate highways is more than 70 percent lower than that of the rest of the roadways in the United States, yet the Interstate handles 25 percent of the volume while representing only 1 percent of the total road surface.[41] In comparison, by connecting to the Internet, it is almost guaranteed the "driver" will experience an "accident" due to one or more preventable defects that were leaked into the global stream of commerce. Connecting to and "traveling" on the Internet is dangerous and expensive.

Strong infrastructure not only lowers costs of production, but results in a safer system, promoting further economic rewards. While the estimated total cost of the Interstate system is $329 billion, the direct economic losses *avoided* due to the use of the Interstate system are estimated at $368 billion.[42] The maxim, "You've gotta spend to save," was never more true. A strong economy requires strong infrastructure.

A Matter of Trust

Traditionally, the telecommunications industry has been regulated as being essential to public health, interest, and welfare. Hence, a core component of its regulatory model was to expand service to give everyone access. In many countries, access to basic service is now considered a necessity of modern life. Historically, the financial services industry has been regulated by the premise that trust and confidence are paramount to the orderly movement of trade, goods, and money. And, given that a special trust is conferred on financial entities, they must conduct their business in a safe, sound, and prudent manner. —World Bank, 2002

Previously in Chapter 2 I stated that only 10 percent of software features are actually used because it requires of users a high tolerance of frustration and malfunction and to be able and willing to explore beyond a certain comfort level. Mistrust is a derivative of malfunction and is compounded by inconsistent behavior. This means software buyers probably do not use software for everything they possibly could. This is expensive for everyone.

If only 10 percent of application features are actually used, this does not speak highly of the level of trust users have in their software systems. But users not only mistrust their computers, they also mistrust the network and other users.

In 2006, the Cyber Security Industry Alliance found in their Digital Confidence Survey that 50 percent of consumers feel the Internet is safe.[43] The survey over the past two years has remained unchanged, showing that neither government nor industry has made significant headway in boosting consumer confidence in the cyber infrastructure.

A 2007 poll conducted by Trend Micro, an anti-virus company, found that 51 percent of users thought the Internet was "very safe." Polled again if they thought the Internet would be safer in six months, the numbers plummeted to 32 percent.[44]

The equivalent "triumvirate of transportation" in cyberspace is the network, the applications, and the users. If any one of these operates sub-optimally or fails completely, the entire "system of systems" falters.

How many networks are cobbled together quickly by organizations who "just want the damn thing up?"

How many applications are built to shoddy specifications just to get it into the marketplace before competitors do the same?

How many organizations allow their users on their networks without the least bit of "driver's education?"

Imagine if roadways were thrown down with the same disregard for design and construction, cars were built with the same indifference, and users were allowed to drive without a modicum of training?

Trust matters when it comes to systems; physical, digital, or otherwise. And mistrust in infrastructure has significant consequences. Trust derives from consistent stable performance, which in turn is derived from standards of design, construction, and skill. U.S. drivers trust their transportation system because the cars, the roadway, and for the most part a majority of other drivers behave consistently and safely. The roadway and vehicles are designed and constructed to specifications by qualified engineers and experienced workers. (As simple as pouring concrete may seem, accounting for environmental conditions and timing of the pour take an experienced hand and can dramatically affect the stability of the concrete.)

There also happens to be considerable oversight, standards, and regulations placed on each of these elements. Car accidents certainly happen and will continue to happen regardless of standards and regulations, but the safety odds are *with* the drivers, not against them. On the Internet, the odds are decidedly against software users. One of the amazing benefits of our trust in the triumvirate of transportation is the democratization of mobility. In, *The Best Investment a Nation Ever Made*, Wendell Cox makes these observations:

In large measure, the interstate highway system has democratized mobility in the United States, providing virtually all Americans with the ability to move quickly to any destination within their communities and to travel throughout the nation, inexpensively, and at whatever time or date they desire.

The large majority of households, including households below the poverty line, have automobiles available and are thus able to access a broader range of employment, shopping, and other opportunities. Indeed, the poor in America generally have greater personal mobility by virtue of the automobile and the interstate highway system than many middle income households in developed nations where quality roadways are less extensive.

America's democratized mobility has lowered retail prices, thus benefiting consumers. As freedom of movement has expanded, people have been able to travel further to shop. At the same time, large discount retailers have been established, placing further competitive pressure on prices. To compete, smaller local retailers have had to become more efficient. One of the most important reasons that people get more for their retail dollar today is that they have more options—they are able to travel wherever they like for bargains or larger selections that would not be available if they were restricted to shopping opportunities in their own immediate areas. And, because they rely on their own personal transportation, they are able to shop at whatever time they desire. This has encouraged longer store hours, more efficient utilization of retail facilities, and created additional jobs.[45]

Expanded mobility allows for a tremendous range of activities that would otherwise not be possible if strong infrastructure did not support it. This is critical. Expanded mobility for all classes of citizens in the United States is possible largely due to the efforts of government to invest and oversee its infrastructure. Certainly, the private sector has contributed to mobility, but contrary to the assumption that the private sector can always do things better than government, the reality is that the private sector rarely spontaneously invests in basic infrastructure or engineering excellence unless there is an overwhelming economic upside. This seldom happens. Regardless, there are some things government must involve itself in or risk benefits to its well-being.

Like the Interstate, the Internet promises a similar democratization effect, only this time, democratization applies to information. The *democratization of information* promises similar benefits to mobility by allowing access to information anywhere in the world, inexpensively, and at whatever desired time or date. And the economic benefits are clear as companies must aggressively compete among themselves in a global market— and an increasingly informed consumer base—placing further downward pressure on retail prices.

If only the Internet were made of concrete and steel. As silly as this lamentation may sound, it rings true. Software makes the democratization of information possible, just as concrete and automobiles made possible democratized mobility. But the Internet—specifically the software that manifests it—simply does not meet the standards nations demand of other forms of infrastructure. Joseph Bazalgette was permitted to replace entire brickworks of the London sewer with Portland cement only after he established Portland cement's suitability through rigorous objective quality controls, controls that are used to this day. In contrast, software is replacing and injecting itself into greater numbers of systems with little, if any, objective evaluation of its suitability. This practice may ultimately threaten the democratization of information just as faulty cement and unsafe cars would threaten mobility. Arguably, information democratization is already being threatened as organizations stifle the flow of information by constructing incredibly expensive and complex systems to protect against intrusion and limit liability.

> *Joseph Bazalgette was permitted to replace entire brickworks of the London sewer with Portland cement only after he established Portland cement's suitability through rigorous objective quality controls, controls that are used to this day. In contrast, software is replacing and injecting itself into greater numbers of systems with little, if any, objective evaluation of its suitability.*

To put this problem in context, when concrete is used for a roadway, it increases the speed cars are permitted to drive. When crumple zones are added to vehicles it does not make the car go slower, nor do the addition of seat belts or airbags degrade a car's performance. Just about every safety feature added to vehicles not only avoids detrimentally affecting the possible speed achieved but increases the speed at which cars can travel safely. In contrast, the security products used to protect our software—firewalls, intrusion protection systems, anti-virus, anti-spyware, and so on—all negatively impact the performance of the network, the computers, or both. This slows everything down, inhibits information people are willing to share, and promotes mistrust of an already mistrusted system.

The argument in software oversight is not that government cannot innovate at market speed, nor even that government cannot provide services better than the private sector. The argument is much more subtle. The problem is that government might fail to regulate the correct things in software production. But the same can be said of the software industry. It is not like the software industry cannot innovate or provide services that support the population as a whole, but that the software industry might fail to innovate on matters that do not have an overwhelming and immediate economic upside but are critical to national and economic well-being nonetheless.

Robust construction increases the velocity at which people, products, and money may travel. Software is certainly faster than manual processes, just as a Ford Model-T is faster than a horse, but like a Model-T, current software development practices are failing to deliver the speeds and safety comparable to the capabilities of a modern, five-star rated automobile. As for the network, well, our two lane farm road does not help matters any.

The question is not whether regulation will come to software. The question is what form oversight will take. But, as David Whyte reminds us, stopping to ask this question means we "might not like the self-appraisal stopping would require." But of course, the thinking is we cannot stop to ask this question because not only might the self-appraisal be unpleasant, but we just might mortally wound our economic well-being, hinder the inevitable march of technology, and endanger all the utopian advantages technology may yet provide.

To be clear, there is nothing intrinsically wrong with traveling at high speed, but the infrastructure must be able to support it and the safety of those who seek it. The triumvirate of cyberspace—the network, the applications, and the people—requires no less oversight than the triumvirate of transportation. The Interstate should teach us that much at least.

One of Skill in the Art

To design and build an Interstate requires engineers—lots of them. Engineers do not spontaneously generate, however. Engineers must be educated and trained, ridding them of the bad habits that come from ignorance, misunderstanding, and the foibles of the craftsmen that preceded them.

As such, engineering is not an art,[46] though it can be considered by some to be an artful science, embracing nature's complexity, yet remaining able to "simplify to nature in its essence."[47] On the whole, however, engineering is about systematic application of scientific and mathematical principles in the design, construction, and pursuit of practical ends such as buildings, bridges, machines, and processes. Engineering, and in particular engineers, must conform to certain requirements that craftsmen and artisans might at times conveniently disregard. Moreover, those who wish to call themselves professional engineers must graduate from accredited universities and be formally licensed and registered in their skill. In this context, the career path associated with software construction challenges the notion that "software engineering" is true to its name.

In fact, software engineering—though perceived as a modern skill—remains firmly entrenched in the craftsmen's discipline, much akin to blacksmiths and textile weavers of the pre-industrial era whose handcrafted items could certainly be considered elegant constructions but could not necessarily be considered feats of systematic engineering. As cherished as the output of craftsmanship may be, the shortfall of the craftsman's discipline is that product quality is largely dependent on the craftsman's talent and expertise—not to mention that a craftsman's work is very, very expensive. Nor is it consistently repeatable. Like any handmade item, software applications that perform similar functions might be entirely unique in design and implementation. The similarities between a hand-woven basket purchased from Wal-Mart and the software residing in the bowels of a financial institution are unsettling.

In short, the U.S. Interstate and the automobiles that travel upon it were not built by craftsmen, nor could they be. Armies of craftsmen certainly built the Pyramids of Giza and the Great Wall of China, but these are considered World Wonders largely because they were not repeatable. In comparison, suspension bridges and skyscrapers that dwarf all previous World Wonders in size, scale, and expenditure are regularly constructed around the globe. These magnificent structures are not considered World Wonders simply because the discipline of engineering has made them commonplace. In contrast, vast numbers of large-scale software applications are one-off creations, and nearly three quarters of those are considered "operating failures" either failing to function as intended or simply not used by their sponsor.[48] The wonder about software is that it works at all.

This does not bode well for global infrastructure. Though cyberspace appears to be one single creation, it is actually a hodge-podge of handcrafted software, each developed by artisans of indefinite qualification and unpredictable talent, using techniques that are neither standardized nor consistently repeatable. If to construct an Interstate requires engineers, the Internet deserves no less. In fact, because of the Internet's reach, it deserves far greater.

Engineers simply work with the laws of Nature and are bound by limitations those laws define. But those who create software define the very essence and fabric of cyberspace. A failure on the part of a traditional engineer may be due to miscalculations within an unchanging Law of Nature, such as force equals mass times acceleration (F=ma). The failure of a software engineer has more profound consequences given that not only might the failure derive from misapplying another software developer's "law," but might be, at base, because the original software creator failed to correctly define the law in the first place. It is one thing Isaac Newton discovering the Second Law of Motion and a future engineer miscalculating the effects; it is quite another if you conceive a law and blunder its creation. It has consequences for the entire universe.

> *It is one thing Isaac Newton discovering the Second Law of Motion and a future engineer miscalculating the effects; it is quite another if you conceive a law and blunder its creation. It has consequences for the entire universe.*

As such, creators of software bear enormous responsibility. Even the smallest bit of software, once connected to the network, becomes part of the corpus of the Law. Yet users of software seem apprehensive about holding the software industry to a standard equivalent to traditional engineering or legal practice.

Since 1994, the debate about licensing software engineers has shown little forward motion. Texas and Ontario are the only government bodies to date that restrict who may wear the title of professional engineer in software development, though other states like California have flirted with the concept. Even at that, Texas provides an enormous loophole that does not require licensure of software developers working at a software company.[49] This is like not requiring a surgeon to be a doctor if he happens to work at a hospital.

The arguments against licensing individuals that construct software are many. States have limited enforcement capabilities. State legislatures have few, if any, engineers on staff creating laws that do not accurately reflect the intentions of the profession. As a new skill, there is considerable debate over what "qualified" software engineers must know and whether software development is in fact an engineering discipline. A "one-size-fits-all" licensure does not make sense for software developers. Licensure will not improve the quality of software—after all, it is still possible to get a bad hair cut by a licensed hairdresser. These arguments and many like them are all perfectly valid—and all distract from the underlying issue.

Society has consistently demanded independent competency validation regardless of political undertones for practitioners engaged in work that impacts health, safety, welfare, or the environment before these individuals enter the marketplace. This is true for doctors, barbers, nurses, electricians, engineers, lawyers, stockbrokers, and even prostitutes.

Prostitution in the state of Nevada is regulated at the county level[50] and has far stricter controls on "houses of ill-fame" and those who work at them than most all of the software development companies that call the state home. State law requires that registered brothel prostitutes be checked weekly for sexually transmitted diseases and monthly for HIV. Condoms are mandatory for all sex acts, and brothel owners can be held liable if customers become infected with HIV after a prostitute has tested positive for the virus.[51]

The irony of software is that it impacts all four categories of health, safety, welfare, and the environment, yet oversight, licensure, and regulation is practically non-existent. If a brothel owner is held liable for infection of a client, is it not reasonable to hold a software company liable for an equivalent infection of a client by virus, or worm, or by enabling the exploitation of the client due to weaknesses in the software product?

In 1999, the Association of Computing Machinery (ACM) recommended against licensing software engineers, citing that "it is premature and would not be effective at addressing the problems of software quality and reliability." ACM recognized that licensure was inevitable, however, and actively supported the deliberations of the Texas Board of Professional Engineers, although they asserted that any help they might provide in the future to developing licensing requirements for other government bodies did not imply endorsement of the licensing movement. Since 1999, ACM has made no public statement altering their stance.

By 2004, the Institute of Electrical and Electronics Engineers (IEEE) continued its effort begun in 1998 to make software engineering a branch of traditional engineering by releasing the Software Engineer Body of Knowledge (SWEBOK) that "does not purport to define the body of knowledge but rather to serve as a compendium and guide to the body of knowledge that has been developing and evolving over the past four decades."

In short, the skill of software engineering desires all the language and credibility of engineering but is plagued by the eccentricities of playwrights and the foibles of craftsmen, while enjoying the immunity of congressional witnesses.

> *In short, the skill of software engineering desires all the language and credibility of engineering but is plagued by the eccentricities of playwrights and the foibles of craftsmen, while enjoying the immunity of congressional witnesses.*

Despite the laudable efforts of ACM, IEEE, DHS, and others, immunity from liability and responsibility will mortally wound any attempt to improve the current state of software engineering. Historically, society has rarely tolerated immunity for long and, in fact, whenever an industry has expanded to affect society at large, some degree of control soon follows regardless of countervailing arguments.

It is ironic that few organizations want to "hurt" the software profession by demanding standards, qualifications, and regulations, while at the same time are being hurt and witness others being hurt by shortcomings in the software development profession. The preservation of innovation and creativity are simply not sufficient counter arguments to excuse the type of disasters we are witnessing on the Internet.

Immunity breeds irresponsibility. Put software in a perfectly safe car, and it becomes perfectly dangerous all over again. Put software in a medical device such as an x-ray machine, and it can become a monster. Should we feel glad that a radiological overdose did not result in death, or a software bug in an air traffic control system merely results in near misses, or that no deaths were reported due to faulty software controlling our car's fuel injection system? When will we exhaust our feelings of relief over tragedies that could have happened because of "bad" software but did not simply because of happenstance?

It does not have to be this way. Software does not have to be perfect, but it must rise to the level of quality expected of something that serves as the foundation for our civilizations and the fabric of our infrastructure. The progenitors of the Interstate expected no less.

Immunity breeds irresponsibility. In order to remove irresponsibility, then, one must remove immunity....

CHAPTER 5

Absolute Immunity: You Couldn't Sue Us Even If You Wanted To

The typical software license reads (no really, read it):

THIS SOFTWARE IS PROVIDED "AS IS" AND ANY
EXPRESSED OR IMPLIED WARRANTIES, INCLUDING,
BUT NOT LIMITED TO, THE IMPLIED WARRANTIES
OF MERCHANTABILITY AND FITNESS FOR A
PARTICULAR PURPOSE ARE DISCLAIMED. IN NO
EVENT SHALL THE CONTRIBUTORS BE LIABLE FOR
ANY DIRECT, INDIRECT, INCIDENTAL, SPECIAL,
EXEMPLARY, OR CONSEQUENTIAL DAMAGES
(INCLUDING, BUT NOT LIMITED TO, PROCURE-
MENT OF SUBSTITUTE GOODS OR SERVICES;
LOSS OF USE, DATA, OR PROFITS; OR BUSINESS
INTERRUPTION) HOWEVER CAUSED AND ON ANY
THEORY OF LIABILITY, WHETHER IN CONTRACT,
STRICT LIABILITY, OR TORT (INCLUDING NEGLI-
GENCE OR OTHERWISE) ARISING IN ANY WAY OUT
OF THE USE OF THIS SOFTWARE, EVEN IF ADVISED
OF THE POSSIBILITY OF SUCH DAMAGE.

Despite my encouragement, my guess is that you glossed over the
language in this license after the third line—and no wonder. It is a
mire of legal language that the ordinary, and even well-educated,
person rarely understands. Unfortunately, this language has
significant impact on our lives in cyberspace and on national infrastructure.

Translating into plain English, this software license sounds
something like the following:

*We don't claim this software is good for anything—
if you think it is, great, but it's up to you to decide. If this
software doesn't work: tough. If you lose a million dollars
because this software messes up, it's you that's out the
million, not us. If you don't like this disclaimer: tough.
We reserve the right to do the absolute minimum provided
by law, up to and including nothing.*[1]

Currently, software manufacturers insulate themselves from liability under legal contract theories by conditioning use of a software application upon the user accepting this language. The
problem is by accepting the language, the user is absolving the
software manufacturer from nearly all forms of liability for any
design or application defects that might result in exploitation by
attackers or any other form of loss or harm. As a result, software users are left to wait anxiously for software patches that
promise to eliminate subsequently discovered vulnerabilities
with little or no recourse for actual damage or losses incurred
in the interim.

Few industries enjoy such a fantastic amount of immunity. In
essence, the language in a typical software license frees the software vendor from any meaningful warranties, removes the ability
of the buyer to seek any recompense except perhaps replacement
or repair costs of the purchased software (heaven help you if it was
"free" software), and completely reallocates all risk of loss from
the software manufacturer to the consumer for any malfunction,
weakness, or failure whatsoever in the software itself.

The software user, by agreeing to the language in a software
license, forgoes any right to pursue legal action against the seller and accepts the full weight and burden of risk for using the
software. The manufacturer, by offering such language, shifts
any and all responsibility to the user, releasing itself from liability for all consequential damages resulting from faulty software.
In the absence of a court imposed duty of care on the manufacturer, declining this license—and therefore use of the software—
is the only chance a buyer has of protecting himself.

By clicking the "I agree" button for a software application,
you are, in fact, agreeing for you, your family, or your business
to act as crash test dummies without any chance of holding the

software manufacturer to account for injuries, harm, damage, or loss. Only in the most extraordinary circumstance—death caused by software malfunction—does the software user have a chance of seeking meaningful compensation. In short, this type of license allows the software vendor to get away with anything short of murder. However, in light of Multidata Systems, which we discussed in Chapter 4, "Myopic Oversight," even this threshold is debatable.

> *By clicking the "I agree" button for a software application, you are, in fact, agreeing for you, your family, or your business to act as crash test dummies without any chance of holding the software manufacturer to account for injuries, harm, damage, or loss.*

To add insult to injury, software buyers might not even realize they are not purchasing software at all, but licensing software, which means that the purchaser is merely a licensee of the software, not the owner. The software manufacturer does not transfer title (ownership) of the software to the buyer but permits the buyer to use its intellectual property contingent upon accepting licensing terms. Permission can be revoked at any time, under rather capricious circumstances, without any recourse on the part of the licensee.

The license terms themselves, outside of completely transferring all risk to the buyer, drastically limit what the software buyer can do with the software, such as make copies of it. The terms might even bypass U.S. federal copyright law regarding the first-sale doctrine, a doctrine that states the purchaser can sell or give away a lawfully made copy without permission once the copyrighted work has been obtained. This continues to be an area of legal confusion given that software manufacturers argue the first-sale doctrine does not apply because software is not sold, but licensed. In the end, this means the software is not yours, and you cannot do with it as you please. The software buyer is literally left with nothing but the risk imposed by the software itself.

Such terms are usually included in a license that is called an adhesion contract, which has become common in the past 20 years particularly in the technology industry. Adhesion contracts are regularly used for mass-market products where companies seek to form binding agreements with large numbers of individual consumers. Adhesion contracts, otherwise known as standard form contracts, are preferred by companies due to their efficiency: the period of negotiations, which is typical in formulating contracts between parties, is entirely eliminated. This not only expedites the purchasing process, given that bargaining is purged from the interchange, but allows the seller to employ dense and confusing boilerplate language that is rarely understood and therefore rarely read by the buyer. Buyers do not typically understand the consequence of accepting such contracts.

Since adhesion contracts do not allow for any negotiation, they are offered on a take-it-or-leave-it basis. The buyer has no option to change the contract terms before signing; therefore, she has two choices, either accept the terms without modification or forgo the purchase entirely. Adhesion contracts are favored by parties in a stronger market position because the contract fundamentally allows the seller to push around smaller and weaker buyers who are internally compelled to satisfy a driving desire for utility. Buyers that fail to coordinate among themselves are like fish that fail to school in the presence of predators, allowing larger fish to pick them off one by one. Individual buyers have little to no power in relationships with larger market entities and therefore must typically mortgage their own well-being in exchange for desired utility.

The current legal trend in the United States is to enforce one-sided software agreements as long as the user has an opportunity to read and "manifest assent" to the terms.[2] When the buyer clicks "I agree," regardless if terms are read or not, agreement is manifested and the contract is as good as signed, sealed, and delivered. The crash test dummy uniform arrives in the mail at a later, undisclosed time (just kidding).

The law in the United States traditionally has had difficulty accommodating adhesion contracts compared to bargained contracts. Bargained contracts are the focus of many books and courses on negotiating, and there is considerable investment made by both parties to achieve a suitable agreement. *You Can Negotiate Anything* and *Getting to Yes: Negotiating Agreement Without Giving In* are just two books among hundreds focused exclusively on building bargaining skills for achieving better outcomes in negotiations. Bargained contracts allow users to clearly state terms both parties must abide by. As long as the terms are not illegal, the courts allow parties to contract for just about anything on any terms whatsoever. In a bargained contract, it is up to you to protect your interests, maximize your advantages, and have it solidified in a signed contract. U.S. courts have been increasingly deferential to adhesion contracts, however, treating them not only as enforceable, but akin to "sacred cows" rather than, as some legal observers have commented, "dangerous animals, likely to do harm unless confined and tamed."[3] And harm they have.

Unlike other manufacturers who are responsible for the quality of their products and have a duty to their consumers to avoid creating products that might cause harm, software manufacturers are free from all liability. Normally, courts do not condone the manufacture and distribution of defective products; relatively inconsequential manufacturers of toasters and lamps can be held liable, yet software manufacturers, who arguably touch almost every aspect of modern life, know no such duty of care. An adhesion contract further releases software manufacturers from any potential residual responsibility or accountability. Not even Superman enjoys this amount of legal invulnerability.[4] Software cannot be harmed nor be found to cause harm, even if it does. Impressive.

The license language at the beginning of this chapter is just the tip of the iceberg regarding the dysfunction, confusion, and the fiasco that is the software crisis. Multiple failures on the part of the courts, government, and the market have brought consumers and citizens a dangerous and expensive status quo, threatening our infrastructure and the welfare of those that depend on it.

In Chapter 4 we discussed rationale for government oversight of the software industry, but such regulation might not be possible in the foreseeable future and therefore not immediate enough to affect meaningful change. It might also be completely ineffectual. This means courts could be the only body flexible and swift enough to make a difference. In fact in 2004, Jeffery Hunker, a special advisor to President Bush, stated, "I think you are going to see reform come through lawsuits. We'll see [vendors] getting sued [because] so much of our infrastructure depends on computers that it's unsustainable to hold software

In 2004, Jeffery Hunker, a special advisor to President Bush, stated, "I think you are going to see reform come through lawsuits. We'll see [vendors] getting sued [because] so much of our infrastructure depends on computers that it's unsustainable to hold software companies blameless."

companies blameless."[5] In short, if regulation fails to improve the situation, and unfair contracts are shielding software manufacturers from the need to improve, legal liability might be the least unacceptable solution.

There are a number of problems with this position, however. At present, there is no defined standard of care for software manufacturers, and therefore a claim for damages against a non-existent standard is impossible. Even if there were a standard of care, statutes like the Uniform Computer Information Transaction Act (UCITA), adhesion contracts, and general disclaimers work against any attempt to prove a software vendor did not use reasonable care.[6] But to top it all off, the United States Congress went so far as to amend the Computer Fraud and Abuse Act in 2001, explicitly forbidding action against software manufacturers for negligent manufacturing of software.[7] To date, despite an epidemic of computer security flaws, no plaintiff has recovered damages for cyber crimes enabled by flawed software under any legal theory.[8]

The remarkable legal invulnerability of the software industry is in part a result of substantial investment by software companies in legal services to protect their interests. But it is also partly luck. The software industry could not have timed its ascent any better. Beginning in the 1980s, there were a number of larger forces at play in the commercial, legislative, and judicial arenas that set the stage for the current state of affairs. In this chapter, we look at these forces and how each unwittingly combined to grant software manufacturers absolute immunity for producing defective software. We then turn to a discussion of legal liability and how to potentially strip the software industry of a once understandable immunity that is now obsolete. In particular, the latter portion of this chapter discusses the arguments of two groups of legal thinkers seeking to establish liability for the software industry.

As one group observed, "The software industry is no longer in its infancy. Its development has moved out of garages and into corporate offices. It has matured to become a dominant sector of the economy. Consequently, it is appropriate to consider liability for defective software in the same light as liability for defective automobiles, pharmaceuticals, and other products."[9]

Indeed, the time has come.

The Forces of Failure

"Government is not the solution; government is the problem." So went the proclamation of Ronald Regan in his first inaugural address in January 1981.[10] What followed was a slow but consistent chain reaction of less government involvement in a wide range of activities, particularly business. For the devout capitalists in the audience, this was a satisfying moment. Less government involvement means businesses are free to establish a wider range of relationships at less cost and less bureaucracy. Moreover, individuals would be better able to pursue self-interest through a freer market. *Less government is a good thing*, so the reasoning goes, and to a certain extent, this reasoning is accurate. However, less government has certain consequences for the market and for the courts.

Economists hold dear to their heart that free people exercising their talents within a free market is the best possible scenario for the economic success of a nation. But economists also hold that an unconstrained market is just as dangerous as an unconstrained populace. The paradox of free peoples and free markets is that they are not without limitation; they are "free" but only within defined boundaries. In other words, *some* government involvement is absolutely necessary. The idea that a free market, left to its own devices, will promote nothing but well-being and joy around the globe is not only wrong, it is ruinous. Some of the most economically devastated regions in the world are due to bad government or no government. Half the African continent serves as a living example. The function and purpose of government therefore, among other things, is to set frameworks and boundaries to create an environment where free peoples and free markets may flourish without unduly burdening either.

Government must constantly balance the needs of its citizens against the needs of the market, suitably protecting each. This is a difficult balancing act.

At times, the balancing act is subtle and elegant. At other times, it is like a sailor thoroughly experienced with drinking, and being drunk, sways drastically from side to side but nonetheless has enough wits about him not to fall down. This appears to be the current state of "balance" regarding the software market.

There are a bevy of laws protecting the software industry and few, if any, protecting software buyers. In fact, in a dispute between software manufacturer and buyer, it is *assumed* the software manufacturer is not negligent. This stance assigns all liability to one and only one party: the buyer. This is an inequitable division of culpability and what makes data breach notification laws like California's Data Breach Law (SB1386) so absolutely frustrating. The frustration is not that buyers should not be held culpable in some way for cyber intrusions, but the law, by omitting mention of software manufacturers, makes buyers essentially *solely and exclusively* culpable despite knowledge and recognition to the contrary. In essence, data breach laws hold the software buyer strictly liable—that is, responsible for stolen data no matter what, regardless of the fact that the data breach might have been due to and could have largely been eliminated by the manufacturer in the production process.

> In essence, data breach laws hold the software buyer strictly liable—that is, responsible for stolen data no matter what, regardless of the fact that the problem might have originated with and could have largely been eliminated by the manufacturer.

This failure to protect the software buyers occurs on multiple fronts. First, statutes like the Uniform Computer Information Transactions Act (UCITA) promote vendor-friendly terms at the expense of all other market participants. Second, in practice, the judiciary and legislative branches of government have failed to appropriately constrain the software industry, and third, the market has responded inefficiently to cyber threats, causing billions to be spent only to have cyber attacks increase.

UCITA is a long, complex law governing contracts for the development, sale, licensing, maintenance, and support of computer software, in addition to contracts for information (such as books) in digital form.[11] UCITA is an attempt to standardize the laws across U.S. states to resolve differences in the legal treatment of computer-related services and the licensing of software.[12] In other words, UCITA is largely an attempt at formalizing what is already permitted by law but not practiced consistently across the entire United States. So far, so good. However, UCITA is heavily backed by software industry lobbyists.[13] As such, it is really just a thin veneer of law over whatever the software industry feels like dictating to the market.

Highlights of UCITA include the following (these should sound familiar):

"No Warranties: UCITA allows software publishers to sell software "as is" the way used cars are sold...meaning there is no warranty that the software works...and the consumer is not entitled to a refund if it does not.

Trapped by Hidden Terms: UCITA allows the consumer to be trapped into agreeing to the "as is" provision and all sorts of terms that the consumer can see only after the consumer pays for the software or the online service. Under UCITA these provisions may be placed in the boilerplate fine "print" that the consumer sees for the first time on the computer screen after the consumer buys the software at the mall and takes it home (or downloads it), unwraps the box, puts the disk in the computer and loads it—when the consumer is ready to use the software for the first time. That is when the consumer finally has the opportunity to see the contract provisions, restrictions, disclaimers, and limitations that UCITA permits. While the proponents of UCITA point to its "right of return" provision, this "right of return" vanishes as soon as the consumer clicks "I agree."

> *Forum Selection: If the consumer and the seller have a dispute over bad software or poor on-line service, UCITA allows the software publisher or Internet service provider to name almost any state in the United States as the state where the consumer's law suit has to be brought.*[14] *For example, it is prohibitively expensive for a Florida resident to file suit against a software company in California. Requiring a consumer to file suit in a distant forum acts as* absolute immunity *[my emphasis] where the cost and inconvenience of filing a lawsuit far exceeds what can be recovered.*"[15]

As bad as UCITA appears, it actually is. To date, only two states have passed UCITA into law. Many states have passed "bomb shelter" legislation, which is, in effect, special laws enacted to protect their consumers from UCITA but not from other legal practices that are already in force that UCITA merely tries to standardize. Multiple professional and consumer groups such as the IEEE and Ralph Nader's Consumer Project on Technology have also strongly opposed UCITA. Due to stringent resistance by multiple pro-consumer groups, UCITA is the least of the imbalance issues. In practice, the judiciary and the legislative branches of the U.S. government have consistently failed to hold the software industry accountable. As such, these forces represent far greater and deep-seated imbalances that are more difficult but not impossible to correct.

Absolution for Dereliction

Robert Pinkney, in the *Albany Journal of Law and Technology*, identified two occasions in which the U.S. Congress foreclosed on holding the software industry liable for programming blunders.[16] The first occasion was the Year 2000 problem (Y2K), and the second was when Congress amended the Computer Fraud and Abuse Act in 2001.

The Y2K crisis, the ultimate mega-event of all recorded history that was to bring the collapse of civilization for the simple reason that software manufacturers had forgotten two decimal places in the year portion of the date, was notable for one thing: *absolutely nothing happened*. Civilization did not collapse, public utilities continued to work, nuclear missiles did not leave their silos unexpectedly, financial systems did not break down, and thankfully, our computers did not fail. Whew. See, there was nothing to worry about all along, or so goes the argument. On the contrary, more happened than anyone could ever comprehend. While the impact was not immediate, the impact was nonetheless significant and inevitable.

Y2K was a classic example of a broken window. Recall from Chapter 3, "The Power of Weaknesses," that a broken window is an element of disorder. Inattention and sloppiness invites disorder. And disorder invites greater disorder, even crime. In the case of software, our systems are broken even before we purchase them. Y2K seems to prove this point in spades. The fact that nothing *obvious* happened on January 1, 2000, is irrelevant. In fact, plenty happened. As a broken window, Y2K sent a message to everyone in the global networked neighborhood that no one was in control of software. Y2K was a message sent round the world heard by everyone: citizens, officials, hackers, and organized crime. Only now are we seeing the results.

> *As a broken window, Y2K sent a message to everyone in the global networked neighborhood that no one was in control of software. Y2K was a message sent round the world heard by everyone: citizens, officials, hackers, and organized crime. Only now are we seeing the results.*

In their panic, Congress, instead of grabbing the software industry by its ear lobe and saying, "You arrogant, sloppy little men, what have you wrought," passed the Year 2000 Computer Date Change Act limiting the liability of the software industry. In essence, the Act was absolution for dereliction. It just goes to show that it is rather difficult to grab someone by the ear when they have you by the balls.

If that weren't enough, Congress missed yet another opportunity to hold the software industry liable in 2001 when it amended the Computer Fraud and Abuse Act (CFAA). In the 1990s, several court decisions were interpreting language in the

CFAA such that it touched software and hardware manufacturers directly; that is, the courts were finding manufacturers in violation of the law for shipping faulty software.

The CFAA is a criminal statute but provides for civil action against anyone who "knowingly causes the transmission of a program, information, code or command, and as a result of such conduct, intentionally causes damage without authorization to a protected computer." Faulty software seems to fit the definition rather well. Two court cases in particular, *Shaw* v. *Toshiba American Information Systems* and *North Texas Preventative Imaging* v. *Eisenberg*, expanded the definition of "transmission" in CFAA to cover market transactions of faulty software.

In 1999, Ethan Shaw and Clive Moon filed a class-action suit under CFAA against Toshiba and its parent company NEC for manufacturing and distributing floppy disk devices that contained faulty software. The software failed to properly detect errors in writing to the floppy disk, resulting in storage of corrupt data and/or the destruction of data without the user's knowledge.[17] Shaw and Moon sought an injunction to prevent the continued distribution of the faulty code.

The court first noted that, although the statute was a criminal law, it provided a private right of action. Reviewing the statute's language along with analogous case law, the court held the statute did in fact apply to the shipment and delivery of faulty software in computer parts. The court held that the manufacturer was liable under CFAA, despite the fact that Toshiba neither designed nor owned the rights to the NEC computer parts on which the software existed.[18] In essence, the court found that Toshiba was *transmitting* faulty code simply by shipping and delivering faulty floppy disk drives.

In *North Texas Preventative Imaging* v. *Eisenberg*, a similar finding protected the software buyer against a logic bomb placed in their software by the software manufacturer. Texas Preventative Imaging is a Dallas-based provider of medical diagnostic imaging. To assist its diagnostic imaging, Texas Preventative Imaging bought a computer system known as the "Scribe system" from Medical Diagnostic Imaging, Inc. (MDI), a California-based software company. The Scribe system performed enhancement of medical images aiding in the diagnosis process of cancer. Texas Preventative Imaging was dissatisfied with the Scribe system, and it sent MDI a letter "canceling" its purchase of the Scribe system and demanding return of its purchase price.[19]

MDI refused and responded with a letter asking Texas Preventative Imaging to enter into a new license agreement and noting that, if the new license was not executed, the software would be disabled on January 31, 1996. When the software was initially installed, it contained no time restrictions or other disabling codes. However, MDI periodically sent Texas Preventative Imaging update disks to keep the Scribe system current.[20]

Here's where it gets dirty. In late 1995, MDI sent Texas Preventative Imaging an update disk which, unbeknownst to Texas Preventative Imaging, contained a time bomb that would render the Scribe system inoperable at a pre-set time and date. Texas Preventative Imaging learned about the time bomb's existence and filed suit under CFAA.

The court found "transmission" to include the development of destructive software by MDI, shipment of that destructive software via disk, and downloading of the destructive software from the disk onto the client's computers. Although MDI had not hacked into the client's computers directly and installed the time bomb, MDI surreptitiously included the time bomb in a regular update disk, which, of course, Texas Preventative Imaging dutifully used to patch its system as any responsible software user should do.[21] To the court, MDI's actions were unacceptable and the court found in favor of Texas Preventative Imaging.

These two cases were important because they set legal precedent regarding the software development practices of vendors. Developing faulty code and then shipping it to customers, as in the case of *Shaw v. Toshiba America*, was interpreted as a violation of CFAA. How much more was a violation of CFAA committed in the second case when MDI developed defective code, shipped it to customers, and embedded a logic bomb in a software update? The legal tide appeared to be turning in favor of software users, not software manufacturers. Fast forward 10 years later.

In 2006, Microsoft included language in its Windows Vista license agreement that essentially permitted Microsoft to "unilaterally decide that [users] breached the terms of the [End User

License Agreement] and can essentially disable the software and possibly deny [users] access to critical files on [the user's] computer without benefit of proof, hearing, testimony, or judicial intervention."[22]

But wait, how could Microsoft fundamentally include time-bomb or drop-dead code in their operating system when courts found in 1996 that MDI was in violation of CFAA by "transmitting" the exact same type of functionality Microsoft was shipping in 2006? Moreover, Microsoft, as well as thousands of other software manufacturers, have released in total thousands of patches each year to repair both software vulnerabilities and software defects alike; yet none have had a judgment against them. What happened to the legal precedent?

It was essentially overridden—not by another court, but by Congress.

In 2001, Congress amended the Computer Fraud and Abuse Act to explicitly include the following language: "No action may be brought...for the negligent design or manufacture of computer hardware, computer software, or firmware."[23] In effect, Congress made it legal for software manufacturers what was unacceptable for everyone else. Injecting logic bombs into software would land a hacker in jail if caught, and creating faulty products would land other manufacturers in court. The new language clearly provided absolution for insufficient software manufacturing practices as well as insulation from any further legal action under CFAA.

While the amended language was a setback for software buyers, the change was faithful to the original intent of the law. The Computer Fraud and Abuse Act was intended primarily as a *criminal* statute with the option of *civil* action against individual hackers that broke into systems, not civil action against software manufacturers that shipped broken systems. Fundamentally, the law was meant to curb computer fraud and abuse resulting from *unauthorized* computer use. CFAA was not intended to address *authorized* abuse, which is in fact what users consent to upon agreeing to the seller's licensing terms.

So while the change in the law is understandable, the amended language left software buyers with no recourse for the damages caused by faulty software. But maybe there was hope.

Seeing that previous courts found in favor of plaintiffs under the original interpretation of CFAA, the logical follow-up question might be, "Did Congress enact replacement legislation to protect users against what was obviously identified by earlier courts as unacceptable behavior on the part of software manufacturers?" The answer is "No." To date, Congress has yet to enact or even seriously consider any statute imposing liability on software manufacturers.[24]

In fact, both the Congress and Senate have moved farther down the path of punishing software buyers for the iniquities of software manufacturers, further insulating the industry. Instead of moving to protect software buyers, both the House and Senate have joined the pervasive self-flagellation movement sweeping the States by proposing a bevy of new data breach notification laws, holding a wider range of private and public organizations liable for cyber intrusions.[25] A federal equivalent of the California data breach law is not outside the bounds of possibility at this point. Yet all the security configuration and firewalls in the world will not mitigate the consequences of insecure software. Think about it. An automobile's crumple zone is not a counterbalance against defects in the vehicle's frame, nor is a seat belt substitution for the quality of the vehicle itself. These are protective features *in addition to* quality engineering not *in spite of* faulty manufacturing.

> *An automobile's crumple zone is not a counterbalance against defects in the vehicle's frame, nor is a seat belt substitution for the quality of the vehicle itself. These are protective features in addition to quality engineering not in spite of faulty manufacturing.*

The Federal Agency Data Breach Protection Act introduced by Congressman Tom Davis marks the height of our dysfunctional relationship with software. The insistence that we, software users, are the only parties culpable for cyber intrusions is misplaced, incomplete, and myopic. Some might even say dangerous. Congress has mistakenly bought into software manufacturers' erroneous argument that cyber crime can be blamed solely on the sophistication of cyber criminals and on haphazard attempts on the part of users to implement adequate security measures. In fact, a majority of cyber intrusions—roughly 70 percent—result from attackers exploiting software vulnerabilities, vulnerabilities made possible by grossly inadequate software engineering practices.[26] Software manufacturers share enormous responsibility for the problems of disorder and cyber crime—a far greater share than laws reflect or Congress apparently is willing to acknowledge. This imbalance must change.

Holding software manufacturers responsible for the consequences of defective and insecure software will arguably provide far stronger incentives for manufacturers to improve their practices and will, at base, address the continuing message of disorder far more effectively than any actions to date. Focus must shift from blaming ancillary elements to the primary source of disorder. While Congress hesitates, the number of cyber intrusions and the incidents of cyber crime only increase.

If Congress will not act in a timely manner, then, will the courts? The answer is complicated.

Victims of a Border War

The next force of failure in the software story is the judiciary. To be completely fair, the courts are not failing, per se. The legal system is doing what it is supposed to do; it just looks like failure to outsiders. Perceived or actual, however, failure has consequences.

- To date, despite an epidemic of computer security flaws, no plaintiff has recovered damages for cyber crimes enabled by flawed software.[27]
- Courts have yet to extend professional standards of care to software designers who develop...code that lacks adequate security.[28]
- No court has recognized strict liability as a cause of action...and there are relatively few cases predicated upon negligence.[29]
- Judges have steadfastly refused to extend strict product liability to software, let alone insecure software.[30]
- Courts have yet to recognize an action for professional negligence filed against software engineers who construct insecure software.[31]

- The evolution of software law has led to the enforcement of adhesion contracts, depriving software buyers of meaningful remedies.[32]

Why should the courts demonstrate the same hesitation toward holding software manufacturers culpable as Congress? The answer is a little more comforting but no less frustrating. As flexible and as swift as the courts might be compared to the well-chronicled sclerosis of political, military, and religious institutions, historically there has been a lag between the common law and good sense.[33] This works for and against society. Legal lag means laws do not change so quickly as to be ephemeral and quixotic or change so slowly as to cripple and stagnate; yet there is a period of confusion in which old laws are not relevant to new environments or technologies and therefore must be revised and updated to keep pace. While this process can be slow, it is by no means as slow or as erratic as other institutional processes.

As a case in point, in 1936 a young law student named Richard Nixon, who would later become President of the United States, observed in *Changing Rules in Automobile Accident Litigation* that an extensive legal lag existed between the widespread adoption of cars and the development of modern product liability laws.[34] In 1905, Nixon observed that all of American automobile case law could fit within a four-page law review article,[35] but by 1935 a "comprehensive, detailed treatment [of automobile law] would call for an encyclopedia."[36] In the 30-year interim between 1905 and 1935, Nixon found that judges were extending the principles underpinning "horse and buggy law" to automobiles as well as applying some creative judicial "special sauce" by stretching current legal formulas to achieve a result that better aligned common law with the notion of "good sense."[37] It was a relatively tumultuous time until a majority of the kinks were resolved and the law could provide equitable remedies for new civil wrongs involving automobiles.

The same tumultuousness appears to be the current state of cyber law. Courts have yet to develop a legal regime, which suitably protects software buyers in general and victims of insecure software in particular.[38] Current cyber-related laws are fundamentally reflexive extensions of old intellectual and copyright laws proving far more favorable to AOL, Microsoft, Walt Disney, and Hollywood than to consumers.[39] In effect, these

> *Courts have yet to develop a legal regime, which suitably protects software buyers in general and victims of insecure software in particular.*[38]
>
> *Current cyber-related laws are fundamentally reflexive extensions of old intellectual and copyright laws proving far more favorable to AOL, Microsoft, Walt Disney, and Hollywood than to consumers.*

laws insulate software manufacturers in the same manner as horse and buggy laws unexpectedly insulated automobile manufacturers. Mix in the growing number of data breach notification laws that essentially hold software buyers strictly liable for failures in cyber security by wholly ignoring software manufacturer culpability, and software buyers are considerably disadvantaged in this new era.

Legal lag is understandable, but in the case of software, legal lag was and is exacerbated by a larger national trend in the United States, starting back in the 1980s. Earlier, I referred to Ronald Reagan's inaugural address that started a chain reaction of less government involvement in a wide range of activities, particularly business. Regan's philosophical stance also resulted in fewer court impositions into the affairs and activities of individuals. Nowhere has this been more significant than the border between contract law and tort law.

In the United States, contract and tort law live within a broader form of law known as *common law*. The United States common law system is a useful remnant from its time as a colony of England. The common law itself dates back to 1154 when Henry II became the first Plantagenet king of England and institutionalized the country's laws by creating a unified system of law "common" to the country; hence, the term "common law."[40]

Common law is made by one of three law-making bodies in the United States. The three law-making bodies are the legislature, executive branch agencies, and the courts. Statutes, such as the Computer Fraud and Abuse Act, Clean Air Act, or Civil Rights Act, are enacted by legislatures comprised of elected officials. Regulations, such as requiring automobiles to be equipped with airbags, are the real and enforceable laws behind

Congressional Acts and are promulgated by executive branch agencies that have been delegated rule-making authority by the legislative body. Examples of executive branch agencies include the Environmental Protection Agency, Department of Transportation, and the Food and Drug Administration.

The third and final law-making body is the courts. Courts create common law. Common law, also known as *case law*, is law based on legal decisions issued by previous courts. In essence, common law is "judge-made law," or laws enacted by judges who must come to a decision by balancing case facts against interpretations of prior court decisions, statutes, and legal doctrines. *Roe v. Wade* mentioned in Chapter 3, or *North Texas Preventative Imaging* v. *Eisenberg* mentioned earlier in this chapter, are examples of case law. Common law is notable for its inclusion of extensive non-statutory law (laws created outside the legislature) that reflects previous courts' decisions known as *precedent* that have been handed down through centuries of judgments by working jurists.[41] This to a large extent makes common law consistent, explicit, and rational. Consistent, since judges are bound to a certain extent by the decisions of previous judges; explicit, since the interpretations, reasoning, and decisions are documented in a court record; and rational because it is self-correcting. Erroneous court decisions can be reversed.

Common law itself is divided into property law, contract law, and tort law. Each of these have central organizing principles that act as basic paradigms for legal action. The central organizing principle in property law is that individuals may do as they please with their own property. For contract law, the central organizing principle is that individuals should be able to freely agree between and among themselves. The contract establishes a structure within which individuals can voluntarily negotiate and reach agreements they feel best serve their own needs or desires. Finally, the central organizing principle in tort law is that people should act reasonably under the circumstances, whatever those circumstances may be, and that if they do not, they should compensate those whom they foreseeably injure due to their unreasonableness.[42]

In the big picture, contract and property law assign responsibility to individuals through actions in the private market.

Unless actions are illegal, individuals can do as they please. The market will encourage or discourage behavior as buyers and sellers see fit. In contrast, tort law imposes responsibility on individuals through courts and juries.[43] In other words, contract law rests on mutually imposed obligations by two or more bargaining parties; there is no outside interference. Tort law rests on obligations imposed by courts. Of the three, contract and tort law are most frequently involved in "border wars," depending on the political ideology of the time.[44] This is why President Reagan's inaugural comments had such far reaching effects.

In Reagan's vision, "...government is the problem because it interferes with individual freedom, particularly the individual freedom to pursue self-interest through the market, the social institution that promotes the best results."[45] In essence, private parties, not courts or government, are best at ordering and coordinating themselves to achieve the greatest benefit. Thus, "private ordering" embodies the ideology of autonomy and consent; assigning decision-making power to individuals and the market rather than courts and government.[46] Between contract and tort law, then, contract law aligns far better with Reagan's vision of individual freedom than does tort law.

As such, the 1980s witnessed one of the most aggressive and widespread law reform campaigns in American legal history.[47] Almost every state in the union enacted one or more limitations on tort rights and remedies.[48] In short, contracts, not tort, became the dominant legal paradigm in the relationship between parties. This tectonic shift would have been fine, except for one significant problem: adhesion contracts.

When buyers sign contracts containing terms they do not even comprehend and for which they have no bargaining power whatsoever to change, their self-interest and well-being is subordinated to the interests of another more powerful party. Instead of abiding by the central organizing principle of contract law, which holds that people are "free to agree...and voluntarily negotiate" among themselves, the situation is less a practice of contract law and more a perversion of its intent. There are only two words to describe this situation: The Sopranos.

The mafia is well known for offering people "a deal they cannot refuse." Of course, software buyers *could* refuse to sign adhesion contracts just as a person could theoretically refuse a deal from the mafia. Both would do so at great personal expense, however. They are free but mordantly so.

To refuse to accept a software license of a single manufacturer means software buyers are essentially forgoing participation in the market all together, considering that every other software manufacturer offers similar terms. If a buyer refused to accept licensing terms from one manufacturer, it seems reasonable to believe they would not accept essentially the same licensing terms from another manufacturer. This leaves the buyer with no suitable or acceptable alternative except not to use software at all. Of course, the immediate counterargument is that buyers, as free participants in the market, can indeed refuse any given software license. The buyer can choose not to accept the license and not to use software. This is true but only in principle. The reality is quite different.

> *Of course, software buyers could refuse to sign adhesion contracts just as a person could theoretically refuse a deal from the mafia. Both would do so at great personal expense, however. They are free but mordantly so.*

Once upon a time, an information technology (IT) system simply gave organizations and companies a competitive edge. For instance, having a computer database crammed with electronic records was not only much easier to organize than a physical filing system, but the database allowed data to be retrieved, aggregated, sorted, and analyzed in a just few minutes traditionally would otherwise take perhaps days just to retrieve. This functionality certainly gave companies a competitive edge over other companies but only for a time. As more and more companies saw the value of and adopted IT systems, these systems went from something that lent an advantage to something that was critical just for survival.

In *Does IT Matter?* author Nicholas Carr makes the observation that IT has largely been commoditized and that anyone can set up a web server, accounting system, or inventory management system. The wide accessibility of IT means that while anyone can set up a web server or inventory system, not many companies can survive without one since competitors can easily acquire the same technology and potentially surpass a company that does not. Considering in 2006 global expenditures on IT exceeded $1 trillion, it is perhaps safe to speculate companies are spending frantically on IT so as not to be surpassed by their competitors. What is true for commercial business is perhaps relevant for government also, only in a different context. As a case in point, the State of California recognized the following:

Without IT, many state operations would be cost-prohibitive or simply unable to meet current service demands. Thus, it is appropriate to view IT as a key component of the state's operational infrastructure. *[my emphasis] In today's state government, computers perform a wide variety of functions including aiding in the design of highway systems, providing local law enforcement officers with criminal history record information, and providing citizens with local employment opportunities.*

The importance of IT has been recognized by the Legislature, which has established in law both policies governing the state's uses of IT and the OIT as the organization responsible for over-seeing the use of such technology in the state.[49]

Without an IT system, not only is an organization at a disadvantage, but it threatens the organization's survival in the case of business and the organization's relevance in the case of government. The State of California recognizes that without software, it would be unable to adequately service the needs of its populace. To forgo accepting a software license could, in effect, cripple its ability to fulfill its fiduciary responsibilities. Considering Microsoft Windows has roughly 90 percent of the desktop market and close to 40 percent of the server market, the State of California, or any other organization for that matter, would be hard pressed to

> *The State of California recognizes that without software, it would be unable to adequately service the needs of its populace. To forgo accepting a software license could, in effect, cripple its ability to fulfill its fiduciary responsibilities.*

find a suitable alternative to Microsoft that did not use nearly the exact same licensing terms. Software buyers have a choice between accepting software license terms or being crippled by irrelevance. It's a deal you cannot refuse.

Much is said about poverty creating a Digital Divide between those who have access to the technology and those who do not. Poverty restricts individuals from partaking in a large and growing portion of the global economy. As a knowledge-based economy displaces the mass production durable-goods economy, the "digital have-nots" are and will remain truly disadvantaged. While there exists substantial sympathy regarding *poverty* in regard to acquiring technology, little sympathy exists for *principle*. Namely, if software buyers decline to leverage information technology by refusing to agree to, on principle, the abhorrence of adhesion contracts, that is unfortunate—but not a tragedy like poverty. But herein lies the problem. Poverty might not be a choice, but it does have a way out. Adhesion contracts are not nearly as kind.

In reality, software buyers are victims of a border war between contract law and tort law. The benefits in reducing tort rights and remedies over the past 30 years are

> *Poverty might not be a choice, but it does have a way out. Adhesion contracts are not nearly as kind.*

offset by the disadvantages introduced by belligerent private ordering allowed by adhesion contracts and used to great effect by the software and technology industries. From this perspective, contract law has failed to provide software users with any meaningful remedies for the consequences of insecure software. If courts are to continue to enforce these one-sided contracts, which by all accounts it appears they are likely to do, the border war between tort law and contract law might need to intensify for the condition of software buyers to improve.

It would be a mistake, however, to consider tort law as a panacea. Contracts are preferred for their efficiency because individuals freely negotiate terms they deem acceptable without any interference from outside parties. Private ordering is just that, private people ordering themselves thusly. Contracts are also preferred given that courts are involved only if a breach of contract terms occurs. Even then, the court's involvement is simplified considering that contract language is the primary basis by which any disputes will be resolved.

In the age of tort retrenchment, statutory immunities awarded through the Computer Fraud and Abuse Act, in addition to the court preference for the private ordering paradigm over tort, the development of torts in cyberspace is extremely slow and difficult. This complicates the remedies tort can provide as well as hinders the speed at which they can be provided. Besides, tort is expensive in time, effort, and resources for everyone involved, including the courts. A number of factors, therefore, must come together to make tort an effective tool to combat the software industry's immunity. These factors are...

Duty, Breach, Cause, Damage

Duty, breach, cause, damage. This is the mantra of tort.

The word "tort" is an awkward word. It derives its meaning from the Latin word *torquere*, which means "twisted or wrong."[50] In essence, tort is a "wrong" that occurs when a party breaches an expectation society has of that party's behavior; in other words, the party in question breaches a societal duty it has to another party. For instance, a doctor has a duty to exercise the care and skill of the average qualified practitioner. If the doctor fails to do so, she is breaching her duty. But a breach of duty is simply not enough in tort. Actual *harm* must have occurred to another party because of that breach, and there must be a *causal* relationship between the breach of duty and the harm inflicted. If that causal relationship is identified and reasonably relevant to the situation in question, the victim can seek compensation for *damages* (the injuries resulting from harm).

Suppose, for the sake of argument, javelin throwers have a duty to exercise reasonable care in conducting their sport and that the intended beneficiaries of that duty include everyone within the stadium who will enjoy the spectacle of javelin throwing but might be put at risk by a javelin thrower's failure to fling with adequate care. If you survived reading that sentence, now suppose two throwers each fling their javelins with reckless abandon at a contest; one causes injury, and the other does not. Both have breached a duty, and in so doing both have committed a wrong, but only the javelin thrower that caused injury is subject to tort.[51]

When this threshold is met, the injured party can attempt to recover damages for his or her losses. In this scenario, the victim of the reckless javelin throw could seek recovery for damages against the reckless thrower. The ultimate measure of damages, and therefore the amount paid to the injured party, is determined by the nature of the tort committed and the type of injury suffered. "Impaled by javelin" would certainly give the victim a rather high likelihood of recovering for damages. Damages generally fall into one of four categories: damages for injury to person (as in our javelin example), damages for injury to personal property (such as a car), damages for injury to real property (such as a home), and punitive damages (awarded in excess of actual damages to "punish" the offender). Alternatively, victims can ask for "injunctive relief" which, if granted by the court, is an instruction to desist from a wrongful activity.

Duty. Breach. Cause. Damage.

What distinguishes tort law from contract law is that in contract law the totality of a party's legal obligations—or liabilities, an obligation to do or not do something—is declared within the "four corners of the contract;" that is, whatever is written on the pages of the contract are the contracting parties' legal responsibilities to each other. If one party disclaims any and all warranties (as with software licenses) and the other party accepts this disclaimer language in the contract, the *injured* party (plaintiff) is blocked from taking action against the *injuring* party (defendant) for breach of contract because, in essence, the injured party has freed the defendant from an obligation not to cause harm. As stated previously, the terms within the contract are up to the parties to determine and agree upon. As long as the contract terms do not violate a law or "shock the conscience" of the courts, parties are free to bargain among themselves without any

> As long as the contract terms do not violate a law or "shock the conscience" of the courts, parties are free to bargain among themselves without any need for court involvement—at least until a breach of the contract terms occurs.

need for court involvement—at least until a breach of the contract terms occurs. By the way, courts have proven to possess extremely tolerant consciences when it comes to contracts; therefore, *shocking* the court is far more difficult than one might think.

In tort law, by comparison, courts recognize society-imposed obligations that parties are expected to abide by. Legislative bodies can define these obligations, but frequently courts and juries identify and determine these duties by way of case law (previous court decisions). The negotiating skills of autonomous parties are not relevant in this process.

For instance, prior to the court case *Elliot* v. *Laboratory Specialists, Inc.*, laboratories conducting tests for the use of illegal drugs by employees on behalf of employers were not responsible to the employees should the laboratory falsely determine the employee was using illegal drugs. Depending on an organization's hiring policies regarding substance abuse, employers will often terminate the individual's employment should a drug test come back positive. This is exactly what happened to David Elliot.

Mr. Elliot was released from his employment after Laboratory Specialists reported his urine sample tested positive for THC, the active ingredient in marijuana.[52] In such a situation, it seems entirely foreseeable that a false finding by a drug testing laboratory could cost an employee his job—but only until a court says so.

This is where tort law gets expensive and arduous. Tort law places the burden of showing a breach of duty on the *victim*. It is up to the victim to connect all the dots for the court, ultimately demonstrating duty, breach, cause, and damage. If the victim fails to do this, the injuring party (the defendant) escapes paying for inflicted harm.

Courts need only look at what is contained within the four corners of a contract in a dispute between parties. However, in first-of-its-kind tort cases courts must look at the "four corners of society," so to speak, to determine if, as a matter of public interest, a duty has been breached. Whereas a contract explicitly delineates the obligations a court will consider in a breach of contract case, society is a mish-mash of implied cultural norms, differing political viewpoints, and philosophical disparities, making the determination of one party's duty to another more difficult.

In the David Elliot case, the plaintiff's attorneys (the lawyers working on behalf of Mr. Elliot) had to build a case against Laboratory Specialists (the defendant) to demonstrate to the court that in fact (1) a duty to Mr. Elliot was breached by Laboratory Specialists, (2) harm was inflicted on Mr. Elliot, and (3) it was foreseeable that harm could be inflicted by the defendant's breach. Note that Laboratory Specialists did not have a direct relationship with Mr. Elliot; Mr. Elliot's urine sample was one of thousands of samples the laboratory handled on behalf of multiple employers. There were no contracts or immediate relations between Mr. Elliot and Laboratory Specialists. In this case, Mr. Elliot was a third party, and yet the actions of the laboratory could have foreseeably harmed Mr. Elliot. This is important.

Judges use the concept of foreseeability to decide whether *proximate cause* exists. Proximate cause is a misleading term because it has nothing to do with proximity of the defendant to the plaintiff; it has everything to do with the scope of liability of the defendant. A judge must ask the question, "Do the injuries in this case bear some reasonable relationship to the risk created by the defendant's actions?" If the defendant should have foreseen that they could have caused injury, the defendant would be held liable for the plaintiff's loss. If a given risk could not have been reasonably foreseen, proximate cause cannot be established, and liability is not imposed.

Testimony by an expert witness during the *Elliot* trial showed the testing procedures used by Laboratory Specialists "cannot under any circumstances, be considered appropriate, scientifically defensible, ethical, or proper at any kind of level."[53] The expert witness also found the chain of custody was "totally inadequate,"[54] meaning that samples could easily be tampered with, mishandled, or contaminated.

The court recognized the reasonableness of imposing a duty and the foreseeableness of injury if the laboratory should breach its duty:

> *We find the elements of tort present, fault, causation and damage...To suggest that [Laboratory Specialists Inc.] does not owe Elliot a duty to analyze his body fluid in a scientifically reasonable manner is an abuse of fundamental fairness and justice. LSI should be held responsible for its conduct.*
>
> *The risk of harm in our society to an individual because of a false-positive drug test is so significant that any individual wrongfully accused of drug usage by his employer is within the scope of protection under the law. Mr. Elliot being labeled an illegal drug user has such emotional, economic and career detrimental effects that failure to find protection under our law would be a step backwards for the protection of the individual. LSI's duty to Mr. Elliot is as obvious as any independent contractor's standard of care to an employee of another.[55]*

Another court agreed with this reasoning in a separate case, *Stinson* v. *Physicians Immediate Care, Ltd.*

> *We agree with* Elliot *[and other related cases] that there is a close relationship between a plaintiff and a defendant which had a contract with the plaintiff's employer if it is reasonably foreseeable that the plaintiff will be harmed if the defendant negligently reports test results to the employer.*
>
> *Here, the injury, that the plaintiff would be terminated from his employment, is not only foreseeable, but also is a virtual certainty in the event of a positive drug test result. In addition, the likelihood of injury is great; the plaintiff allegedly lost his job and was hindered in his efforts to find other employment because of the false positive drug test report. The first two factors favor imposing a duty.*

Again, foreseeability is as critical here as is the imposition of a duty. The court goes on to state

---

We agree with Elliot ...that public policy requires the imposition of a duty here. The drug-testing laboratory is in the best position to guard against the injury, as it is solely responsible for the performance of the testing and the quality control procedures. In addition, the laboratory, which is paid to perform the tests, is better able to bear the burden financially than the individual wrongly maligned by a false positive report. We therefore hold that a drug-testing laboratory owes a duty of reasonable care to persons whose specimens it tests...

In addition to illustrating duty, harm, and foreseeability, both the *Elliot* and *Stinson* cases demonstrate a central notion to tort law, which is the moral notion of "ownership" as opposed to the notion of "blame."[56] Tort law establishes a mechanism for recognizing a party's ownership of the harm their behavior generates. It does this by imposing a duty to compensate the victim for the costs of such behavior. Rather than ascribing blame to the defendant, tort seeks to shift at least some of the costs of the victim back to the liable party; therefore, tort law imposes a *duty of repair* in addition to a *duty of care*. Tort allows a defendant to *take ownership of their responsibility to another*.

> Tort law establishes a mechanism for recognizing a party's ownership of the harm their behavior generates. It does this by imposing a duty to compensate the victim for the costs of such behavior.

At bottom, tort law provides victims with an avenue of redress for a party's violation of a duty; however, tort law does not guarantee recovery. Tort law places steep requirements on victims in order to satisfy due process—that is, to remain fair to the defendant. The more sophisticated and complicated a situation (as it is in the story of software), the more difficult it becomes to satisfy the mantra of tort. As such, victims must not only be willing to satisfy these requirements, but must be willing to invest significant amounts of time and money to do so. It is no wonder many victims opt to "grin and bear it" and move on.[57] In the case of software, resignation only adds to manufacturer's immunity.

Still, tort law serves an important function in society and fills in where either no contractual relationship exists between parties or where contract law fails to provide meaningful remedies. To understand how this might be possible, two more aspects of tort law must be discussed.

Teleporting Tigers

Tort law distinguishes between two basic kinds of liability: fault liability and strict liability. Fault liability is further divided into two categories: *intentional* wrongs such as battery, defamation, and invasion of privacy, and *unintentional* wrongs, otherwise known as *negligence*. A large number of tort actions fall under negligence claims, and much of what we discussed so far in this chapter relates to negligence. Negligence is conduct that falls below the standard established by law for the protection of others against unreasonable risk of harm.[58] Doctors can be found negligent as well as lawyers, electricians, motorists, Nevada brothel owners, or even drug testing laboratories.

Strict liability is another aspect of an unintentional wrong but is a completely different animal than its sibling, negligence. Strict liability is a legal doctrine that imposes liability on a party irrespective of the amount of care or diligence exercised. In essence, it is liability without a wrong; there is no requirement to demonstrate fault in the case of strict liability. Likewise, there is no defense in strict liability that the defendant followed a commercial, judicial, or legislative standard of care. In strict liability, if, as the saying goes "shit happens," the defendant owns the failure. Period.

Strict liability is a public policy stance for the protection of society for certain risky, but beneficial, activities. In other words, strict liability is reserved for those who engage in risky, for-profit activities that might be useful and necessary for society but are nonetheless dangerous to society and its members.

The traditional examples of strict liability include demolition (or blasting), generating or transporting hazardous materials, or harboring wild animals as in the case of a zoo or circus. In these examples, no matter how much care and diligence are exercised by the defendants, they will be held strictly liable if blasting harms someone, a nuclear processing plant irradiates a town, or a tiger jumps its enclosure and mauls somebody. It does not matter if the tiger's cage is made of titanium bars no futher apart than one centimeter and hung 1000 feet in the air. If the tiger magically teleports himself to the ground and mauls somebody, the circus is strictly liable. Even though the circus did nothing wrong and took all available precautions, a tiger on the loose is a hazard to society.

> *Strict liability is a public policy stance for the protection of society for certain risky, but beneficial activities. In other words, strict liability is reserved for those who engage in risky, for-profit activities that might be useful and necessary for society but are nonetheless dangerous to society and its members.*

This same notion of "liability without wrong" applies to manufactured products as well but not until the last half of the twentieth century. It was not until the 1960s that *strict product liability* was introduced in force. Before then, manufacturers could release defective products into the stream of commerce without any liability, typically hiding behind the doctrine of the *privity of contracts*. The privity doctrine limited manufacturer's responsibility to their distributors (to whom they were contracting) and did not extend protection to consumers that were purchasing the products from the distributors. In essence, manufacturers were using the doctrine of privity to shield themselves from third-party claims for injuries caused by defective products. As could be expected, much of the case law surrounding this fiasco involved, you guessed it, automobile manufacturers.

In 1916, the case *MacPherson* v. *Buick Motor Co.* chipped away at the doctrine of privity. Judge Benjamin Cardozo allowed a consumer to recover for injuries caused by a collapsed wooden wheel on his automobile, stating that if the manufacturer is negligent, "where danger is to be foreseen, a liability will follow."[59] It was not until 44 years later in *Henningsen* v. *Bloomfield Motors* that the shield of privity was completely removed. The court stated the following in 1960:

The obligation of the manufacturer should not be based alone on privity of contract. It should rest, as was once said, upon the demands of social justice. When a breach of the warranty results in personal injury to the buyer the law is clear that such damages are recoverable...it is settled that where the buyer...suffers injuries because of negligent manufacture or construction of the vehicle, the manufacturer's liability exists.[60]

So far, so good, but complete consumer protection under product liability was not yet fully realized. Three years later in 1963, *Greenman* v. *Yuba Power Products, Inc.* solidified strict product liability as we know it today. The court found that a "manufacturer is strictly liable in tort when an article he places on the market, knowing that it is to be used without inspection [by the buyer] for defects, proves to have a defect that causes injury to a human being."[61] In other words, the sophistication of products had evolved to the point where normal consumers could no longer be expected to inspect products beyond a casual observation before use.

Most importantly, the court refused to "permit the manufacturer to define the scope of its own responsibility for defective products make[ing] clear that the liability is not one governed by the law of contract warranties but by the law of strict liability in tort. Accordingly, rules defining and governing warranties that were developed to meet the needs of commercial transactions cannot properly be invoked to govern the manufacturer's liability to those injured by its defective products..."[62]

The *Greenman* case signified recognition by the courts that the consumer product market had fundamentally changed. First, a wide variety of sophisticated mass market goods meant no single consumer could reliably inspect products before purchase and use. Second, complicated distribution chains created a labyrinth of intermediaries between the manufacturer and the consumer, removing any possibility for a direct relationship and, therefore, a direct contract between the buyer and manufacturer. Finally, the court recognized that product-related injuries were resulting in significant social costs to both victims and society.

The intersection of these three factors helped the court conclude that manufacturers were in the best possible position to prevent defects and therefore the injuries caused by them. While the cost to the manufacturer of improving quality and reducing liability was inarguably high, the cost was justified by the courts simply on the grounds of good public policy.

After *Greenman*, manufacturers became strictly liable for any injuries that resulted from placing defective products into the stream of commerce regardless of the amount of care exercised in manufacturing the product or whether the consumer entered into a contractual relationship with the manufacturer. Moreover, plaintiffs were freed from the onerous task of establishing proof of negligence as well as being released from contractual limitations on warranties and related victim-oriented expectations. Such is the power inherent in the doctrine of strict liability.

> *After Greenman, manufacturers became strictly liable for any injuries that resulted from placing defective products into the stream of commerce regardless of the amount of care exercised in manufacturing the product or whether the consumer entered into a contractual relationship with the manufacturer.*

A party subject to strict liability must bear the full costs of their activities as well as the costs imposed on others for engaging in the activity. Whether it's an automobile, lamp, or toaster, the manufacturer of a product is liable for defects that cause harm. As such, parties engaged in risky activities must be willing to ensure the safety of others as a price of doing business.

In cases involving wrongs due to negligence, the costs of accidents that are the fault of no one (for example, shit happens)—or are not worth preventing on the part of the defendant—are borne by victims. In contrast, strict liability dictates that all costs, no matter what they are, are borne by the party engaged in the risky activity. This means demolition teams must take every possible precaution when destroying a building, transportation companies carrying hazardous waste must acquire the most advanced equipment and take the most circuitous routes around populated areas, and zoos must build the very best tiger enclosures. Even if they do everything right, they must still be willing to accept the cost if something should go wrong. The risk of not doing so is too high for society.

Why, then, would one party be subject to negligence while another might be subject to strict liability? As with most things, money is a big issue.

The Least-Cost Avoider

From the economist's perspective, whether to impose negligence or strict liability amounts to determining the magnitude of incentives inducing individuals to take necessary cost-justified precautions and based on that research, identify which party is the least-cost avoider. The more risk inherent in the behavior, the greater the liability and therefore the greater incentive to take precautions. As such, economists tend to consider tort law a system of incentives for inducing parties to behave in socially efficient ways; that is, what liability rules are most likely to have the greatest impact on reducing accidents at the least-cost?

> *Economists tend to consider of tort law a system of incentives for inducing parties to behave in socially efficient ways.*

For instance, suppose a neighborhood allows outdoor wood-burning fireplaces.[63] If a spark should land on the fireplace owner's roof or fly through an open window, it might catch his house on fire. For the sake of argument, the damage caused by this event is $20,000 but it only has a 1 in 100 chance of occurring. The *expected loss* from this event, then, is $200; the total cost of the event ($20,000) *multiplied by the probability* the event will occur (1 percent).

If the fireplace owner could purchase a wire screen for the outdoor fireplace for $50, he would incur a $50 expense for preventing an expected loss of $200. In this case, the benefit of the wire mesh far outweighs the costs—that is, spending $50 to avoid incurring $200 in expected loss. The fireplace owner would be demonstrating socially efficient behavior.

However, if the wire mesh was purchased from *Frontage* magazine for $250, the fireplace owner would be acting socially inefficient; the cost of the wire mesh exceeds the dollar amount he is trying to protect. It would be much better to either try to find a less expensive wire mesh or opt to increase the coverage of his home insurance as long as the added expense was less than the expected loss.

A more interesting problem exists, however, when, because of the distance from the fireplace to the house, sparks do not threaten the fireplace owner's home but instead threaten the homes of his neighbors. In this case, the total damage caused by the event might still be $20,000 (depending on the grandeur of the surrounding homes) with a 1 in 100 chance of occurring. The expected loss is still $200, but the incentives have changed. Compared to the built-in assumption of the incentive to protect his own home, would the fireplace owner spend $50 to protect his neighbors? How much does he like them, and what responsibility does he feel toward them?

In the absence of an obligation to protect his neighbors from damage, the fireplace owner might forgo purchasing the wire screen and therefore not choose the socially efficient precaution. In this case, the neighbors are depending on whether the fireplace owner (1) likes them and (2) is capable of simple multiplication. This might be far too erratic for the neighbors' liking, in which case legal intervention could be necessary.

In this case, negligence is most applicable because while backyard fires are certainly risky, outdoor fireplaces do not pose nearly the same magnitude of risk as keeping a tiger. Sparks and cinders fly out of fireplaces frequently, and a majority do not result in secondary fires; however, tigers rarely escape their zoo enclosures, but if they do, the tiger will most likely attack or harm someone as wild animals trapped in suburbia often do.

In the fireplace example, sparks *might* cause harm but *probably will not* if the wire screen is not purchased (there is a 99 percent chance damages will not occur). The obligation to purchase a wire screen is for social responsibility and efficiency rather than mitigating a clear and imminent hazard like housing a wild animal. In the outdoor fireplace situation, though, neighbors *could* protect themselves by purchasing fire-retardant shingles, paint, and so on. In short, the neighbors have the opportunity to mitigate the risk to some degree.

In the caged tiger example, if failure happens at all, irrespective of precautions or probability, it will most likely cause harm; hence, strict liability is most appropriate. Potential victims literally have no opportunity to protect themselves except to forgo going to or anywhere around a zoo. This behavior on the part of zoo goers defeats the purpose of the zoo for keeping a caged tiger in the first place; people pay admission to see a tiger.

The interesting thing here, though, is that the zoo can spread the cost of precaution across the paying population; that is, if excellent tiger enclosures cost $2,000,000, the zoo can increase its ticket price from $20 to $21. In essence, this is a "tiger tax" imposed by the zoo on customers curious enough to visit. As such, a "tiger tax" is socially efficient because the zoo is the best regulator of its behavior, not the general population. The population could only choose to visit or not to visit, but the zoo can invest in precautions that permit many visitors to safely view the tiger. Besides, it would be unreasonable—and a considerable disincentive for visitors—to expect each zoo visitor to pay $2000 for individual protective tiger suits.

In this case, the zoo is considered the *least-cost avoider*; that is, the zoo is in the best position to implement precautions and can do so in an economically efficient manner (spreading a small tiger tax over a large population such as 3.2 million visitors per year as with the San Diego Zoo[64]).

You can think of the strict liability rule as the "no brainer rule;" it is obvious the event will cause harm if any precaution fails for any reason, and it is obvious the defendant (the one that could cause harm) is in the best position to take precautions.

In summary, strict liability is assigned if defendants are the parties that can best adjust their behavior at the least-cost. Negligence is best assigned when plaintiffs have *an opportunity to adjust their behavior* outside of forgoing an activity entirely (not going to the zoo, or not buying software) or drastically altering their way of life (avoiding cities that have zoos, or avoiding all computers).

Negligence Versus Strict Liability

There are debatable aspects in negligence versus strict liability, however. Each has its drawbacks and advantages. Strict liability has three drawbacks. First, it is considered to be a regressive tax that punishes low-income market participants. Second, strict liability is seen as inefficient where both plaintiff and defendant should demonstrate some modicum of care. Finally, strict liability tends to over-deter risk taking, reducing the number of people involved in a beneficial but risky behavior. Negligence, on the other hand, has high administrative costs, can result in under-deterrence, is prone to error and might not recognize situations where the plaintiff is the best least-cost avoider.

When a zoo raises ticket prices from $20 to $21, the increase tends to disproportionately affect families with low incomes than it does families with higher incomes. This means that a $1 price increase has a greater effect on families for whom disposable income is already under considerable pressure, if disposable income exists at all. The additional $1 cannot possibly be spent because the family would need to forgo a basic necessity, and therefore a responsible low-income family would be deprived of the ability to go to the zoo. Wealthier families, in contrast, will not feel a $1 increase quite as acutely because the family would probably not think twice about the extra amount for zoo tickets, given the assumption that a richer family enjoys a considerable amount of disposable income. For instance, if a poor family made $10 per year, and a rich family made $100 per year, the "tiger tax rate" of the poor family would be ten percent of total income for a $1 increase of zoo tickets. For the wealthy family, a $1 increase would merely represent a one percent tax rate. As such, the costs imposed by strict liability are borne by everyone regardless of income, but the effect is not considered "fair" because of its unevenness. If the activity or product in question is sought more frequently by the poor and less frequently by the rich, the price increase or tax is considered a regressive tax and carries all sorts of political ramifications.

Second, strict liability might over deter risky behavior by making it too expensive for any party to engage in the activity. If parties bear the risk of all foreseeable and unforeseeable harms, parties might elect to avoid possible benefits—and therefore deprive society of possible benefits—because the radius of risk is largely unknown. This can have a particularly negative influence on new and emerging products or technologies. For instance, if a biomedical company were considering a new cancer treatment using a variant of genetically modified Bubonic Plague, the company might forgo pursuing the technology due to the large number of unforeseeable events. Not only might the company lose out on potentially enormous profits, but society would lose out on a potentially revolutionary medical treatment.

Finally, strict liability is considered inefficient if in addition to the defendant, plaintiffs also need to demonstrate a certain amount of care. In the case of the caged tiger, visitors to the zoo do not need to demonstrate any additional care because the enclosure is not only designed to keep the tiger in but to keep visitors out. However, consider a product like a chain saw. If a buyer knew that the chain saw was covered by strict liability and there was no need for him to demonstrate care in using it, the buyer might use the chain saw in an unsafe manner. For instance, if after an afternoon of heavy drinking, the chain saw's owner decides to accept the challenge of his friends to see how quickly he can cut down the tree in his front yard, he would obviously not be demonstrating proper care. Without a requirement of care on the part of the plaintiff, the strict liability rule is considered inefficient. Often times strict liability must be complemented with comparative or contributory negligence (placing a separate but related burden on the plaintiff to demonstrate care) in order to be considered efficient.

In the paradigm of negligence, administrative costs are significantly higher than in strict liability. Plaintiffs must collect as much evidence as possible to argue for duty, breach, cause, damage, and the courts must consider this evidence to determine the level of care that would be appropriate and optimal under the circumstances brought forth by the plaintiffs. In contrast, the strict liability rule merely requires the court to determine if the defendant caused the plaintiff's injuries. This is far less onerous and therefore far less expensive for all parties concerned, including the court.

Second, the expense of pursuing a negligence suit can act as a disincentive to plaintiffs that should otherwise be willing to file suit for actual harm. This can result in under-deterrence because defendants are not being held liable for that which they should and therefore are not bearing the full cost of their risky activities.

For example, consider a situation where a mining company fails to stop a leak in its sludge lake and pollutes a nearby stream. For the sake of argument, one thousand downstream residents each experience a loss of $100 because of the pollution. It would cost the mining company $50,000 to stop the leak. The total damage to downstream residents is $100,000, which is far greater than the cost of stopping the leak. A court would most likely find the defendant liable for not plugging the leak, so to avoid that liability it would be reasonable to assume the mining company would act in a socially efficient manner and invest in stopping the leak. However, if the mining company reasons that only 20 percent of the population is environmentally-conscious enough and has the funds (and desire) to pursue civil action, the defendant will likely avoid plugging the leak given that the cost of liability ($20,000) is far less than the fix ($50,000). In this situation, the defendant will not act socially efficient because paying the judgment is cheaper than addressing the problem.

Third, in determining negligence the court might be prone to error in determining the level of appropriate care. If the court sets the standard too low, a larger number of injuries can occur, leaving plaintiffs with fewer situations for action. If the court sets the standard of care too high, defendants might be paying too much for precautions. This balance can be further impacted by the ideological predisposition of the court in which the case is brought forward—that is, whether the court tends to be pro-plaintiff or pro-defendant.

Finally, the court might not recognize situations where the plaintiff, not the defendant, is the least-cost avoider. If it costs a plaintiff $10 to avoid harm, but it costs the defendant $100, the plaintiff is clearly the least-cost avoider. This can and does come down to the quality of the legal arguments which, in turn, returns us to the first problem with the negligence paradigm: high administrative costs.

Stripping Immunity

Let's return to our question, "If Congress will not act, will the courts?" This depends largely on the willingness of victims to pursue tort actions. Sadly, the software industry's immunity is

> *Sadly, the software industry's immunity is granted not simply from statutory immunity or the court's preference for the private ordering paradigm, but in part by the reluctance of software buyers to engage in tort battles.*

granted not simply from statutory immunity or the court's preference for the private ordering paradigm, but in part by the reluctance of software buyers to engage in tort battles. The better question to ask therefore might be, "If Congress will not act, will you?"

The lengthy discussion of legal concepts was necessary to highlight a number of important aspects regarding the software crisis. The *Elliot* case is an example of negligence and illustrated that the drug testing laboratory had a duty of reasonable care because a false report of drug use could foreseeably affect a person in a detrimental manner. It also demonstrated that the laboratory was in the best position to guard against injury as it was solely responsible for the performance of testing and the quality control procedures. As such, the lab was better able to bear the financial burden (the least-cost avoider) than the person wrongly maligned by the lab's inadequate processes.

This case offers interesting parallels to software. Software manufacturers are in the best position to guard against vulnerabilities as software manufacturers are solely responsible for testing their software and implementing internal quality control procedures. As such, software manufacturers are better able to bear the financial burden of addressing software weaknesses than buyers of software. In short, it makes more sense to assign the task of securing software to a relatively small number of software manufacturers compared to burdening the software's 500 million potential users with the responsibility. It is also far cheaper in financial and social costs to make software manufacturers the least-cost avoider. Finally, assigning a duty of care to software manufacturers seems reasonable because in a networked world, it is highly foreseeable attackers (such as cyber criminals) will discover and exploit software weaknesses. Based on this, it can be safely argued that software manufacturers owe their customers a duty of reasonable care to produce software that does not make them susceptible to exploitation and enable criminal or warlike behavior.

The *Greenman* case supports this reasoning but from a strict liability perspective, thereby eliminating the requirement for plaintiffs to "connect the dots" for the court. The case signifies recognition by the courts that the consumer product market had fundamentally changed. Products could no longer be inspected by buyers for suitability due to products' increasing sophistication. If a user cannot reasonably inspect a chain saw or lawnmower before purchase, it is safe to assume that those same buyers would not be able to inspect software either. Nor should they. Consumers must rely on the manufacturer to make a product that is safe for its intended use, no matter how complex or unforeseeable an intended use might be. Testing the product after purchase, or worse, the expectation of software manufacturers for users to test the products for them, is unacceptable.

The *Greenman* court also recognized that product-related injuries were resulting in significant social costs to both victims and society. The epidemic of cyber crime has been made possible largely in part by grossly inadequate software engineering practices, incurring a high cost to both victims and society. As such, by stipulating that automobile manufacturers were in the best possible position to prevent defects and therefore the injuries caused by them, the court gives a potentially helpful platform by which to impose the same level of responsibility on software manufacturers. Software manufacturers are in the best possible position to prevent defects and the disorder created by software vulnerabilities. Based on current statistics, firewalls, anti-virus, and other security products are not and cannot successfully fulfill a protective role that should belong primarily to software manufacturers.

While the cost of improving quality and reducing liability was inarguably high for automobile manufacturers, the cost was justified by the courts simply on the grounds of good public policy. With cyber crime at epidemic proportions, an ascendant China and Russia abusing software vulnerabilities to support their own political and commercial agendas, and no clear or effective mechanisms for law enforcement agencies of different countries to coordinate on capture and prosecution, it is reasonable to assert that while the cost to software manufacturers of improving quality and reducing vulnerabilities might also be extraordinarily high, it is justified simply on the grounds of good public policy. This cost will not bankrupt the software industry any more than it did other industries before it. While the added production costs will inevitability result in an increase in software prices, the market has proven extremely resilient to such shocks. Automobile sales are higher than ever before.

After *Greenman*, manufacturers became strictly liable for any injuries that resulted from placing defective products into the stream of commerce regardless of the amount of care exercised in manufacturing the product or whether the consumer entered into a contractual relationship with the manufacturer. Moreover, plaintiffs were freed from the burden of establishing proof of negligence as well as being released from contractual limitations on warranties and related expectations of the victim to make their case.

In other words, the decision of the *Greenman* case gives cause to ignore blanket excuses or even well-reasoned arguments by software manufacturers why "something can't be done" simply on the grounds that good public policy dictates protection of the public, no matter how difficult it proves to be. Surely an industry known for innovation can look this challenge squarely in the eye. The failure of contract law to provide meaningful remedies for the victims of software vulnerabilities also provides compelling arguments for strict liability for software manufacturers given that dense and obfuscated licensing terms are made moot.

Finally, the *MacPherson*, *Henningsen*, and *Greenman* cases together show that even parties enjoying a significant amount of immunity, like the pre-1960s automobile industry, can eventually be brought to task for irresponsibility no matter how strong the prevailing legal precedents and no matter how seemingly unrelated previous court decisions might have been. Software manufacturers might indeed enjoy absolute immunity, but as history has shown, it will not, and should not, last forever.

The ultimate objective of liability for software manufacturers is the proper demonstration of care and diligence supported by incentives that promote and encourage quality and security, rather than excuse and absolve grossly inadequate software engineering practices. Tort law allows software manufacturers to take ownership of their responsibility to society. If immunity breeds irresponsibility, then the process of stripping immunity is the first step to promoting preventative vigilance and care by software manufacturers. How then to strip immunity?

One of the first potential decisions is whether negligence or strict liability is most appropriate. Each has its advantages and disadvantages as discussed previously. While the *Greenman* and *Elliot* cases provide a suitable foundation for investigating software manufacturer liability, two groups of legal thinkers have each separately pursued negligence and strict liability for software manufacturers in great detail. In May 2005 Frances Zollers, Andrew McMullin, Sandra Hurd, and Peter Shears argued for strict liability where software defects result in physical injuries to users. They based their arguments in part on what would appear to be completely unrelated to software: aeronautical charts. Later that same year, Michael Rustad and Thomas Koenig authored an article in the *Berkley Law Journal* that argued for tort action against software manufacturers when negligently designed software enables cyber crime. The following sections discuss each group's line of reasoning, and then the chapter concludes with a possible action plan for software buyers.

Strict Liability and Aeronautical Charts

The Zollers group argues that strict liability is now appropriate for the software industry on two counts. First, the software industry is no longer in its infancy and has become a dominant multi-billion dollar sector of the economy. While initial legal protection might have been understandable so as not to stunt the growth of the fledgling industry, software has long since left its nest and now walks among the largest and most influential enterprises on earth. Second, given the significant number of cases where defective software has resulted in death or injury and the likelihood this number will only increase as software embeds itself further into the foundation of civilization, it is well within reason to "consider liability for defective software in the same light as liability for defective automobiles, pharmaceuticals, and other products."[65] In truth, software has as much capacity to do harm as products from all other industries, yet the software industry faces none of the liability exposure as does its counterparts.

The conditions under which the *Greenman* court established strict product liability are precisely the conditions found today in the software market. Namely, software is typically a mass-market good demonstrating "a significant propensity for harm if the product is defective." Additionally, "an injured buyer...has no bargaining power to negotiate a deal with the manufacturer...different from the rest of the buying public...and [there exists] a large disparity in knowledge about the product...between the manufacturer and the affected party."[66]

The use of adhesion contracts means that buyers have no ability to negotiate and must accept whatever level of protection the manufacturer feels is appropriate, even if that level is deficient or non-existent. As mentioned earlier, the knowledge required to construct software makes it nearly impossible for software buyers to inspect software, regardless if the application's source code is proprietary or made openly available. As such, injured parties cannot possibly pinpoint exactly what went wrong or where in the software the defect might be. This poses a significant barrier to the consumer for protective action as well as creates a broad shield for the manufacturer. Previous court cases have established this is unacceptable and that, as decided in the *Greenman* case, "it is sound policy to place the burden on the one who is in the best position to avoid the defect in the first place [software manufacturers] even though doing so may pose an extreme hardship on one producer or another."[67] The fact that software *inevitability* contains bugs is not a valid defense by software manufacturers. On the contrary, that software defects are inevitable explicitly dictates the need for applying strict liability.

> "It is sound policy to place the burden on the one who is in the best position to avoid the defect in the first place [software manufacturers] even though doing so may pose an extreme hardship on one producer or another."

The Zollers group bases their reasoning on multiple court cases, each of which addresses many of the hurdles that have historically limited legal action against software manufacturers. The court cases cited by the Zollers group include cases of false information contained in books, cases involving defective navigation charts, and cases involving failures on the part of other industries to practice due care.

A central question Zollers puts forward is whether information in a computer program is analogous to information in a book. Zollers argues it is not based on the intent behind the First Amendment. While software enjoys copyright and intellectual property protection, it is not information in the same way the content of books is information and therefore should not necessarily be held to the same standard or afforded the same protection as literary works. Because of these assumed similarities, however, First Amendment issues such as freedom of expression have often arisen in the software arena. Citing multiple court cases involving false information in books, Zollers highlights that the distinguishing aspect between errors in books and defects in software is that while books contain the thoughts and expressions of an author, for which they should not be held liable under the First Amendment, the value of software lies not within expressions made by the software programmer, but within the software's behavior itself. In short, books do not *behave*; software does.

As such, errors in books can arise not only because of the author's mistakes, but because of misinterpretations by the reader, making strict liability inappropriate. Errors in software, on the other hand, are due solely to software engineering error because computers are incapable of "misinterpreting" software instructions. In fact, computers do exactly what software engineers instruct the computer to do through software—no more, no less.

The inherent functionality of software is an aspect that distinguishes it from books and makes it more a product than an expressive work of art; therefore, First Amendment concerns should not affect nor protect the software industry as it does literary works. To establish this reasoning further, Zollers cites another set of court cases involving defective navigation charts used by the aviation industry.

The information contained in navigation charts is similar to information in books insofar as it is a printed medium that transmits information to the reader. However, unlike with books, courts have routinely held that navigation charts are products for purposes of product liability and that strict liability can be applied due to functionality inherent in navigational charts and the harm that can occur if charts are inaccurate. The court's findings on these cases are important to Zollers because the similarities between navigation charts and software provide a critical avenue for establishing strict liability in software cases resulting in injury or death. The critical similarities between software and navigation charts are that they are works intended to be *functional* and *useful*. In comparison, books are works that are primarily expressive and literary. Zollers cites four separate cases where inaccurate navigation charts led to airline crashes.

In *Aetna Casualty and Surety Co. v. Jeppesen & Co.*, the court found the defendant, Jeppeson & Co., "strictly liable for injuries caused by a defective product."[68] In this case, a commercial airplane crashed on approach to Las Vegas airport, killing all on board. What is so interesting about this case is that neither party disputed that Jeppesen's approach charts were accurate. In fact, Jeppesen's charts were accurate in every respect.[69] The defect lay in the ambiguities in the graphical representation Jeppesen used for its 3-mile and 15-mile approach charts. The court stated

---

The "defect" in the chart consists of the fact that the graphic depiction of the profile, which covers a distance of three miles from the airport, appears to be drawn to the same scale as the graphic depiction of the plan, which covers a distance of 15 miles.

...when faced with the Las Vegas chart [pilots] would assume that the altitude shown on the profile as proper for three miles distant would, reading it as drawn to the same scale as the plan, be proper for 15 miles distant...the crash was due to pilot reliance on this faulty assumption, invited by the difference in scale...this difference in scale created a conflict between the information conveyed by the graphics of the chart and that conveyed in words and numbers, and that this conflict rendered the chart defective.[70]

In other words, even though the charts were individually and completely accurate, the scale used by Jeppesen in each chart made it difficult for pilots to easily differentiate between the 3-mile and 15-mile approach charts. The court found that the Las Vegas chart "radically departed" from the usual presentation of graphics in other Jeppesen charts. The conflict between "the information conveyed by words and numbers and the information conveyed by graphics rendered the chart unreasonably dangerous and a defective product."[71] The court also stated that the purpose of navigation charts was to translate the chart's information into "an instantly understandable graphic representation."[72] This is what gives charts their usefulness.

The second case Zollers identifies in support of imposing strict liability for software is *Saloomey* v. *Jeppesen & Co.* In *Saloomey*, the court held Jeppesen & Co. strictly liable for manufacturing a faulty navigation chart that led to a private airplane crash in West Virginia that took the lives of the pilot, his father, and the pilot's six-year-old son.[73]

The pilot of the aircraft had an area chart for the Washington D.C. area, but he did not have an approach plate for the Martinsburg airport. At the time, the Martinsburg airport did not possess a full instrument landing system (ILS); it was equipped with a localizer beam but not a glidescope beam.

A localizer beam provides lateral guidance on approach to the runway, informing the pilot whether the aircraft is too far to the right or too far to the left of the runway. In other words, the localizer beam keeps the plane centered on the midline of the runway. A glidescope beam provides vertical guidance that directs the aircraft to follow the typical 3-degree descent path to the runway for a smooth, "glide in" landing. However, glidescopes are normally designed assuming the site around them is flat and might need to be adjusted for uneven terrain. If a pilot were to assume a normal glide path using a non-existent glidescope in hilly or uneven terrain like the terrain around the Martinsburg airport, the "normal" glide path could intersect with a large stationary object such as a mountain.

The tragedy was that the Jeppesen aeronautical chart for Washington D.C. showed the Martinsburg airport as indeed employing a full instrument landing system when, in fact, it did not. The National Transportation Safety Board report on the crash noted that the plane wreckage was located at 1400' on the west side of a 1600' mountain ridge.[74] The plane apparently struck the ridge at a normal descent angle in virtually exact alignment with the runway and the localizer beam.

Again, the chart's functionality and accuracy was the primary issue of this court case. While certainly conveying information, the chart was far from the notion of artistic free expression because a chart must correctly instruct pilots, not invoke emotions. As such, a chart is more appropriately classified as a product rather than a literary work, even though it looks and smells like a picture. The court stated

---

There was certainly adequate evidence to sustain the jury's specific findings that Jeppesen's ... chart was defective...and that Jeppesen was negligent in the manufacture or inspection of that chart.

By publishing and selling the charts, Jeppesen undertook a special responsibility, as seller, to insure that consumers will not be injured by the use of the charts; Jeppesen is entitled—and encouraged—to treat the burden of accidental injury as a cost of production to be covered by liability insurance...the mass production and marketing of these charts requires Jeppesen to bear the costs of accidents that are proximately caused by defects in the charts.[75]

While Jeppesen & Co. was found strictly liable in *Saloomey*, the next court case Zollers cites demonstrates the full power and consequence of strict product liability.

In *Brocklesby* v. *United States*, another Jeppesen chart was at fault for an airplane crash near Cold Bay, Alaska. But in this case, the Jeppesen chart was accurate insofar as it did accurately portray an instrument approach procedure as provided by the Federal Aviation Administration (FAA). Unfortunately, the FAA's data that Jeppesen used to manufacture the chart was wrong.[76] In other words, the defects in the Jeppesen chart were a result of the FAA's faulty procedure and not a typo or error on the part of Jeppesen. As would be expected, Jeppesen argued that it should not be held liable for a problem caused by the government.

Recall from our previous discussion, however, that strict liability does not depend on fault, yet this did not stop Jeppesen from pointing the finger at its "supplier," the government, for creating the defect. Jeppesen's position resembled the "contract specifications" defense in which the defendant's contract with the plaintiff states that the manufacturer cannot be held liable for producing a product in accordance with specifications that are beyond its control.[77] This also happens to be a classic defense used by software manufacturers—that they cannot he held liable for third-party software included in their own. This argument is a kind of "dodge the bullet" defense by which the manufacturer attempts to side-step any responsibility for defects caused by a supplier.

However, the court pointed out that Jeppesen did, in fact, have an opportunity to inspect data from the government and that "Jeppesen's manual requires its employees to contact official sources to resolve apparent discrepancies in information."[78] More fundamentally, however, the court stated that

---

...existing products liability law is contrary to Jeppesen's position. Assuming that the Government's instrument approach procedure was defective, the literal requirements of [product liability] are met. Jeppesen's chart was a "product in a defective condition unreasonably dangerous to the user" [and that] strict liability is appropriate even though "the seller has exercised all possible care in the preparation and sale of his product."

A seller is strictly liable for injuries caused by a defective product even though the defect originated from a component part manufactured by another party. Accordingly, the appropriate focus of inquiry is not whether Jeppesen caused the product to be defective, but whether the product was in fact defective.[79]

A seller is strictly liable for injuries caused by a defective product even though the defect originated from a component part manufactured by another party. Accordingly, the appropriate focus of inquiry is not whether Jeppesen caused the product to be defective, but whether the product was in fact defective.

The last sentence of the court's statement is most critical. Regardless of what defects Jeppesen *could have detected* and whether or not Jeppesen *caused the defect to occur*, the product manufactured and released by Jeppesen *was defective*. Period. It does not matter how the defect occurred, even if the cause of the defect could be attributed to a process or product completely outside the control of the manufacturer. Strict liability dictates responsibility for a defective product released into the stream of commerce irrespective of the cause, reason, or excuse. The court reiterated that strict liability does not depend on fault and that sellers are strictly liable for injuries caused by a defective product even if they have exercised all possible care:

The justification for strict liability has been said to be that the seller, by marketing his product for use and consumption, has undertaken and assumed a special responsibility toward any member of the consuming public who may be injured by it;

...that the public has the right to and does expect, in the case of products which it needs and for which it is forced to rely upon the seller, that reputable sellers will stand behind their goods;

...that public policy demands that the burden of accidental injuries caused by products intended for consumption be placed upon those who market them, and be treated as a cost of production...

...and that the consumer of such products is entitled to the maximum of protection at the hands of someone, and the proper person to afford it are those who market the product.[80]

The last case cited by Zollers is *Fluor Corp. v. Jeppesen & Co.* In *Fluor*, a plane crashed into a hill on approach to Adirondack Airport in New York, killing all on board. The Jeppesen chart failed to show the hill, even though it was the highest point in the area.[81] Like previous cases, the court found that

> *[Jeppesen's] position that its navigational charts provide no more than a service ignores the mass-production aspect of the charts. Though a "product" may not include mere provision of architectural design plans or any similar form of data supplied under individually-tailored service arrangements, the mass production and marketing of these charts requires Jeppesen to bear the costs of accidents that are proximately caused by defects in the charts.[82]*

The higher court went on to clarify that "the policy reasons underlying the strict products liability concept should be considered in determining whether something is a product within the meaning of its use...rather than...to focus on the dictionary definition of the word."[83] In essence, the court held that charts should be considered products whether or not charts are actually products under the strictest definition of the word since charts *are used as products.*

The fact that a navigation chart is a piece of paper with information on it is irrelevant. As all these court cases have shown, a chart is functional and useful. The court stated that "although a sheet of paper might not be dangerous, per se, it would be difficult indeed to conceive of a salable commodity with more inherent lethal potential than an aid to aircraft navigation that, contrary to its own design standards, fails to list the highest land mass immediately surrounding a landing site."[84] Moreover, the court insisted that

> *...characterizing [Jeppesen's] instrument approach charts as products served the public policy to relieve plaintiffs from the problems of proof inherent in pursuing negligence and warranty remedies, and thereby to insure that the costs of injuries resulting from defective products were borne by the manufacturers that put such products on the market rather than by the injured persons who were powerless to protect themselves.*

•

As such, the deceased pilot should not be found negligent, nor should the pilot's survivors need to establish the pilot was not negligent. By simple fact the Jeppesen chart failed to accurately show the hill in which the pilot crashed, Jeppesen was strictly liable relieving the victims from the onerous task of proving themselves non-negligent and the defendant liable.

All four court cases demonstrate the court's stance on the functionality and usefulness of navigation charts as a product rather than as an artistic expression or literary work. The courts repeatedly struck down notions that aeronautical charts were merely "information" or "expressions of an author." The courts applied strict product liability to something that certainly would look and smell like information to an ordinary user, but in practice acted like a product.

As such, Zollers believes the court's reasoning on strict product liability for charts is a more perfect analogy for understanding software rather than the traditional thinking of copyright and intellectual property. Namely, software, like navigation charts, is functional and not literary. There is no other purpose for navigational charts than to instruct pilots in the function of flying. Likewise, software has no other purpose than to instruct microprocessors in the function of computing. Even though software might look and smell like information, in practice it is *used* like a product. In other words, software's value lies in its behavior, not in its text.[85]

> There is no other purpose for navigational charts than to instruct pilots in the function of flying. Likewise, software has no other purpose than to instruct microprocessors in the function of computing.

The functional aspect of navigation charts makes free expression in navigation charts an undesired quality.[86] Information contained in navigation charts must be factual and accurate. There is little cause or reason when manufacturing a navigation chart to take literary license, make a political statement, or exercise artistic expression.[87] Hence, the court's interpretation was that navigation charts are a product. The same is true of software.

Software must be accurate, and it must work.[88] Computers are logical morons and cannot deal with ambiguity in the same way as humans. Free expression is not a desired quality in software of any import. As such, software is exclusively functional, not literary, political, or artistic. Besides, van Gogh did not build the Brooklyn Bridge, nor did Robert Ludlum construct the U.S. Interstate system. Software *is* infrastructure; books and artwork are culture.

The final important point the Zollers group highlights especially from the *Saloomey* case is that the term "mass-marketed" should not be confused with "marketed to the masses."[89] Whereas navigation charts are used by a very small segment of the population and are not available in book stores or local retail shops, a defect in a chart can extend consequences far beyond the user of the chart.[90] This means even software that is not shrink-wrapped, such as software in medical devices, software used in monitoring nuclear reactors, or software embedded in automobiles, can cause a wide and devastating impact on those who were not the intended purchasers.

As case in point, Zollers goes on to argue that while millions of automobiles are purchased every year by a wide range of consumers, the impact of defective software embedded in an automobile is not much different from that of defective software in an air traffic control system, which is sold to a very small group of purchasers.[91] It is not, then, the number of units sold that defines "mass-market," but the *scope of the impact* a defect would have on the populace.[92] Connect software, no matter the type, to a network, and the impact is simply magnified.

In summary, Zollers believes that current market conditions are suitable to impose strict liability on software manufacturers. First, buyers are unaware of and unknowledgeable about software's inner workings. Second, the buyer is not a bargaining party in the sale of software; subsequently, the buyer has no ability to negotiate the allocation of liability if something should go wrong. Third, in instances where software is embedded in "traditional" products such as automobiles, microwave ovens, traffic lights, or medical devices, there exists a significant likelihood of grave injury should the software be defective or because of defects be exploited specifically to cause harm.[93] And finally, software is no longer in its infancy. Software is everywhere, embedded in just about everything, used for just about any purpose. Defect can no longer be tolerated.

The imposition of strict liability on the software industry removes the incentive to place defect-ridden software into the stream of commerce especially where faulty software can have high human costs. While perfect software is not possible, strict liability removes the notion that software may be "incrementally improved" at the expense of consumers and national infrastructure. It is no secret software companies rush product to market to gain competitive advantage, but this rush-to-market is not the same as being unable to attain excellence; one is an excuse and the other an engineering limitation shared by every other product on the market and accepted as the cost-of-doing-business by every other manufacturer. Strict liability merely balances the equation in favor of the software buyer and places responsibility, as it did with navigation charts, back onto the party best in position to avoid defects.

Faced with strict liability, software manufacturers might give pause when releasing software with the intention of letting buyers tease out defects. Zollers presumes that software that can cause serious injury or death would not be employed so cavalierly by the software industry, yet in general when software manufacturers are held to a mere negligence standard of liability, this might be exactly the case as it was with Multidata Systems mentioned in Chapter 4.[94]

In the end, the Zollers group limits the scope of strict liability to software defects that result in physical injury or death but stops short of imposing strict liability for lesser harms. There remains, then, the epidemic of cyber crime for which Zollers' arguments for strict liability do not apply. To address this shortfall, a different group of legal thinkers proposes a liability regime for software manufacturers that aid and abet cyber criminals by releasing defective software into the stream of commerce.

The Tort of Negligent Enablement of Cyber Crime

According to Michael Rustad and Thomas Koenig, the software industry has simply abdicated to third parties its responsibility for limiting high-risk defects in software through one-sided licensing agreements.[95] As discussed previously, this allows software manufacturers to shift potential losses they might incur due to defective software to weaker contracting parties who must accept the entirety of all risk. This practice has resulted in an epidemic of cyber crime because cyber criminals often exploit vulnerabilities in software applications that should have been corrected by software manufacturers but were not because the necessary incentives for doing so were absent. The failure of contract law to provide minimum consumer protection and meaningful remedies to victims of cyber crime simply exacerbates the situation, making the use of tort law a necessary imposition for reducing the number of defects in software. Thus, Rustad and Koenig propose a new tort on software manufacturers for the negligent enablement of cyber crime.

Under Rustad and Koenig's proposed tort, software manufacturers would owe a duty of reasonable care to software users for protecting them from highly foreseeable cyber crime. The duty would entail eliminating negligent software design, grossly inadequate software engineering practices, and poorly implemented software applications, thus producing software with reduced vulnerabilities and a greater likelihood of withstanding exploitation. This in turn would inhibit the growth of cyber crime, in that fewer vulnerabilities means fewer avenues by which cyber criminals can attack victims. Surely, there will be other avenues by which attackers might exploit the unsuspecting, but closing down the avenue provided by software blunders is a critical measure. The negligent enablement tort would also provide remedies to victims when defective software "paves the way for highly foreseeable cyber crime."[96]

The negligent enablement tort is not just aimed at software manufacturers, however. The proposed negligent enablement tort would also allocate responsibility to both software manufacturers and end users where appropriate. Software manufacturers would certainly be held liable for distributing software with preventable security flaws, but computer users would also be accountable to a certain extent for failing to take minimum precautions such as protecting passwords or not responding to email promoting on-line scams or duping users into providing sensitive personal information. The failure of a software user to do so would make the user *comparatively negligent*; that is, any damages the plaintiff might collect would be reduced by the degree of their own negligence. This would not absolve software manufacturers from a majority of liability; on the contrary, it merely reflects the *shared* responsibility of protecting computer systems and assigns responsibility where appropriate.

For a new tort to succeed, however, it must be anchored in well-established principles of common law. The negligent enablement tort has its foundations in premises liability, negligence-based product liability, and professional malpractice.[97] Each is used to construct a modified duty of care for software manufacturers. As with any tort, however, the mantra of tort—duty, breach, cause, damage—must be satisfied by plaintiffs if they hope to recover damages as victims of cyber crime. This makes the proposed tort not nearly as easy to employ as Zollers' strict liability arguments but nonetheless provides a possible avenue for redressing the ills of cyber crime.

Of the three legal theories, premises liability is perhaps the most interesting to investigate considering we have already touched on product liability and professional malpractice in other sections of the book. To summarize the other two, then, product liability in a "bad software" case would be based upon "claims that personal injury, death, or property damage was caused by a manufacturing defect, design defect, or failure to warn software users of a known danger."[98] Software engineers could be held liable for malpractice based on failure to develop reasonably secure software. Even if software engineering is not held as a "profession," as is medicine and law, even members of a skilled trade can be held to standards of care and practice for that trade.[99] Courts would need to work out, then, exactly what an acceptable standard might be; a topic I address in Chapter 7, "Moving Forward."

Rustad and Koenig reason that protecting software users from the actions of cyber criminals is similar to the concepts undergirding premises liability. In premises liability, an owner of property is legally responsible for accidents and injuries that occur on that property. If an owner invites the public onto his property for business purposes, the owner is potentially liable if those invitees are harmed by the attacks of third parties. For instance, Rustad points out premises liability lawsuits are often brought against owners of hospitals, colleges, day care centers, shopping centers, and other properties whose inadequate security measures fail to prevent criminals from attacking customers.

This is in large part why retail shoppers see mall guards at the local shopping center, gate guards and security cameras at public parking garages, and other defensive measures taken by owners of retail establishments.

Just as retail establishments must employ security measures to protect their customers, so too, reason Rustad and Koenig, should software manufacturers:

The seller of inadequately configured software may expose its customers to predators just like a retail establishment that fails to employ security guards in a high crime area. A software vendor may owe a duty of care to its customers as well as to third parties that makes it liable for enabling the conversion of credit card numbers, the invasion of privacy, identity theft, or the misappropriation of trade secrets. Courts may find a vendor liable for rushing poorly tested software to market.[100]

In essence, through their actions, owners send a message into the environment either of disorder or control; subsequently, that message either attracts or repels criminals. According to the authors, what is true for landlords might also be for software manufacturers. Rustad and Koenig's reasoning also appears to tie in rather neatly with the mantra of broken windows: Inattention invites disorder. And disorder invites greater disorder, even crime. So just as landowners "may create dangerous conditions that attract robbers and murderers,"[101] software manufacturers may, by producing vulnerabilities in software, create equally hazardous conditions that attract cyber criminals.

Rustad and Koenig's reasoning also appears to tie in rather neatly with the mantra of broken windows: Inattention invites disorder. And disorder invites greater disorder, even crime. So just as landowners "may create dangerous conditions that attract robbers and murderers," software manufacturers may, by producing vulnerabilities in software, create equally hazardous conditions that attract cyber criminals.

The use of premises liability is novel, but as Rustad and Koenig point out, premises liability would need to be heavily modified by the courts to make it usable within a tort action. The problematic aspect of the premises liability theory as applied to software manufacturers is that cyberspace is borderless and does not involve land, the basis of premises liability. This means premises liability must be extended or expanded by the courts in order to be useful in the negligent enablement tort. Whether a court would be willing to do so in practice remains to be seen.

Rustad and Koenig argue the negligent enablement tort will create essential incentives for the software industry. "Just as the auto industry enacted safety audits after the imposition of product liability, the software industry will respond to the proposed tort by allocating more resources to preventing cyber crime through better design, fortified product warnings, and more thorough testing."[102] While Rustad and Koenig are hopeful the negligent enablement tort will significantly change the status quo, Rustad and Koenig recognize the tort will not eliminate cyber crime, rather reallocate the associated costs to the parties in the best position to prevent cyber crime.

The Verdict...

The beauty of the American legal system is that it is largely a grass roots system where anyone can seek redress for harm at any time. Of course, this can also be argued that it is a weakness of the system given that frivolous lawsuits can potentially clog the courts. Regardless, the courts are not in the habit of seeking out wrongs and acting on them; that is the job of a vigilant populace. As such, a certain amount of frivolousness is to be expected, even tolerated. The courts are merely an avenue for correcting wrongs, not the impetus.

That being said, taking legal action against another party is an unpleasant affair and is not to be taken lightly. The reader should not assume undertaking legal action against software manufacturers, or any party for that matter, is desirable. In the absence of relevant legislative statutes, regulatory laws, and meaningful protections through warranty, legal action is oftentimes considered the least unacceptable alternative.

Imposing liability on software manufacturers is not unreasonable. To date, laws such as the Computer Fraud and Abuse Act make hackers completely accountable for breaking into computer systems, even if they are rarely caught. Data breach notification laws make software buyers completely liable should the sensitive data they possess, like mailing addresses, social security numbers, and so on, be illegitimately accessed by cyber intruders. But no statute, or any regulatory law for that matter, imposes any liability whatsoever on software manufacturers for the defects that oftentimes make the other two parties accountable. In reality, liability rests only on software buyers, regardless of whether a software manufacturer could have eliminated the underlying defect, a firewall could have prevented an intrusion, or law enforcement could have apprehended a cyber criminal. This is essentially strict liability for software consumers. As such, culpability for disorder and resultant cyber crime is not properly shared. The imbalance should rightfully be corrected.

> *In the absence of relevant legislative statutes, regulatory laws, and meaningful protections through warranty, legal action is oftentimes considered the least unacceptable alternative.*

The benefits of imposing liability on software manufacturers is three-fold. To be sure, there are more possible benefits of imposing liability on the software industry, but these are just a few. First, the number of defects in software will decrease, and the quality of software will subsequently increase. History has shown that when manufacturers are subject to product liability, defects tend to be exposed more quickly both during and after production; subsequently, defects tend to be resolved more quickly, reducing the overall impact those defects might have on consumers in the marketplace. Prior to the development of product liability, automobile manufacturers employed contract disclaimers, releasing them from much of the consequences of their design defects. Auto manufacturers clouded the issue at hand by blaming the epidemic of driver injuries solely on driver error. To date, software manufacturers blame the epidemic of cyber crime primarily on hackers and on inadequate security precautions taken by software buyers when, in fact, like automobile manufacturers, their defects are largely to blame. Product liability changed the equation for auto manufacturers as it will most likely do for software manufacturers. The attempts at deflection will stop, and defects will decrease. This benefits consumers and civilization.

Even though software, under intellectual property and copyright law, might be thought of more as a "piece of information that can be licensed for use" rather than a durable product that can be purchased, Frances Zollers points out that, like aeronautical charts, software is *used like a product* and therefore could be potentially treated for legal purposes as a product. This makes the possibility of successfully imposing product liability on software manufacturers more likely.

Second, imposing liability on software manufacturers will reward socially responsible manufacturers that are currently at a competitive disadvantage with other manufacturers less concerned with the social costs of defective software. Socially responsible software manufacturers who otherwise might practice due care by reducing defects before releasing the product into the stream of commerce are forced under an absence of a liability regime to lower their standard of care to match that of other manufacturers in order to compete effectively.

For instance, if it costs a socially responsible software manufacture $100 to produce software, but it costs another manufacturer that does not practice due care $50, the manufacturer not practicing due care can under-price the socially responsible software manufacturer, potentially driving the socially responsible manufacturer from the market. To compete and avoid bankruptcy altogether, the socially responsible software manufacturer will be forced to some extent to lower quality to the level of their competitors. In short, the absence of a legal liability regime punishes those companies who would like to practice due care but cannot because of the realities of market competition. This behavior simply drives up the number of potential and actual software defects, increases the message of disorder, and subsequently invites greater cyber crime. In short, under a liability regime, the message "Don't worry. Be crappy," will no longer be tolerated.

Finally, imposing liability on software manufacturers will redistribute the cost consumers have traditionally paid for protecting software from exploitation back to software manufacturers where the cost belongs. Software manufacturers are the least-cost avoiders. This is true, if for no other reason than they are in the best position to know what their software does even if in actuality they do not. It is far more logical to assign the task of securing software to a relatively small number of software manufacturers compared to burdening 500 million software users with the responsibility. As the *Elliot, Greenman, Saloomey, Brocklesby,* and *Fluor* cases demonstrate, courts have regularly found that the producer, and not the consumer, is in the best possible position to prevent defects and therefore the injuries caused by them.

> *Software manufacturers are the least-cost avoiders. This is true, if for no other reason than they are in the best position to know what their software does even if in actuality they do not.*

While imposing liability will inevitably raise the cost of producing software and therefore the price to the consumer, the price increase will, like every other industry subject to liability, be spread evenly across the user base. In essence, such an increase would be seen as a "flat tax." A flat tax would be considered acceptable by economics because economists tend to favor taxes that are broad, simple, and fair. Besides, a relatively small increase in software prices compared to the enormous individual cost of protecting software from exploitation (which to date has failed to stem the tide of cyber crime) seems far more rational. In short, liability will not bankrupt the software industry any more than liability has bankrupted any other industry. Individual software manufacturers may disappear, this is true, but a whole new crop of software manufacturers will appear ready to satisfy the requirements good public policy dictates. It is simply the Law of Churn as described in Chapter 4, but employed to a more socially responsible end.

Stripping immunity from the software industry will not be easy, however. The complexities of tort law combined with an incomplete understanding of what software does and how it does it will make civil action suits expensive and complicated. Software manufacturers will undoubtedly contend that imposing liability on the industry is impractical because software manufacturers cannot possibly create defect-free software. Liability, so the argument goes, will stifle innovation and would therefore only serve to cripple the industry. Yet if software manufacturers are not held liable for the impacts of reasonably preventable software defects, there is an economic incentive for the vast majority of software manufacturers to use lowest care; this will hurt everyone else.

A second contention by software manufacturers might be that liability will simply introduce a flood of frivolous lawsuits, clogging the courts, and ultimately increase software prices due to software manufacturers' increased cost for insurance, improved manufacturing and production processes, and defending against lawsuits, frivolous or otherwise. This is only partly true. The "litigious society" America seems to be known for has little empirical basis. Only two percent of Americans ever file lawsuits, and of those, only 10 percent seek compensation for injuries.[103] At $152 billion per year, the entire American civil justice system is less expensive to operate than the specific costs imposed on the United States by cyber crime ($117 billion) and lack of software testing ($60 billion).

The claim that frivolous lawsuits result in increased insurance, manufacturing, and production costs for manufacturers sounds plausible, but in reality is far from a compelling argument. On average, the cost of product liability insurance for other industries amounts to 16 cents per $100 of retail costs, or 2/10 of 1 percent; an increase to be sure, but hardly an overwhelming burden.[104] And despite claims that the American legal system is "out of control" deterring manufacturers from marketing worthwhile, innovative products making American products less competitive in world markets, the United States remains the leader in almost every technology field.

But what manufacturers might fail to mention is that corporate defendants have historically employed tactics designed to increase the cost of litigation, not just for themselves but for everyone else. Michael Jordan, the counsel for R.J. Reynolds in the tobacco class action suits, commented, "[T]he aggressive posture we [the tobacco industry] have taken regarding depositions and discovery in general continues to make these cases extremely burdensome and expensive for [victim's] lawyers,...To paraphrase General Patton, the way we won these cases was not by spending all of [big tobacco's] money, but by making the other son of a bitch spend all of his."[105]

Like Big Tobacco, many software manufacturers are flush with money and have more than enough resources to engage in extensive, drawn out, and prolonged tort battles. But if size matters, consumers have historically had the advantage...*if they coordinate.* So the question remains, if legislatures will not act, will you?

Open Source Software:
Free, But at What Cost?

If you've ever used Google or Yahoo! to search the Web or been amazed by the special effects in movies like *Lord of the Rings*, *Cars*, or *Happy Feet*, you've witnessed the power and capabilities of a particular type of software called "open source software." Successful open source software projects bear names like Linux, Apache, and BSD. It is not necessarily different from other types of software such as Microsoft Windows, QuickBooks, or Intuit's TurboTax. Developers who create open source software use the same programming languages and can put their software on the same kinds of devices like personal computers, automobiles, or mobile phones as do other software manufacturers.

But open source is not just running search engines or creating special effects; it is being adopted—and in some cases mandated—by governments to run e-government initiatives that provide public services. The U.S. Government has adopted open source software for large aspects of defense, energy, and other critical infrastructure projects. Open source software has even found its way onto satellites and the Mars rovers. It is being injected into national, state, and municipal infrastructure as much as any other type of software and is often touted as a suitable and more secure replacement for proprietary software. As far as you, the user, are concerned, however, you would not and should not be able to tell the difference between open source software and another type of software unless someone told you.

Where open source software is distinct from other types of software, however, is *how* open source software is created and *what* intellectual property restrictions are enforced. These distinctions have ramifications for consumers, for the software market, and ultimately for the security of national infrastructures. In which case, knowing whether or not software is "open source" can matter greatly.

In 2006, the Department of Homeland Security (DHS) initiated a program dubbed the "Vulnerability Discovery and Remediation, Open Source Hardening Project." This program granted $1.5 million for identifying vulnerabilities in open source software.[1] What was interesting about this project was not the security weaknesses discovered *in* open source software, but what the project unwittingly highlighted *about* open source software. It could be that the great benefit of open source software, which is discussed in this chapter, might also be its great undoing.

Open and Shut

To understand the essence of open source software, it is helpful to step back for a moment from the immediate discussion and recall our previous description from Chapter 1, "The Foundation of Civilization," regarding the use and adoption of Portland cement. Portland cement is used all over the modern world in nearly every physical infrastructure project. This is possible because the composition of Portland cement is not secret; nor is the method for making it. Anyone can make cement if they have the inclination and the materials. Although the formula for this cement was once protected by patent, it can be considered "open" insofar as everyone knows—or can find out—what cement is compromised of and how to make it.[2]

Because the formula for cement is open and well-known, people have experimented with mixture ratios and manufacturing techniques over the years. Such experimentation has ultimately made cement more durable, resilient, and broadened the range of conditions in which cement can be used. In the past 40 years, the biggest improvements to cement include chemical and plastic additives, known as admixtures, which the United States now requires in the construction of highway pavements and structures.[3] In the long run, modern admixtures make concrete less expensive for taxpayers because they prolong the life of cement by reducing susceptibility to wear and tear as well as the stresses associated with freeze-thaw cycles.[4] It has also made the market more competitive because buyers can potentially select from a wider range of cement and cement manufacturers. From this perspective, the openness of cement's formula has benefited society substantially.

Now contrast the openness of cement's formula with the recipe for Coke, for instance, which is a trade secret the Coca-Cola Company has kept under guard for almost a century.[5] Although billions of people drink Coke, only a select group of individuals know the actual recipe. As such, the formula for Coke is proprietary to the Coca-Cola Company and is therefore considered a "closed" formula.

Though the Coca-Cola Company has fiddled with the secret recipe over the years (recall the blunder of New Coke), the company has largely forgone improvements to the original Coke formula, opting instead to acquire other beverage companies to expand its market share. The $4.1 billion acquisition in 2007 of Glaceau, the maker of Vitamin Water, is one such example.[6]

Because the recipe for Coke is closed to the public and has not been widely experimented with, it can be argued that Coke has not "improved" for nearly 100 years. But the formula is a success nonetheless. The Coca-Cola Company is the only company in possession of the secret formula, and consumers all around the world exuberantly drink Coke—as well as all the other drinks manufactured by the company—propelling Coca-Cola's profits into the billions year after year. From this perspective, the "closed-ness" of Coke's formula has also benefited society substantially because investors and shareholders have been able to share in the Coca-Cola Company's continued success.

The comparison between Portland cement and Coke highlights some important differences between "open" and "closed" formulas. Whether open or closed formulas are *better* depends on your point of view, your definition of "better," and who it might be better for. On one hand, closed formulas protect the intellectual property of the manufacturer. This restricts who can compete with the company and in turn maximizes the company's potential profits. On the other hand, open formulas, free from intellectual property restrictions, tend to promote improvements of a given formula. Because anyone can experiment with a formula in any manner they choose without fear of legal reprisal, creativity is given a whole new range of possibilities.

> *Whether open or closed formulas are better depends on your point of view, your definition of "better," and who it might be better for.*

Open formulas appear to possess a problem, however. Without legal protections such as patent, copyright, and other legal structures, the incentives for first-time innovators are questionable at best making an open formula a risky avenue for new, unique ideas to enter into the market. If protections for intellectual property did not exist, a competitor could acquire a newly developed, but unprotected formula, improve it, and compete with the original innovator well before the originator could enjoy the full fruits of his labors. If this were the case, an innovator would have little rational incentive to innovate in the first place because any advantages related to innovation (such as profits) would be reduced, if not lost entirely to a larger, more aggressive competitor. This is what traditional intellectual property law seeks to preserve: the incentive to innovate in the first place.

Open formulas, then, tend to do best when an innovation has already been widely adopted and legal protections have expired (such as the patent on Portland cement) or are non-existent (such as aggregating enormous quantities of publicly available information into a single collection such as an encyclopedia). In other words, open formulas appear to be best positioned to build upon things others have already done.[7] Openness promotes *further* innovation, but it does not necessarily promote *initial* innovation. Proprietary software manufacturers like Microsoft, Oracle, and Quicken favor the "closed" paradigm for just such reason. Proprietary software companies allow buyers to purchase their software but not the recipe that makes the software original. Just as consumers can drink Coke but do not have access to the formula for Coke, software buyers can consume (that is, install and use) Microsoft Windows but do not have access to Microsoft's recipe—the source code—for Windows.

Source code is certainly similar to a recipe, but this analogy has its limitations. Recipes are simply not functional in the same way as source code is functional. In this respect, source code is more like the script for a theatrical play than simply a recipe; that is, a play's manuscript tells actors what to do, how they should act, and what they should say. Likewise, source code instructs a computer what to do, how to act, and even sometimes, what to say to the audience—the computer user.

But a computer cannot do or understand all these things directly from source code. In fact, computers do not understand source code at all. Source code, which is written in a wide variety of programming languages just as manuscripts may be written in many different human languages, simply allows software developers to express what they would like the actors—the computers—to do. The "actor" cannot directly read what the playwright has written. Therefore, the "script" software developers create must be transformed into instructions computers—or more specifically the microprocessor—can understand. This is accomplished with the help of a special software application called a *compiler.*

A compiler transforms source code into a string of ones and zeros computers can read and "act to." This string of ones and zeros is called a *binary*, and this binary is the actual "software" you purchase from a software manufacturer. In other words, binaries are what software manufacturers in the business of creating proprietary software allow buyers to purchase. There is a very good reason for this.

While a binary is easy for a computer to read, it is tremendously difficult for a person—even the original developer—to understand. So just as it is nearly impossible for a curious soda drinker to decompose Coke into its original formulaic parts, it is equally challenging for a curious software user to reconstitute binaries into the original source code. As such, distributing binaries is an effective way for proprietary software companies to restrict what buyers can do with their software. Without the original source code, buyers cannot change their software, cannot understand the internal workings of their software, or experiment with different ways of making their software function in new and unique ways. This also means competitors cannot do the same, which is really the whole point. Proprietary software manufacturers would not release source code any more than Coca-Cola would publicly release the formula for Coke.

> *So just as it is nearly impossible for a curious soda drinker to decompose Coke into its original formulaic parts, it is equally challenging for a curious software user to reconstitute binaries into the original source code.*

This restriction is at the heart of intellectual property protection for software manufacturers. It allows software vendors to protect their initial investment of making unique and original software as well as earning the necessary profits and revenue needed to reimburse software developers for their creativity and reward shareholders and investors for their faith.

The essence of open source software is the exact opposite of proprietary software. Open source software is largely an innovation *after-the-fact*; that is, open source builds upon an idea already in the marketplace that can be easily replicated or copied. For instance, while the source code for Microsoft Windows is proprietary, the *concept* of an operating system is not. While the Encyclopedia Britannica is copyrighted, the *idea* of an encyclopedia is not. In each case, the open source community has taken what was already in the marketplace—commercial operating systems and encyclopedias, respectively—and simply made cheaper versions of each; Linux or BSD in the case of an operating system and Wikipedia in the case of an encyclopedia.

This same situation applies to many of the most successful open source projects: MySQL regarding databases (Oracle is the proprietary equivalent), Apache regarding web servers (Microsoft's Internet Information Server is the proprietary equivalent), and Firefox regarding web browsers (Microsoft's Internet Explorer is the proprietary equivalent).

It would be a mistake, however, to assume since open source projects are "mere copies" of previous products, open source software should somehow garner less respect. In fact, as "mere copies," this does not mean Linux, Wikipedia, or any of the other open source software projects are any less potent competitors in the market. In fact, open source is a significant challenge to downstream revenue for any market competitor. Open source cannot only do what others have done, but can do so cheaper and on a larger scale because open source projects can leverage forces that cannot be as easily tapped by their proprietary cousins, such as using thousands of volunteer software developers that would be otherwise too expensive to hire and employ.

> *In fact, open source is a significant challenge to downstream revenue for any market competitor.*

First, as an innovation after-the-fact, open source projects do not need the same legal strictures to protect first-time innovators considering first-time innovation is the exception rather than the rule in open source. This means binaries and associated source code can be released with few, if any, intellectual property restrictions, allowing anyone to use, study, modify, and re-release her own "new and improved" version of the software.[8] In other words, both the software and source code are non-proprietary and open to the public. This freedom applies to users and competitors alike. The advantage of this regime is that once an idea such as an operating system, web browser, or word processor is in the market, the idea can be aggressively evolved, beyond perhaps what even the original innovators ever thought possible.

A second advantage of open source projects is the cost and availability of labor. Instead of paying software developers for their ideas and contributions as do proprietary software vendors, the open source movement is largely volunteer-driven with rewards pertaining to merit rather than pay. Anyone can contribute. Anyone can be praised. Individuals donate their programming skills and ideas to a software project of their choice. In a way, one could think of the entirety of the open source movement as one would any other volunteer organization such as Habitat for Humanity.

Individuals involved in Habitat for Humanity donate materials as well as their carpentry skills to build or refurbish homes for disadvantaged families around the world. Likewise, software developers donate their programming skills free of charge to a particular software project either building a new software application or refurbishing a pre-existing one. But whereas Habitat for Humanity must look for local sources of material and labor close to the building site, open source projects can leverage the experience of developers located anywhere in the world. As long as volunteers have an Internet connection—and if they are software developers they probably do—volunteers can find a project to contribute to and do so from the comfort of their home. This model drastically expands the pool of labor that can be drawn upon for any given project at essentially no additional cost. Traditional manufacturing firms can only dream of such labor liquidity across national borders.

A third advantage of open source projects relates directly to the issue of software security. Given the number of contributors to an open source project and given that source code is open to the public, the number of available people to inspect the software for quality and security far exceeds the number available to proprietary vendors. Proprietary software vendors simply cannot release their source code for review by a broad population given that the very act would increase chances of their intellectual property being disclosed. As such, distribution of proprietary source code must be tightly controlled, if allowed at all.

In comparison, a cherished adage in the open source community is "given enough eyeballs, all bugs are shallow."[9] The reasoning is simple; as the number of people who use and inspect the source code increases, so too does the likelihood of discovering a weakness or blunder. This means that while a potential problem in software—a "bug"—might be difficult for a handful of people to discover over a given period of time, the same bug might be found quickly when thousands of people analyze and use the source code in question—hence, the metaphor of "shallow." In effect, given a large enough population, *someone* is going to find and report a defect *eventually*.

The advantages of open source over proprietary software sound compelling. But just as it would be a mistake to assume open source is inferior to proprietary software, it would be an equally large mistake to assume open source software does not come with certain disadvantages. For instance, if software and source code are free, traditional economic models and incentives that drive proprietary software vendors do not apply to open source projects. This might not be a disadvantage per se, but what then are the incentives that maintain the momentum of the open source movement and, in particular, the individuals that make the open source movement what it is? Second, if anyone from anywhere can contribute to an open source project, how can accountability be enforced through some legal or regulatory regime? These questions are difficult to answer and require a certain amount of context in order to do so.

The History of Free and Open

In January 1956, the Department of Justice set about on a course of action that would eventually ignite the open source software movement. The Department's legal action had absolutely nothing to do with software, however, and everything to do with corporate structure, specifically the monopoly of AT&T.

For much of AT&T's history, it operated as a legally sanctioned, government regulated monopoly under the principle, formulated by its 1907 company president Theodore Vail, that robust telephony was most efficiently achieved via singular control by a fully integrated provider of telecommunications services.[10] Under the umbrella of AT&T, Western Electric manufactured communications equipment, Bell Operating Companies (BOCs) provided local calling services, Bell Telephone Laboratories (BTL or "Bell Labs") researched future industry developments, and AT&T connected it all with long distance services.[11]

The U.S. Government largely accepted this principle and AT&T's corporate structure for a number of years, but as political philosophy evolved and in light of a growing number of alleged company abuses, President Truman's administration filed an anti-trust lawsuit against AT&T in 1949.[12] This lawsuit was resolved in 1956 by a consent decree signed by the Department of Justice and AT&T that restricted AT&T's activities to that of the regulated business of the national telephone system. In other words, the decree effectively banned AT&T from entering markets having nothing to do with telephones as well as mandated AT&T to license its patents to competitors.[13] This would eventually have a significant impact on a group of Bell Labs researchers in 1969.

Ken Thompson, in a fit of summer-time creativity—and in part due to frustrations with an earlier failed attempt by MIT, Bell Labs, and General Electric to collaborate on a new computer operating system—created in the course of one month by himself what the three entities could not create in a five-year period.

Creating an operating system is no small feat, especially creating one alone. An operating system is a piece of software that sits between a computer's hardware and the applications employed by a user. In effect, an operating system is a governor, ensuring no single application devours the limited resources of the computer's microprocessor (the micro chip) or any of the other connected electronics (like the monitor, keyboard, hard drive, and so on). Without an operating system, a computer is rather unusable.

The summer of 1969 was the beginning of Thompson's new operating system. Thompson called his creation UNICS; an acronym that stood for "uniplexed information and computing services." This rather awkward name would eventually evolve over the following years into UNIX—what some might call "the mother of all operating systems."[14]

The use of UNIX was primarily restricted to within Bell Labs, totaling roughly 16 installations by 1973. In 1974, the situation was dramatically different. Due to a paper presented by Thompson to hundreds of software programmers in October 1973 at a professional symposium on operating systems, requests for copies of UNIX flooded in from universities, research departments, and eventually commercial and military users. UNIX was taking off. From a business perspective, nothing could be better. However, the demand for UNIX made AT&T lawyers skittish.

Despite the 1956 consent decree, AT&T's relationship with the Department of Justice was tenuous at best. As software, UNIX was decidedly outside the business of telephony. Not wanting to draw the attention of the government again (there were many other problems brewing on the horizon), AT&T lawyers made it excruciatingly clear that although the company was the creator of UNIX, AT&T renounced any intention of pursuing software as a business. So AT&T washed its hands of UNIX, so to speak, by offering licensed copies of UNIX—as well as the source code—"as is" to any interested party without providing support, bug fixes, or any other potentially business-oriented interest in its unfortunately successful innovation.

This renunciation resolved AT&T's legal consternation over its new operating system but created a whole new set of technical problems for the operating system's adopters. Without support or bug fixes from AT&T, adopters of UNIX would have to collaborate among themselves to simply maintain, let alone evolve, the operating system. Because universities were already in the habit of collaborating among themselves, the academic environment proved the best soil in which UNIX could seed.

Without support or bug fixes from AT&T, adopters of UNIX would have to collaborate among themselves to simply maintain, let alone evolve, the operating system.

The 1970s saw an explosion in the variations and capabilities in UNIX but especially from Berkeley University in California. In fact, the Internet largely owes its existence to a particular version of UNIX called Berkeley Software Distribution, or BSD. By the end of the 1970s, however, AT&T knew UNIX was a winner, and though it could not "cash in" on UNIX's success, the company's mood was shifting, and licensing became more restrictive and limited during that decade.

The 1980s saw a pivotal event in the software world. Again, however, this had nothing to do directly with software itself. Another anti-trust lawsuit initiated by the Department of Justice in 1974 for monopolistic behavior on the part of AT&T finally came to trial in 1981. By January 1982, AT&T had agreed to divest itself of its local calling services (the Bell Operating Companies). In essence, the 1982 consent decree broke up AT&T, and after the smoke cleared after two years of haggling, Western Electric was dissolved, Bell Labs was a separate and distinct entity, and seven independent regional Bell operating companies remained.[15] By 1984, the new AT&T emerged competing against multiple telecommunications players for the same market share it once took for granted. This was not nearly as bad as it seemed.

In return for agreeing to the break up, the Department of Justice agreed to lift the constraints imposed on AT&T by the 1956 consent decree. Now all of sudden, the "unfortunately successful" UNIX was no longer something to keep at arm's length, and AT&T aggressively entered the software business. The first order of business was to drastically change the pricing for UNIX from the sublime, around $20,000 in the early 1980s to the

ridiculous, more than $200,000 by 1989. This pricing funda-
mentally cut off all universities—including Berkeley—that were
not already excluded from AT&T's increasingly restrictive
licensing.

Concurrent with the story of AT&T and UNIX was the
proliferation of other software companies each doing what
companies do best, competing among themselves by out-inno-
vating and out-thinking each other. But any company at that
time could not survive if it were to release its source code to the
public, not even AT&T. And so the short-lived, moment of
openness in the software world came to an end in the 1984—
an odd coincidence of Orwellian import.

The end of openness did not sit well with the research and
academic communities. In fact, openness was not seen as a
momentary phenomenon at all, but a constant of the academic
environment. To imply that software could thrive in anything
but an open environment is anathema. This was odd, given the
early days of computing were largely comprised of proprietary
operating systems running on proprietary hardware.
Accustomed to, and indeed dependent on, openness, sharing,
and collaboration for continued, mutual enrichment, the academic and research communities found detestable that corporations would bastardize and pollute what was the normal course
of their professional existence. But the academic and corporate
worlds have perhaps always been at odds when it comes to
intellectual ideals and business realities. Nowhere was this
bifurcation of ideals and reality felt more strongly than perhaps
at MIT, by one gentleman in particular.

The reproprietization of software (among other industry
trends) resonated deeply with Richard Stallman. Coinciding
with (but not necessarily because of) the drastic change of
UNIX licensing and pricing, in 1984 Stallman resigned his position at MIT to form the Free Software Foundation. The Free
Software Foundation was not about offering software for free,
that is, at no cost, but free from standard intellectual property
laws. The organization's slogan, "think free speech, not free
beer" was an attempt to clarify this important distinction.

To Stallman, software was not merely a set of instructions
to control a computer, but an expression of human creativity

wrapped in an interactive, collaborative process to achieve a certain beneficial end. Standard intellectual property laws such as patents and copyrights morbidly retarded this human interaction as well as the creativity such interaction provoked. More importantly, it detrimentally affected the reason why communities work together in the first place.

Stallman's libertarian feelings went deeper than mere displeasure with proprietization; proprietary software was to be opposed on moral grounds. In effect, proprietary software was a "moral bad" because standard intellectual property laws interfered with community efforts to solve problems for the public good. As Stallman put it,

> *Stallman's libertarian feelings went deeper than mere displeasure with proprietization; proprietary software was to be opposed on moral grounds. In effect, proprietary software was a "moral bad" because standard intellectual property laws interfered with community efforts to solve problems for the public good.*

The easy choice was to join the proprietary software world, signing nondisclosure agreements and promising not to help my fellow hacker. Most likely I would also be developing software that was released under nondisclosure agreements, thus adding to the pressure on other people to betray their fellows too. I could have made money this way, and perhaps amused myself writing code. But I knew that at the end of my career, I would look back on years of building walls to divide people, and feel I had spent my life making the world a worse place. Another choice, straightforward but unpleasant, was to leave the computer field. That way my skills would not be misused, but they would still be wasted. I would not be culpable for dividing and restricting computer users, but it would happen nonetheless.[16]

From Stallman's perspective, a software application is only free if

- You have the freedom to run the program for any purpose.
- You have the freedom to modify the program to suit your needs.
- You have the freedom to redistribute copies either with or without a fee.
- You have the freedom to distribute modified versions of the program so that the community can benefit from your improvements.

Each of Stallman's points implicitly relies on unconstrained access to source code by any interested party. This implicit reliance, however, introduced a complication for the free software movement. If software were released without any restrictions whatsoever, what possible mechanism would prohibit some future actor from leveraging free software to create a proprietary software application and thus restrict access to source code? In short, the answer was nothing.

The free software movement, then, did not necessarily promote the negation of standard intellectual property law, but required a rethinking of what intellectual property law was used for. As opposed to preserving the right to exclude property from non-owners, as standard intellectual property law imposes, the free software movement sought to enforce the *right not to exclude*—that is, to ensure free software remained free, open, non-proprietary, and widely distributable. To accomplish this, Stallman created the General Public License, known as the GPL, which was the first of many (and often times conflicting) open software licenses.

Again, instead of negating intellectual property law, the GPL sought to ensure that free software could not be restricted, even to the point of excluding software licensed under GPL to be included in any proprietary software application whatsoever. The GPL ensured that once software was free, it could never be made proprietary by accident or on purpose, including any derivative works of the original or later versions. But GPL took a revolutionary step further by dictating that any software created under GPL could not be mixed with proprietary software unless the entire mixture was released under the GPL. In effect, this made GPL infectious, forcing any mixture of free and proprietary software to adhere to the distribution mandates of the free software movement: Free software shall always be free. Period.

Such a strong legal and moral stance was not exactly welcomed, even by some of Stallman's own colleagues. Just as proprietary software licenses restricted what developers could do with a given piece of software, so too did the GPL just in a different, if novel, way. The stark ideological stance that all software licensed under GPL must remain free was, in its own way, just as restricting as proprietary licensure. The lack of flexibility in GPL tended to offend more pragmatically inclined developers who wanted to leverage "good code" regardless of whether it was proprietary or not. With the pillars of black and white firmly ensconced—proprietary on one side, free on the other—a spectrum started to form in between.

> *Just as proprietary software licenses restricted what developers could do with a given piece of software, so too did the GPL just in a different, if novel, way. The stark ideological stance that all software licensed under GPL must remain free was, in its own way, just as restricting as proprietary licensure.*

The most notable middle ground was found by a group of developers that created the Open Source Initiative (OSI), a movement also based on the notion of free but without the moral fervor of the Free Software Foundation. OSI defined what is now widely known as the definition of "open source" software. Like free software, open source software is distributed along with its source code to any interested party. The Open Source Definition, or OSD as it became known, is based on three essential principles:

- Open source software allows for the unrestricted redistribution of software without licensing fees or royalties paid to the author.
- Open source software requires that source code be included at no additional cost other than the cost of the distribution media.

- Open source software allows anyone to modify and/or derive software from it and to redistribute the modified software under the same terms.

The critical distinction between GPL and the Open Source Definition lays in the last principle. While the Free Software Foundation *requires* distribution under the same terms of the GPL, the OSD license *allows* distribution of modified software under the same terms. This was an important distinction because open source software could not only be used with proprietary software, but derivative works based on open source software could in fact be made proprietary. Free software shall be free, but only when it made sense. This did not sit well with Stallman, who continued to stress the theme of "freedom, community, and principles" as more important than simply good software.[17]

The history of open source software is far more nuanced and detailed than described here. Nonetheless, the open source movement represents a critical difference in the way software is developed, distributed, and controlled. This has both positive and negative consequences.

An Incentive to Itch

The split between Free Software Foundation and the Open Source Initiative is similar in flavor to the schism between the Roman Catholic and the "more tolerant" Protestant church. Just as both churches are grouped beneath the banner of Christianity, so too are the "free software" and "open software" movements grouped under the banner of Open Source.

And like its religious counterparts, schisms in the open source community have proven to be rather common. Within 30 years of open source's beginnings, the 130,000 or so open source projects not only represent distinct technology projects, but reflect 130,000 *different ways of thinking*. The tendency for schism leads literally to holy wars over technical minutia, piddling philosophical differences, and dissimilar licensing terms that are incomprehensible to outsiders and even, unfortunately, to some within the movement itself. As much as the free and open source communities may be focused on technical aspects of software, these communities are primarily social movements with distinct agendas complicated by the narcissism of small differences. As Steven Weber observed in *The Success of Open Source,* "The open source phenomenon is in some ways the first and certainly one of the most prominent indigenous political statements of the digital world."[18]

As a social movement, the open source software community exhibits not simply political overtones, however, but exhibits all the lineaments of a religion, complete with creed, prophets, sacred texts, and the promise of a better world made possible by non-proprietary, open source software (or at least providing a decent alternative to the shenanigans of commercial software manufacturers). Open source projects are led by sacerdotal lead developers that are heaped with reverent adulation by disciples seeking to rise in the meritocratic priesthood of open source. As one commentator observed

> *The tendency for schism leads literally to holy wars over technical minutia, piddling philosophical differences, and dissimilar licensing terms that are incomprehensible to outsiders and even, unfortunately, to some within the movement itself.*

[Open source is] all about Eric, and Linus, and RMS [Richard Stallman], and Tim, and Bruce, and Tom and Larry. These are charisma guys. They're like...guys who dress up with halos and wear wizard hats. The widows and orphans are telling you, "Thank you for not letting us starve, kind sir!" They're all grateful to you, they're touching the hem of your garment.[19]

The unshakable quasi-religious faith that permeates much of the open source movement is hard to ignore. But aspects of faith, politics, and social structure within the open source movement introduce complications, especially regarding how to clearly distinguish the incentives of open source participants. If the open source community were simply a socially-conscious volunteer organization like Habitat for Humanity, altruistic tendencies by themselves might easily explain participation. But involvement is not based just on altruism, but on self-interest both in a personal and commercial sense.

As previously mentioned, the open source community is largely made up of volunteers from around the world. These volunteers do not in general receive payment for contributing to open source projects. Volunteers donate their creativity and genius to the project of their liking based on their desire and ability to contribute. In the absence of monetary compensation, volunteer software developers are largely driven by self-interest and ego, rather than, or in addition to, remuneration. This model creates rather potent consequences considering that members of the community will invest time and attention in building features only he or she is interested in, considers appealing enough, or is deemed sufficiently worthwhile. In any case, whatever task is undertaken by a contributor must in some way showcase the technical capabilities of a contributor to their peers, thus establishing suitable credentials of an individual contributor among the community as a whole. Put more succinctly, contributors will dedicate time and effort on features that "scratch an itch" while also "upping their geek cred," otherwise known as improving personal credibility among technical peers.[20] This practice has at least three effects.

Open Source is as much a social movement as it is a Darwinian meritocracy.[21] Whereas commercial vendors inject features to satisfy client demands (real or imagined) as well as to differentiate their products from the products of competitors, open source software projects often experience the same relentless drive to inject features but due to significantly different incentives than market differentiation alone.

As a contributor's credibility increases, so too does the contributor's name and reputation. Thus the contributor climbs the ladder of meritocracy by demonstrating sufficient talent and ability in a given software project. Talent and ability are central to any meritocracy. In the case of open source, talent and ability are demonstrated largely by adding features or new functions to a software project. As more features are added to a software project, more opportunities are available for contributors to demonstrate talent and ability. Thus, features might be added to a software project more in part due to the incentive of a contributor to distinguish himself among his peers, and not necessarily because a particular feature is actually needed in the first place.

This makes sense because failing to add a feature, or improve a function, means a contributor essentially forgoes distinguishing him or herself in the open source community and therefore forgoes climbing the ladder of meritocracy. Volunteers who fail to contribute, then, or do not contribute anything worthwhile, languish at the bottom of the ladder; their "geek cred" is miniscule or non-existent.

Thus, features might be added to a software project more in part due to the incentive of a contributor to distinguish himself among his peers, and not necessarily because a particular feature is actually needed in the first place.

So the first effect of a "personal itch" means that features for any given software project might not be added based on formal requirements, formal specifications, or even client need. A feature is added because it behooves the contributor to do so in order to earn greater "geek cred." The "personal itch" motivation also distinguishes community software from commercial software in that the needs of users in any given open source project may be satisfied if and only if those needs happen to coincide in part with the whims of the volunteer software developers.[22] This is not to say that community or open source software will not respond properly to the needs of others, only that any stated need has the best chance of being satisfied if contributors believe the feature is interesting enough to add, gives contributors the opportunity to demonstrate their talents, and the need does not conflict with features contributors have already decided upon. If, by implementing a new feature, a higher rung in the meritocracy can be achieved, the requestor's needs are more likely to be met.

The second effect of a "personal itch" means that the practice of maintaining an open source project; that is, providing bug fixes or necessary improvements for inferior or incomplete sections of code, depends on the time, effort, and inclination of one of the contributors. In some instances this may happen very quickly when a contributor's passion for a project is high, but as the passion wanes (the "itch" doesn't need as much scratching anymore, so to speak), or the project starts losing its popularity, the incentive and the desire to do the "boring" but necessary work of proficient software manufacturing can trail off significantly.

The third effect is a tendency for significant enlargement of a software application, otherwise known as "code bloat," a phenomenon not limited to commercial software that nonetheless adds more complexity to software and therefore adds greater potential for mistakes to be made and vulnerabilities to be created.

Given the interests and incentives of developers, there is a strong incentive to add functionality and almost no incentive to delete functionality, especially as this can irritate the person who developed the functionality in question. Worse, given that peer esteem is a crucial incentive for participation, deletion of functionality in the interest of benefiting the end user creates a strong disincentive to future participation, perhaps considered worse than having one's code replaced by code that one's peers have deemed superior.

The project maintainer, in order to keep volunteer participants happy, is likely to keep functionality even if it is confusing, and on receipt of two similar additional functionalities, keep both, creating options for the user of the software to configure the application to use the one that best fits their needs. In this way as many contributors as possible can gain clear credit for directly contributing to the application.[23]

> *The desire to keep everyone happy leads to a kind of "pork barrel" development model where lots of features are added, few are deleted, and value is diluted.*

The desire to keep everyone happy leads to a kind of "pork barrel" development model where lots of features are added, few are deleted, and value is diluted. In fact, volunteers *must* contribute even when it does not make sense to do so; there are simply few, if any, alternative avenues for gaining credibility.

So the effects of scratching a personal itch are three fold. First, features are added to a software project based more on the

incentive to increase personal credibility than on formal requirements. Second, features which should be removed are not. This
adds both size and complexity to a software project which not
only hinders maintainability, but also threatens to introduce
more latent defects and vulnerabilities. Third, once an itch has
been scratched, the desire to maintain a piece of code may be
non-existent. If another contributor cannot be found having the
need to scratch the same itch as the previous contributor, the
software may languish due to inattention.

Against the background of individual incentives are larger
commercial incentives at work. While open source is known for
its volunteers, this does not prevent commercial companies from
building services around, and indeed investing directly in, an
open source project. IBM, Red Hat, and Canonical are just a
few of the companies that either hire developers to work on a
particular open source project, or have taken an open source
project completely under their wing. While the software remains
free, both in a monetary and ideological sense, and volunteers
may still freely contribute, the companies hope to benefit in
some way from the project's success either through service contracts or through advertising revenues.

In any case, open source projects are almost always threatened by foreclosure. The lead developer might lose interest, his
"day job" ultimately takes up too much time and hinders his
ability to volunteer, the group of volunteers working on the
project reach a philosophical or design impasse, or the project
itself does not draw enough support to maintain momentum. Of
the 130,000 or so open source projects, only a few hundred are
active. The remainders are simply artifacts of a personal itch
long ago forgotten.

Ideas are important, but for ideas to see the light of day
requires funding of considerable depth. As an example, when
Mahatma Gandhi (who was famous for his asceticism and message of peaceful resistance) was Mrs. Sarojini Naidu's guest and
required supplies of goat milk, fresh fruit, juice, and other rari-
ties on the Indian subcontinent, she reputed to have exclaimed,
"You've no idea, Mahatma, how expensive it is to provide you
with the wherewithal to fast."[24] Nor is it apparent to the
disciples of open source how expensive it is to keep software free
or open. Software of any significant import, commercial or

otherwise, requires tremendous resources to maintain and improve the software. The ideology of open source is unmistakably positive—it is hard to argue against the philosophy of people working together to improve the common good—however, just as with Gandhi, positive ideology is simply not enough. Ideas require sponsors or benefactors that believe something profitable or beneficial may come out of the work.

So the intermixture of personal and commercial incentives makes it difficult to pin down exactly what drives any particular open source project toward success, nor is it a guarantee that those drivers remain constant, or relevant for any extended period of time. In the end, all these unknowns and uncertainties make quality and security in some open source projects difficult to reliably enforce. Although statistics tend to show that open source software manufacturers tend to patch faster than their proprietary cousins, the act of patching simply demonstrates the lack of attention paid during the initial design and development process by the software manufacturer. It is hard to compliment a practice for any type of software manufacturer which fundamentally demonstrates a shortfall in due care before the product is released into the stream of commerce.

> *So the intermixture of personal and commercial incentives makes it difficult to pin down exactly what drives any particular open source project toward success, nor is it a guarantee that those drivers remain constant, or relevant for any extended period of time.*

The Question of Sustainable Security

In 2006, the Department of Homeland Security (DHS) initiated a program dubbed the "Vulnerability Discovery and Remediation, Open Source Hardening Project." This program granted $1.5 million for identifying vulnerabilities in open source software using a proprietary automated source code scanning solution created by a commercial company called Coverity.[25] Automated source code scanning uses a software application that reviews the source code of a given software application looking for mistakes made during the manufacturing process. Think of source code scanning like the spell-checker of a word processor, but one that also looks for logical errors not only in sentence structure, but in the line of reasoning by the author. In the ideal, automated scanning of source code promises to cover larger sections of code, in a shorter time period, and with fewer idiosyncrasies, inconsistencies, or false positives than in a manual review by experienced, individual software developers.

At first, the DHS program for "hardening" open source—that is, to improve the security of open source software—was welcomed by the open source community because, in theory, the database of vulnerabilities constructed by the Coverity tool would help open source software become more secure. This would obviously benefit organizations employing open source software, including national infrastructure, by purging latent defects missed by open source developers and volunteers during the manufacturing process. But two significant criticisms arose, both of which were levied by Ben Laurie, director of the Apache Foundation, an open source group responsible for creating and managing the most successful open source web server on the market, called Apache.

The first criticism pertained to the availability of the Coverity tool.[26] The open source community, comprised of volunteer software developers around the world, would simply have access to the results of the tool—the list of discovered vulnerabilities—but would not be able to use the Coverity tool directly.

Historically, open source developers have not had the same access to automated source code analysis tools as commercial software vendors because these tools are expensive, and open source projects—even the most successful—are largely without substantial revenues or investment capital to draw upon (even with corporate sponsors). As such, open source developers manually "eyeball" each others' source code, which is a notoriously incomplete, subjective, and tedious process prone to error. Access to an automated tool would dramatically improve the community's capabilities, reduce much of the community's inherent inefficiencies, and reduce the number of weaknesses within the code base. Most importantly, though, access to an automated tool would, as stated by David Park, co-founder of Coverity, "...help put open source on par with commercial software efforts."[27]

The second and more profound criticism from Mr. Laurie was that DHS was subsidizing a private commercial vendor to search for and identify vulnerabilities in "public" software, yet DHS was not allocating funds to open source groups to *fix* discovered defects. Mr. Laurie noted, "It is regrettable that DHS has decided once more to ensure that private enterprise profits from the funding, while the open-source developers are left to beg for scraps from the table. Why does the DHS think it is worthwhile to pay for bugs to be found, but has made no provision to pay for them to be fixed?"[28] To date, DHS has not responded to this criticism, nor provided funds to fix discovered defects in open source projects that were scanned with the Coverity tool. Without additional funds, the open source community is put in a rather unfortunate position: Volunteers might receive a long list of defects and have the inclination to fix them but will have neither the time nor money to do so.

> *"It is regrettable that DHS has decided once more to ensure that private enterprise profits from the funding, while the open-source developers are left to beg for scraps from the table. Why does the DHS think it is worthwhile to pay for bugs to be found, but has made no provision to pay for them to be fixed?"*

Dawson Engler, a professor at Stanford University, defended the DHS program. "The [DHS] money is going to provide them [open source developers] with things they need to fix the bugs, which is bug reports. That is a lot better than they have now, which is nothing."[29]

This unfortunate scenario highlights the greater dangers of open source and why in its current instantiation, open source is problematic for national infrastructure. "Open" is not sufficient criteria for adjudging the suitability of software; it is the standard of construction that matters, and without a standard, openness may be promising, but largely specious. The argument is simple. Commercial software vendors might not exactly have the public interest in mind when they create a particular software application. Remember, markets do not necessarily make what we need, simply what we are willing to buy. Satisfying the needs of public interest is orthogonal to most commercial ventures. That being said, though commercial software vendors might possess the necessary resources to protect consumers if public policy dictates, they simply might not want to and could even vehemently resist; however, they can be forced to if need be. And this is an important point: Commercial software manufacturers can be compelled to allocate additional funds to improve software when public policy dictates. In contrast, open source might have public interest in mind but lacks the funds, resources, and therefore the ability to protect the public should public policy require it.

> *In contrast, open source might have public interest in mind but lacks the funds, resources, and therefore the ability to protect the public should public policy require it.*

Think about it this way, should public policy change tomorrow and software manufacturers are *required* through some external government intervention to reduce the number of vulnerabilities in software by 50 percent, commercial software vendors would need to dramatically modify their pricing models to pay for the additional burden of meeting this onerous requirement. Open source, on the other hand, has no pricing model, or where a pricing model does exist it is in relation to services and not manufacturing. Where would the money come from to pay for the additional resources necessary to meet the government's mandate on improved security when open source cannot currently afford to fix vulnerabilities discovered by the DHS program? To re-quote Mr. Laurie, "Why does the DHS think it is worthwhile to pay for bugs to be found, but has made no provision to pay for them to be fixed?" Indeed, this is worrisome.

And so the question of the sustainability of security in open source software remains open, but far from promising. Commercial vendors can be forced to pay for improved security and in doing so, pass their additional costs on to the consumer. Open Source has no such option should the demand be made.

A countervailing argument to this line of reasoning returns us to the cherished adage in the open source movement, "Given enough eyeballs, all bugs are shallow," which from an earlier description refers to the practice that given enough people doing different things with a given piece of software, a greater amount of bugs will be discovered. This sounds reasonable and as such has become practically axiomatic.

Open source software enables improvement to software quality because open source software removes the asymmetric information problem. Anyone can look at the code, at any time; however, there is no guarantee that such review will occur, that it will be conducted by sufficiently talented or trained individuals, or the funds, resources, and inclination will exist to fix identified vulnerabilities.

With so much emphasis on features and "geek cred," there is a high likelihood that fundamental aspects of software development might be ignored or completely forgotten.[30] This makes "many eyes" blind to only what they want to see based on the filter of ego and reward, and not what *must be seen* based on diligence and proficiency. In the ever-expanding code base and ever increasing complexity due to expansion, the likelihood of manually discovering software vulnerabilities decreases proportionally. This practice does not address the fundamental issues with software quality or its construction; it is simply acquiescence to the fact that software manufacturers have failed to exercise the full extent of their creativity and genius on this critical issue of our time. Such shortfalls make automated source code scanning almost mandatory but no less financially impractical for a majority of open source projects.

Distributed Immunity: No Body to Kick, No Soul to Condemn

In January 2007, Alan Cox, a distinguished contributor to the open source operating system called Linux (on which Google runs its search engine), told the British House of Lords that it would be difficult to make open source developers liable for their code because of the nature of open source software development.[31] As developers share code around the community, responsibility is collective. "Potentially there is no way to enforce liability."[32]

From a legal perspective, the open source movement puts the users of software in an even more precarious position than does proprietary software manufacturers. The notion of open source's distributed community of collaboration simply deepens and extends the blanket of immunity across software manufacturing because in addition to "as is" licensing agreements, the "who developed what, when" questions are not always easy to answer under the open source manufacturing paradigm. This means if a standard of care for software developers should come to fruition, the contributors to open source software applications would in many respects remain unaccountable for any breach of that standard. This complicates modifying incentives for open source contributors since a standard of care could be applied only to those companies that sponsor open source projects, are themselves commercial wrappers around a particular open source project, or directly invest funds into those projects.

> *From a legal perspective, the open source movement puts the users of software in an even more precarious position than does proprietary software manufacturers. The notion of open source's distributed community of collaboration simply deepens and extends the blanket of immunity across software manufacturing.*

Mr. Cox's discouragement of liability simply because of open source's organizational structure is questionable at best. It would be like refusing to prosecute terrorist or criminal organizations simply because their hydra-headed structures do not lend themselves easily to capture. This thinking should cause everyone to pause.

The organizational structure of open source should not preclude it from social responsibility and more importantly, public accountability. If liability is to be considered as a viable incentive for improving the sorry state of software manufacturing, as was discussed in Chapter 5, "Absolute Immunity," the wide adoption of open source by public and private industry could tip the difficult into the impossible.

Doffing the Wizard Hats

The advantages of open or closed software are still a matter hotly debated. Which is "better" is mixed up in a boiling cauldron of personal politics and predisposition. As Steven Weber observed in *The Success of Open Source*, the open source movement has become a kind of Internet era Rorschach test.

People tend to see in the open source software movement the politics that they would like to see—a libertarian reverie, a perfect meritocracy, a utopian gift culture that celebrates an economics of abundance instead of scarcity, a virtual or electronic existence proof of communitarian ideals, a political movement aimed at replacing obsolete nineteenth-century capitalist structures with new "relations of production" more suited to the Information Age.[33]

As such, preferences toward open or proprietary software tend to be tightly coupled to one's political stance. But such thinking, frankly, misses the point. In fact, it is a potentially deadly distraction to the technocrats involved in infrastructure because normal users typically do not know or care about the politics of open source software. The politics of "open" or "closed" is confounding the issue at hand. It is arguable if moral fervor and/or high-handed politics have any place in the construction of infrastructure. It is not that morality is not important, or politics unhelpful, but these should largely be irrelevant to the practice and discipline of construction. Without well-defined professional and construction standards, there is an enormous amount of effort not only getting open source software to work, but to get open source initiatives to work together. Infrastructure requires engineering discipline largely free from personal foibles and philosophical disputes. In the end, an engineer wears a hard hat, not a wizard hat.

> The politics of "open" or "closed" is confounding the issue at hand. It is arguable if moral fervor and/or high-handed politics have any place in the construction of infrastructure. It is not that morality is not important, or politics unhelpful, but these should largely be irrelevant to the practice and discipline of construction.

If open source is to live up to its promise, it must overcome weaknesses in its methods, practices, and philosophies. Open source lacks objective mechanisms for ensuring quality; it is largely driven by developer self-interest to "scratch an itch" rather than relentless diligence for completing tedious but necessary tasks. The strength and weakness of open source is that anyone can contribute, and unfortunately sometimes anyone does. Imagine an automobile built by community members. It might sound like a great idea until you realize the janitor with no formal engineering training is now adding components to the car and cannot be held accountable for his blunders.

Successful open source projects like Apache, Linux, and MySQL, while empirically establishing that large complex systems can indeed be built by loosely organized and non-compensated volunteers, are the exception rather than the rule. Those open source products that are marketable are wrapped by a service model that does not require payment for software; rather, payment is required for all the talent and experience needed just to get open source software to reliably work in a commercial environment.

Regardless, neither open nor proprietary software abides by any meaningful, objective construction standard; software quality is really just a mish-mash of subjective measurements as to what is and what is not "good code." In contrast, Cola-Cola, though it tightly protects the formula for Coke, must still abide by health standards in bottling its drinks. Both concrete and Coke must abide by certain safety standards. Even though Coke is secret, it must follow health and safety guidelines regarding how it is created, stored, and transported. Even though cement is open, it must follow quality assurance requirements. While traditional manufacturing companies such as Toyota may be emulating the philosophy of the open source model in some of its production processes, it is only doing so within a well-defined structure of corporate and engineering standards, regulations, and oversight that must be adhered to when the end product is shipped to consumers. In the case of open or proprietary software, neither abides by a public standard regarding health, quality, or any other objective measurement.

This is an important distinction. Open software does not necessarily mean "open standards" because there is no standard for software development. This calls into question whether open source is any more suitable for national infrastructure than commercial software. In fact, it may be less so. The problem is not whether software is open or closed, but whether a standard on software itself or those who manufacture it can be enforced at all.

Moving Forward:
Rational Incentives for a Different Future

The question is, indeed, Which is to be master? Will we survive our technolo-
gies? We are being propelled into this new century with no plan, no control, no
brakes. Have we already gone too far down the path to alter course? I don't
believe so, but we aren't trying yet, and the last chance to assert control—the
fail-safe point—is rapidly approaching.

—Bill Joy, Founder of Sun Microsystems, April 2000.

Software is a human creation. As such, very little about software—its benefits or its dangers—is preordained. But one
aspect is fairly clear; software will play a large part in modern
civilization's well-being and ultimately, perhaps, its sustainability.
As world populations grow, the need for efficient infrastructure
will grow proportionally. Software promises to deliver much of
that needed efficiency. What is unclear, however, is the real cost
software will impose.

As a human creation, software is not magical, nor should it be
mysterious, but it is complex and extremely powerful. This makes
software both blessing and bane. It is the nearest thing we have to
a universal tool. The radical malleability of software allows us to
make of it what we will. But this malleability also means we have
few precise analogies in the physical world from which we can
articulate coherent frameworks for dealing with it. Like nuclear
technologies before it, software simultaneously benefits and
imperils our welfare on a global scale. And like nuclear technologies, software challenges how we relate to an environment that is
fundamentally altered by its introduction. This creates pressure on
our legal and political systems to adapt to the changes. To date,
our systems—and the traditional ways of thinking on which they
are based—appear ill-prepared to cope.

There is no going back. We cannot and should not rid the world of software, but neither can we tolerate software that endangers our well-being. We can only move forward.

If software allows us to make of it what we will, what then will we make? Will it be a robust, global, software-driven infrastructure capable of servicing the needs of our growing populations or simply another avenue for the malicious and opportunistic? To answer this question we cannot simply look to technology alone; we must look at, and into, ourselves. If we are truly being propelled into the twenty-first century with no plan, no control, no brakes, what is stopping us from changing the story? Are we truly not trying yet?

> *If software allows us to make of it what we will, what then will we make?*

This book has argued that the story of software is the story of *us* and our incentives; therefore, to change the story requires changing the incentives. But which incentives should be changed?

In Chapter 2, "Six Billion Crash Test Dummies," we saw that software buyers want features and usability—they want *utility*—yet software buyers inconsistently value their security. This inconsistency means that software manufacturers have an incentive to make software high in features and low in most everything else. We have also seen that manufacturers have a perverse incentive to reduce software quality—or at least not pursue it with sufficient zeal—thus encouraging the need for extensive patching by software buyers. Because patching allows manufacturers to tune new licensing agreements to their benefit, higher quality software would preclude, to a significant extent, this lucrative avenue.

In Chapter 3, "The Power of Weaknesses," we saw the incentives that disorder creates for attackers, both for individuals, or large organized bodies such as nation states or crime syndicates. Disorder—namely our lack of control regarding software manufacturing—creates incentives for the corrupt and predatory. The lack of jurisdictional coherence across the globe also means that even if attackers can be found, they most likely will be beyond the reach of law enforcement. In Chapter 4, "Myopic Oversight," we discovered the incentives government has *not to become involved* given that few governments want to hinder or in any way hamper a lucrative segment of their economies and even when they do become involved, it is far from optimal. In Chapter 5, "Absolute Immunity," tort law was described as a system of incentives for inducing people to behave in socially efficient and responsible ways. In Chapter 6, "Open Source Software," we saw that while the open source movement may indeed provide numerous benefits, its danger lies in its lack of resources to improve software and an even greater immunity than enjoyed by closed-source software manufacturers.

So which incentives to change? It is difficult to know for sure which incentives are the "right" ones to change and which lead to an optimal outcome. In such cases, the best we can hope for is to have as many people involved as possible who understand the problem and are willing to think critically about the issues confronting us. This is not easy, but it is necessary to move forward. This chapter, then, is not about "answers" in the strictest sense. Instead, this chapter introduces a number of topics for continued discussion, from doing nothing (not interfering in the current state of affairs) to heavy government involvement, to a middle ground somewhere between the two. The suitability of each argument is up to debate—as it should be. Whatever our choices, the software crisis will be hugely expensive, either in the real cost of ignoring it or in the real cost of mitigating its impact. It is up to us to determine what costs we are willing to bear and the results we are willing to accept.

Hands-off

Perhaps one avenue lies not in trying to forcibly improve software, but to continue following a "hands-off" policy and let software evolve naturally, much like DNA has evolved over the eons. Software, like DNA, might be absolutely atrocious from an engineering perspective, but in the end, DNA accomplishes some pretty amazing feats. The fact you are reading this book is proof enough.

To investigate the structure and design of DNA is to realize Mother Nature was wildly inebriated when she wrote the Code of Life. DNA represents everything an intelligent engineer would not do. There is no sense of hierarchy or organization in DNA, there is no version control, many parts have lost their function yet remain nonetheless (more than 90 percent is thought to be junk), vast sections of DNA have been overwritten or "patched" by invasive bacteria, and the lack of optimization in DNA is striking.[1] As far as "bad" software goes, DNA is arguably the worst on the planet. Mother Nature might no more deserve the title of engineer than any other software developer. As one observer put it, "No intelligent designer would have put the genomes of living organisms together the way that evolution has."[2] In a philosophical sense, then, the bumper sticker sentiment of "Life's a bitch, and then you die," might be all too accurate, but from an engineering perspective, Life is also a kludge—an inelegant, clumsy solution that works despite itself.

But if "bad code" in the form of DNA is good enough for Life on this planet, why then should software be any different? To a certain extent, this reasoning could have some merit. Mother Nature might not be an engineer, but she sure can make things that work. As a creative force, there are few things that can compare with DNA. So while bad DNA could certainly kill by any number of horrific genetic disorders, on balance, DNA wins in the category of software that achieves astounding results despite obvious, even dangerous, shortcomings. Likewise, so the reasoning goes that software engineers might never achieve—or need to achieve—the status of "true" engineers as long as their creations keep evolving to meet the demands of the market environments. Software vulnerabilities, like genetics disorders, could simply be the price to be paid for existence.

> But if "bad code" in the form of DNA is good enough for Life on this planet, why then should software be any different?

On the surface, the DNA argument seems appealing. For one, it plays on the technology industry's love of finding rationalizations for its behavior in natural phenomena, such as our discussion in Chapter 4 regarding the idea of *churn* being part of the natural ecology of the planet. If it's good for nature, it must be good for us. But more importantly, the DNA argument also means we don't have to do anything different than what is being done now regarding software. Debates need not be engaged, legislation need not be written, and court battles need not be fought. We simply need to stay out of the way of inevitable evolutionary changes.

There are a number of aspects the software-is-like-DNA argument overlooks, however. For one, DNA is not networked the same way software is networked. Weaknesses in DNA cannot be targeted with the same speed and ferocity as can weaknesses in software. While there is certainly a growing fear of genetic weapons—biological weapons that can target specific ethnic minorities based on their genetic makeup[3]—these weapons remain largely in the imagination. Software weapons that take advantage of weaknesses in our software are employed widely and to great effect right now. Networks magnify these weaknesses to a far greater extent than anything seen in the natural realm of DNA.

Moreover, a genetic weakness is just that, a *weakness*. While a genetic weakness might make someone more *susceptible* to certain diseases, it does not give infectious diseases special access to your thoughts, memories, or identity. Weaknesses in software, on the other hand, can give access to anything stored in an electronic file, whether it be a credit card number, family picture, medical information, or love letter. As such, a weakness in software is more far reaching compared to a genetic weakness; it is an avenue for predators to wield power over more than just the organism itself, but to aspects outside the organism, to the organism's identity, history, and social connections.

Finally, the mechanism of natural selection appears warped in the software world compared to the natural world. Bad DNA, *really* bad DNA like the kind that makes muscular dystrophy, cystic fibrosis, hemophilia, or Tay-Sachs disease tends to vote the individual out of existence earlier in life than those without the disorder. Bad code can and will kill you. But in the software world, this doesn't seem to be the case, at least in one particular sense. While bad software can certainly kill "you" in particular by causing your car to stall or airplane to crash, it does not seem to kill the manufacturers that make it. Manufacturers that produce software that lacks features might be driven out of the market, but manufacturers producing software rife with latent defects appear immune to any negative consequences. In fact, as this book has argued repeatedly, it is software buyers that are risking their existence by using the code, not the manufacturers. This seems to turn the survival of the fittest on its head. Software buyers are not necessarily trying to compete with each other for existence...they just want to use software to gain utility and competitiveness may be only one aspect of many. In comparison, it is software manufacturers that are competing against each other for survival. There are plenty of examples in the software industry of repeated, critical weaknesses made by software manufacturers that did not vote the manufacturer out of existence. In short, DNA does not give organisms a choice; you get the DNA you inherit; luck may or may not shine on you. Software, on the other hand, is all about choice. You get what you tolerate.

> In short, DNA does not give organisms a choice; you get the DNA you inherit; luck may or may not shine on you. Software, on the other hand, is all about choice. You get what you tolerate.

A hands-off argument, whatever its form, augurs ill for civilization. That governments and the market have attempted to address the software crises, no matter how ineffectually, shows there is real concern as to what software can and is doing to us. However, the responses by government and the market have, to date, been inadequate. Reducing external involvement or maintaining status quo promises to worsen, not improve, the situation. But so too does inadequate involvement.

For instance, since enactment of the CAN-SPAM Act in 2003—the Act criminalizes sending more than a threshold number of unsolicited, commercial email in a given period of time— spam has increased three-fold, accounting for nearly 80 to 90 percent of all emails in 2006.[4] Other criminal statutes, such as the U.S. Computer Fraud and Abuse Act and Britain's Computer Misuse Act, have not fared any better. Since their enactment, cyber crime has reached epidemic proportions. The attempt to disincentivize criminal behavior through legislative action has clearly not worked.

Both Congress and Parliament are considering increasing the penalties associated with cyber crime, increasing jail time for cyber crimes to 10 years in some instances. However, as long as there remains a plethora of software vulnerabilities that are inexpensive to exploit, and the likelihood of being apprehended by law enforcement remains practically non-existent, increasing criminal sanctions seems rather vacuous. Ironically, the low probability of capturing an attacker tends to argue in favor of, not against, increasing criminal sanctions. In a *Georgetown Law Journal* article, Mary Calkins argues that as the likelihood of capture decreases, the penalty must increase in order to provide any deterrent whatsoever:

Given the large number of hackers and the high costs of detecting, tracing, capturing, and potentially extraditing each hacker, the costs of catching all or most hackers would be prohibitively high. This case is analogous to the situation of antitrust deterrence, where enforcement policy does not attempt to deter every violation because the cost of deterring some violations would exceed the harm they create. This enforcement-cost problem is efficiently solved if authorities "hang" a violator now and then—that is, if a low level of enforcement is coupled with a penalty of large magnitude when the law is enforced. The current criminal punishment model is akin to "hanging" because only a few hackers are caught and prosecuted, but those who are caught and prosecuted are subject to large penalties, such as prison.[5]

So the less likely a criminal will be apprehended, the more appropriate severe sentences appear to become. In such a situation, the notions of efficiency and effectiveness collide, however. Severe criminal sanctions appear most efficient when the amount of harm is difficult to calculate for any given cyber attack. When the amount of harm is difficult to calculate, society is imposed with the high cost of trying to figure out the magnitude and the cost of the harm. Using a criminal sanction is simply easier and cheaper than having to work out the math; hence, criminal sanctions are more efficient from an economic perspective. But efficiency does not imply *effectiveness*. While criminal sanctions might be easier and cheaper to employ, the lack of effectiveness of criminal sanctions also imposes high costs on society because other mechanisms (such as technology solutions or data breach laws) must be introduced to counteract ineffectiveness. Criminal statutes will be an important part of moving forward, if but to simply make a moral stand on the issue of breaking into and hijacking computer systems; however, it is equally important to keep in mind that criminal activity is not the root cause of software vulnerabilities; it is manufacturing blunders. Criminal statutes might simply serve to complement other mechanisms but are not sufficient in and of themselves.

Legislative action is not the only arena in which government has provided inadequate responses to inadequate software security. To date, government has largely taken the role of information provisioning—that is, acting as a clearing house for information to the market about identifying and counteracting software vulnerabilities. Government has largely avoided exercising any of its "negative power" in this process, opting for the softer, gentler approach of a "friendly hand" that does not *touch* but merely *guides*. This approach is acceptable insofar as that it is a necessary component, but again effectiveness is the objective.

Jean Camp and Catherine Wolfram at Harvard University argue that government's effectiveness in this field is questionable at best.[6] According to Camp and Wolfram, the U.S. government encourages information provisioning via four avenues: information coordination, defining taxonomies for secure systems, setting standards for certain security technologies, and finally through subsidies for incident response and research. In all cases, argue Camp and Wolfram, none has adequately addressed the problem of insecure software.

In this case of information coordination, the 1997 President's Commission on Critical Infrastructure Protection sought to encourage information sharing by restricting what information could be shared. That wasn't a mistype. In the Commission's opinion, it was important to restrict what information might be shared with the public because vulnerability information might contain sensitive proprietary or trade secret information.[7] Given that the federal government is bound under the Freedom of Information Act (FOIA) to make available information in the possession of the federal government to the public upon request, it was important to provide assurances to potential participants their information would remain confidential if shared with the federal government. This much makes sense. The recommendation of the Commission was to allow an exemption from the Freedom of Information Act. The exemption meant that certain information pertaining to the program's participants was restricted from public discovery. This also makes sense, but only to a point. According to Camp and Wolfram, "Thus, the few selected players would have greater information, but the majority of computer users would not only have no additional information but would also be barred from seeking federal information."

Information sharing, particularly between public and private organizations, is complicated by the nature of proprietary and trade secret information. This does not mean this information should not be protected. On the contrary, the recommendation for FOIA exemption was the most responsible recommendation the Commission could make. But Camp and Wolfram hit on a very important point. The problem stems from the fact that certain information cannot and should not be made publicly available. This is a real barrier, one that ultimately lessens the effectiveness of information sharing for the majority of vulnerable software users. In effect, FOIA exemptions would hurt everyone involved in that privileged players might have additional information to protect themselves but might still be overwhelmed by attacks launched from systems owned by the uninformed majority. The irony of such a scenario highlights the issues magnified by our interconnectedness.

> *In effect, FOIA exemptions would hurt everyone involved in that privileged players might have additional information to protect themselves but might still be overwhelmed by attacks launched from systems owned by the uninformed majority.*

The second critique noted by Camp and Wolfram regarding information sharing is that the information that is shared—in the form of best practices for protecting vulnerable systems—is more relevant for large corporate networks rather than small businesses, home users, or ecommerce websites. In short, the information made available to everyone is only meaningful to a few. Small businesses and home users would be hard-pressed to follow—let alone understand—the guidance provided by many best practice recommendations. The players in national infrastructure protection tend to view infrastructure as large intranets controlled by large organizations. In fact, software infrastructure is far more pervasive than this limited view. A network-enabled refrigerator once connected to the Internet is just as much a part of national infrastructure—and potentially impacts national infrastructure no less than—any other computer system. The country of Estonia has already experienced this profound realization. The nature of the modern network means that if you're connected, you are part of the whole no matter how insignificant you might first appear or think you might be. If the country of Estonia could not withstand the onslaught of a hundreds of thousands of hijacked home and business computers, it would not stand a ghost of a chance against a similar attack launched from one million hijacked network-enabled home appliances. Requiring a majority of software users to follow intricate self-protection gymnastics that only large players have the time, money, and talent to pursue is not scalable, realistic, or effective.

The next area where government has proven inadequate is in defining taxonomies for building secure systems—in other words, defining the things that need to be addressed to build a computer system that the U.S. government will call "secure" and will therefore purchase. In essence, this information provisioning mechanism is a way of informing manufacturers what the U.S. government is willing to accept. By leveraging its buying power, the government hoped to alter the market in a positive way.

In fact, the initial statement that the government has proven inadequate in defining taxonomies for building secure systems is not quite accurate. The government has proven quite adept at defining taxonomies for secure systems; only these taxonomies have achieved little in changing the story of software. The U.S. government has defined taxonomies twice under the Trusted Computer Security Evaluation Criteria (TCSEC) in the 1980s and its follow-on, the Common Criteria in the late 1990s. Where the U.S. government has proven less than adept is getting the market to care in any meaningful way about these taxonomies or to have these taxonomies address software manufacturing practices in any notable manner. This is a shame, given that these taxonomies were created specifically with the intention of providing a market incentive for commercial vendors to improve security throughout their product lines. What the heck happened?

According to Carl Landwehr, the attempt to leverage market through government-imposed requirement had some good effects but failed due to three major aspects.[8] First, the carrot of lucrative government procurements of systems evaluated against the taxonomies never really materialized. Apparently, government software buyers fell under the same hypnotic spell as did everyone else regarding software features. Instead of using their market power to demand the systems they wanted, government procurement officers demanded the latest and greatest operating systems and features as long as there was some modicum of evidence *hinting* at the vendor's *intention* to have the product evaluated—*eventually*. This certainly provided vendors with the incentive to initiate the evaluation process, but little incentive to ever finish it. But this scenario has wider implications. Government procurement officers were not using their market power to demand the systems they wanted. Why? Were purchasers guilty of impatience, or was it indicative of a bigger issue? As it turns out, government procurement officers were not leveraging their buying power for lack of patience; they were not leveraging their buying power because it was not nearly as significant as they thought. This brings us to Landwehr's second point and a point we previously discussed in Chapter 2.

Prior to the 1970s, government was by far the biggest purchaser of software. By the 1980s, the situation had changed entirely. Instead of government being the largest purchaser of software, the private sector began buying software in massive quantities. The private sector had decidedly fewer security requirements than the government, if any, and much, much more money on balance. In short, as the commercial software market exploded, government became just another buyer, and a small one at that compared to the market as the whole. As such, government's buying power—and therefore its influence over the market—declined dramatically. So for government procurement officers to withhold their money in an attempt to persuade the market would have been a futile and rather embarrassing gambit. The only way not to fall hopelessly behind the private sector was to set the minimum threshold of looking for evidence the software manufacturer at least demonstrated the intention of getting their software evaluated for government use. But even this minimum threshold was difficult to maintain as speed and churn only increased.

In short, as the commercial software market exploded, government became just another buyer, and a small one at that compared to the market as the whole. As such, government's buying power—and therefore its influence over the market—declined dramatically.

Landwehr's third point is shortest, but perhaps most damning for government's influence in the software market. Since the private sector inconsistently valued security, but on the whole had a far lower standard of security and far greater purchasing power, software manufacturers could not justify, in economic terms, the effort and time required in order to meet the government's evaluation criteria. In the span of a decade or so, government had gone from the largest influence in software systems, to just another software buyer. Why does the U.S. government buy insecure commercial software? Because it has no other choice.

This, then, is the point of Camp and Wolfram's statements about government taxonomies being inadequate. While government taxonomies are widely taught in introductory university classes on computer security, the effort has largely been a failure. Government taxonomies have questionable market power. The basic concepts of government taxonomies are employed in some commercial systems, but inconsistently, and on the whole are largely ignored by the market. Now, this does not mean all vendors completely ignore government buying requirements altogether; it is just not nearly the compelling market incentive some would make it out to be nor have the ancillary benefits of improving software in general as some would hope. While the Common Criteria came into effect in 1999,[9] it was not until

December 2005 that Microsoft finally got its Windows 2003 and XP operating systems evaluated—*after* these operating system had already been designed, built, and released into the stream of commerce. Other operating system vendors followed suit months later. The actual configuration Microsoft used to pass the Common Criteria evaluation remains unclear, which is of little help to those who must deploy the systems according exactly to the evaluation's assumptions (and for the EAL rating to have any meaning).[10] Besides, lack of evaluation did not stop the U.S. government from using Microsoft's operating system or any other commercial or open source operating system, for that matter, in the interim. The pregnant question, of course, is what if any of these operating system manufacturers failed to pass the evaluation criteria? What then?

The third critique of information provisioning noted by Camp and Wolfram is tied closely to previous critique; namely, the government has provided certain standards that have attempted to improve security from a network perspective but has not provided the necessary standards to address software in particular. The National Institute of Standards and Technology (NIST) is a non-regulatory agency of the Department of Commerce. The mission of NIST is to promote U.S. innovation and industrial competitiveness by advancing measurement science, standards, and technology in ways that enhance economic security and improve quality of life.[11] To date, NIST has issued multiple standards regarding network security and cryptography but has avoided issuing any standards regarding software security in particular. The closest NIST has come to making a statement about software security is in its Voluntary Voter System Guidelines, a set of guidelines adopted by the U.S. Election Assistance Commission for the certification of software-based voting systems. The NIST document states

---

Experience in testing software and systems has shown that testing to high degrees of security and reliability is from a practical perspective not possible. Thus, one needs to build security, reliability, and other aspects into the system design itself and perform a security fault analysis on the implementation of the design.[12]

In other words, while testing is important, it cannot accomplish to the same effect as building security into the software manufacturing process from the start. Building secure software from the beginning is paramount (as are the incentives that encourage this); not relying on the populace to crash test software after it has been released into the stream of commerce. However, NIST has remained silent on how to do this as well as what a standard for software might look like. There might be some very practical reasons why this is so, but part of the organization's mission is to continually refine the science of measurement, making possible "the ultra-precise engineering and manufacturing required for today's most advanced technologies."[13] Software has not been entirely included in that mission to date.

The final critique noted by Camp and Wolfram regarding information provisioning is the inadequate results obtained through subsidization of incident response teams, security products, and research projects—specifically, the lack of widespread adoption of optimal security practices by the public and private sectors. It is understandable the market might choose to ignore the government's statements if research findings are simply presented as informational and lack any formal enforcement, but even the U.S. government has proven incapable of listening to itself. The Department of Homeland Security is the U.S. agency responsible for securing the nation's infrastructure, and yet in 2007 DHS received a "D" letter grade on its statutory obligation to comply with the Federal Information Security Management Act (FISMA)—an Act intended to improve computer and network security within the U.S. government by mandating yearly security audits. This "almost failing grade" is actually good news given that it is the first time since 2003 DHS did not fail outright.

So government's response to the software crisis has been largely a learning process into what *does not* work. Statutes have failed repeatedly to disincentivize attackers and to properly incentivize public agencies. Why have software manufacturers been left out of the equation? The failures of government in addressing the software crisis speak strongly against getting government too heavily involved in the software market. Unfortunately, the blunders of government are matched almost equally by the blunders of the market itself, if not more. The market does not need government to mess it up; it can do that quite properly itself.

The point here is not to repeat all the arguments in Chapter 2 regarding irrational innovation and perverse incentives, but to observe the market actions and the subsequent results. In no case has a commercial security technology been introduced into the market that did not substantially increase the entropy of the system as a whole. In other words, we are attempting to fight the software crisis by adding more and more disorder through a greater array of products. And disorder invites more disorder, even crime. Put simply, the more security products we introduce into the market, the more talent, money, and management needed by purchasers to maintain these products' effectiveness. These products and solutions certainly do not run themselves.

For instance, the simple firewall—a device intended to act as the "front door" to the network—remains notoriously difficult for a vast majority of organizations to keep configured properly. But the firewall is but one security technology in a dazzling panoply of technologies. Anti-virus solutions, anti-spyware solutions, anti-spam solutions, intrusion detection systems, file integrity monitors, hard disk encryption, vulnerability scanners…the number of moving parts for a "successful" security architecture is so great, it is no wonder that the message of disorder—and the problems it brings with it—gets more pronounced with each passing year.

The painful irony of this situation is that unlike safety devices on our automobiles, which allow the vehicle to travel ever faster, every security technology we introduce into the market simply slows down the applications and systems we are trying to protect. Imagine if the seatbelt in your car slowed it down by 5 percent, or the crumple zone slowed the vehicle by 10 percent. This is exactly what happens when we introduce security products into our computer systems. Performance starts to lag. Firewalls slow down network traffic, anti-virus sucks down processor cycles on our laptops, intrusion detection systems consume network bandwidth with their logging information. In almost every case, the benefits of security technologies are fairly well matched against their costs. Added in sum, the costs start looking rather ridiculous. When we consider we are paying this money simply to further crash test yet more software applications, the costs seem utterly foolish.

> *The painful irony of this situation is that unlike safety devices on our automobiles, which allow the vehicle to travel ever faster, every security technology we introduce into the market simply slows down the applications and systems we are trying to protect.*

As bad as government's blunders may be, the market's blunder is that much more severe: the current crop of security products is working from the wrong paradigm. Security should not interfere with the performance of the network or computers any more than safety devices should interfere with the performance of a vehicle; yet, this is exactly the situation.

In light of significant failings of both the market and government, it is hard to imagine a clear path forward. Government seems to stumble over its own feet, and the market seems blinded by its own vision. It should be more apparent at this point that a hands-off policy regarding the software market is questionable practice. Despite government's many failings, the market is not responding adequately to the software crisis and cannot be left to its own devices. The incentives are simply not in place that would result in significant change from the status quo. With this in mind, government's many deficiencies argue against heavy government involvement. A forceful incentive such as government control of software production is perhaps out of the question. But other unattractive incentives remain—namely, litigation. What the government may be incapable or unwilling to do, the populace might be more than ready to undertake.

An Inconvenient Tort

Chapter 5 discussed how software manufacturers insulate themselves from liability. Under contract theories, software manufacturers condition the use of an application upon the user accepting a one-sided licensing agreement—called an adhesion contract—that fundamentally absolves the manufacturer from any liability whatsoever for latent defects. The lack of liability means that software manufacturers have few incentives to correctly design and deeply examine their applications before release to market, letting software buyers serve as crash test dummies without any meaningful remedies for damages or loss.

As a matter of public policy, software litigation—any litigation, really—is a particularly unpleasant option, but it could be the only option that leads anywhere. A public policy regime holding software manufacturers liable for defects would significantly alter status quo because incentives for software manufacturers would dramatically change. In the desire to avoid lawsuits, software manufacturers would be considerably more thorough in the design, construction, and release of their products. Most importantly, however, adhesion contracts would largely become unenforceable, making lawsuits based on tort theories an evolutionary path for the software industry.

The evolution would certainly be cataclysmic for many software manufacturers, but arguably, liability would not bankrupt the software industry any more than product liability bankrupted the automobile industry, the food industry, or the pharmaceutical industry. The software industry is now such a large part of the economy that its fledgling status is no longer warranted, and as Zollers argued in Chapter 5, it's time to stop treating the software industry with kid gloves.

In Chapter 5, Rustad argued that liability would not solely fall on the shoulders of software manufacturers. This is important. To a certain degree, software buyers are still rightfully responsible for protecting their systems. Secure software merely stops exploitation via malicious code; it cannot stop users from acting irresponsibly. When it comes to choosing good passwords or configuring security settings, the user is the least cost avoider. This means that liability with a finding of contributory negligence would limit the supposed "litigious free for all" that some argue might happen if the software industry is exposed to liability. Will lawsuits increase dramatically in the early stages? Yes. Will there be frivolous lawsuits? Absolutely. But historically, these are the same challenges faced by every other industry. And every other industry has adapted and most importantly, improved how it conducts itself in the market. Software might be special among the product categories due to its complexity and radical malleability, but software manufacturers are not so special that they should not be held accountable for defects leading to malicious exploitation, cyber crime, physical injury, or death.

> *Software might be special
> among the product
> categories due to its
> complexity and radical
> malleability, but software
> manufacturers are not so
> special that they should not
> be held accountable for
> defects leading to malicious
> exploitation and cyber crime.*

To reiterate, litigation is an ugly, unpleasant, and expensive option. No one should be under the impression that litigation will solve every manufacturing problem within the software industry, nor should anyone assume courts will not make mistakes. Two things are clear; the legal system, particularly the American legal system, has proven itself as adaptive, responsive, and innovative. It certainly isn't perfect, but then again, neither is software. The legal system will face this situation as it has every other technology that has challenged our traditional ways of thinking and acting. The second point is that the software industry will fight with every ounce of its strength. The software industry is flush with cash, has extensive lobbying power in Washington, and has substantial reserves to battle even the most prolonged court cases. The industry is a formidable opponent, but this need not be entirely adversarial either.

Short of litigation, contracts are the next best legal option software buyers can leverage in addressing the software crisis. Under the paradigm of private ordering, the courts allow individuals to negotiate whatever they want as long as it is not illegal. The contract forms the legal relationship between two or more parties. It is extremely important, then, that the contract says what you want it to say; that is, if you do not ask for security, if you do not ask for quality, if you do not ask for metrics *and put it in the contract*, you, the software buyer, will not get any. Moreover, a contract defines the remedies each party can seek should the terms not be met in practice. To date, consumers, and particularly commercial organizations, have accepted adhesion contracts because they feel they do not have any options. For single, isolated entities this could be the case. As Mr. Landwehr observed, even the U.S. government had to confront its lack of market influence as a lone buyer. But if software buyers coordinate and uniformly press for terms that are more agreeable and sane, well, something just might change.

As the next best option to litigation, contracts come with their own set of problems—namely, the amount of time and money required to negotiate a suitable contract. For complex contracts involving highly technical elements, expenditure in time and money can be substantial. It is more than likely, then, that businesses might shortchange their negotiating power in order to meet their short-term requirements without fully considering the long-term consequences. State governments are holding organizations strictly liable for not securing their software-drive systems. A viable place to mitigate this risk is to negotiate contract terms with software manufacturers that link organizational liability to the software manufacturer's performance. It's your contract; negotiate for what you want.

Whether liability or contract options are exercised depends on the resolve of buyers. Software buyers are shouldering a tremendous burden, a burden that promises to become heavier and less manageable as time goes on. How long this goes on depends on how long buyers are willing to tolerate the status quo.

It is too bad that legal battles could be a second-best route to a safer and more secure world, but sometimes industries need a shock to break their sclerosis. Liability depends on an important component, however. The mantra of tort is duty, breach, cause, damages. In the absence of strict liability for software manufacturers, a breach of a standard of care must be established in order to pursue civil action. Without a standard of care, the liability option is a long way off. In the next two sections, we look at the standard of care for software developers and a standard for software itself.

One Ring to Rule Them All

Graduates of Canadian engineering schools are given an iron ring as part of a ritual written by Rudyard Kipling called "The Ritual of the Calling of an Engineer."[14] The ritual was created in 1922 at the request of a civil engineer named Herbert Haultian who felt the community needed an obligation or a statement of ethics to which new graduates in engineering could subscribe. Engineers who wear the ring have obligated themselves to the highest professionalism and humility of their profession. The ring itself is intended to be a constant reminder to the wearer of their obligation and of the social significance of their profession.

Legend has it that the original rings were made from the beams of the Quebec Bridge, which collapsed during construction in 1907 due to poor planning by the overseeing engineers, killing 57.[15] The ring, then, serves as intimate proof of the tremendous power the engineer has not only over nature, but the tremendous responsibility the engineer has to their fellow human beings. The role of the engineer, like the role of doctor or lawyer, is socially significant.

An iron ring is not a symbol of professional qualification— qualification remains the purview of licensing bodies—but the ring is a symbol of pride and humility for the engineering profession.

The Iron Ring is but one example of an obligation played out against the larger background of society's need to define our responsibilities to each other, not only in our individual actions, but in our professional conduct. From Aristotle onward, the question of how people should treat each other according to some ethical code has been repeatedly asked and pursued. It appears that as the importance of the societal role increases, so too do the responsibilities associated with that role. In other words, the more power someone has over another by nature of his or her role, there arises a proportionate obligation for the fair and prudent use of that power.

> *The more power someone has over another by nature of his or her role, there arises a proportionate obligation for the fair and prudent use of that power.*

For instance, the relationship between a bartender and his clientele is less differentiated than the role of a psychologist to her patient. A bartender can certainly offer advice regarding the travails of one of his customers, but realistically, the customer could get the same advice from one of his friends or relatives. Moreover, if the bartender's advice is wrong, like "Have another gin and tonic," the bartender hasn't done anything unethical. The psychologist, on the other hand, is specifically educated to deal with issues of the mind and has special knowledge outside the bounds of normal everyday experience. If she were to offer the same advice as the bartender without undertaking an examination, her advice to "drink it out" could certainly be seen as unethical.

The bartender arguably has some influence over his customers, but not nearly the same influence a medical professional has over her patients. As such, society does not necessarily recognize the bartender as having an obligation to use his knowledge to the best of his abilities to care for the well-being of his customers; bartenders give plenty of advice, both good (sometimes surprisingly witty) and horrifically misplaced. A bartender giving bad advice may be troublesome, but society does not recognize the role of bartender as necessary to serve the need of mental health. In contrast, society does expect a psychologist, by nature of her training, knowledge and the power that training and knowledge confers, to use her skills to the best of her ability for the benefit of her patients. This means she cannot "guess," at least not without exhausting most of the resources at her disposal. In short, the more sharply differentiated the role, whether through experience, training, or education, the greater the expectation of society on the person fulfilling that role to behave ethically and in the best interests of their clientele.

Against this background, then, plays out the specific issue of whether software developers are "professionals" in the same sense as engineers, lawyers, and doctors. Is the role of software developer/engineer so differentiated from other roles in society and the knowledge required to fulfill their role so outside the realm of everyday experience, that they should be held to equivalent obligations adhered to by other professions? Should licensing be required analogous to licensing for doctors and lawyers? This book argues yes.

> *If software is law, then software manufacturing is more than just an engineering discipline; it is a legislative act that has implications for the whole of the environment it creates and all those who depend on that environment.*

Those who are able to create and manufacture software are and will be an increasingly powerful segment of society. If software is law, then software manufacturing is more than just an engineering discipline; it is a legislative act that has implications for the whole of the environment it creates and all those who depend on that environment. This unique combination makes software development/engineering a strongly differentiated role. Just as doctors have enormous power over those in their care, software developers/engineers have tremendous power over how, when, and to what extent societies can express themselves socially, commercially, economically, financially, and politically. This point is borne out by NIST's concern over malicious code purposefully injected into electronic voting machines:

While [proposed] changes [to voting systems], in theory, could make and could yield voting systems that are reliable and secure against certain threats, they would not mitigate the threat of malicious code inserted by an insider at the voting machine company *[my emphasis]. Assertions [against fraud] do not hold up against the enormous evidence of computer fraud that has occurred in other areas of IT and that has or is likely to occur in voting systems, given the billions spent on elections as well as the rich history of electoral fraud. If a software...voting system...cannot be tested to determine whether malicious code exists...or whether fraud has occurred, then one cannot make the argument that [intentionally-introduced malicious code or fraud in voting systems] hasn't occurred and the election procedures are effective at preventing it.*[16]

As evidenced by this excerpt, software developers/engineers have enormous power, even potentially over the machinery of democracy and whether your vote counts or not. The ability for a malicious insider to inject software into a voting system that could alter the course of a local, state, or federal election is real and probable. That the system could be exploited due to a flaw is almost certain. And the ability to detect this activity is questionable at best given that even other technically-oriented and gifted programmers would have difficulty uncovering even a moderately sophisticated attack. This scenario is not limited to voting machines; it is true for financial systems, accounting systems, defense systems, and other critical and non-critical portions of infrastructure. Software manufacturers literally not only have the keys to the kingdom, but they can make as many keys as they like, when they like, and give them away—intentionally or unintentionally—to all sorts of people. This marks the software profession one of considerable power and influence. With this power and influence should come increased responsibility for its fair and prudent use.

> *Software manufacturers literally not only have the keys to the kingdom, but they can make as many keys as they like, when they like, and give them away—intentionally or unintentionally—to all sorts of people. This marks the software profession one of considerable power and influence.*

Even with general agreement that the software "profession" should adhere to equivalent obligations adhered to by other professions, there remains the substantial issue of the extent to which software developers/engineers should be bound to a code of ethics and who would bind them. At present, the two largest technical associations—the Association of Computing Machinery (ACM) in joint venture with the Institute of Electrical and Electronics Engineers (IEEE)—publishes a code of ethics for software developers called "The Software Engineering Code of Ethics and Professional Practice." The Code specifies eight principles that software engineers must adhere to in accordance with their personal commitment to the health, safety, and welfare of the public.[17] This much is good. Compliance with the code of ethics is entirely voluntary. This is less comforting.

A code of ethics is as much an obligatory framework for behavior as it is an educational tool for the public; that is, while the code instructs professionals on how they should behave, the code also helps inform the public as to what they should expect from the professionals themselves. Moreover, the code provides justification for disciplining adherents that have strayed from the principles contained in the code. A code of ethics, then, is meaningful if and only if the public reasonably expects the professionals to adhere to the code and an enforcement mechanism exists to discipline the wayward. Not only does a voluntary code of ethics lack weight and impact, but neither the ACM nor the IEEE has any meaningful way of enforcing their code of ethics. Whereas public accountants and attorneys must pass ethics exams in order to become licensed, software engineers have none. What value, then, does such a code provide to the profession or the public?

If ACM and IEEE are overly lenient regarding software engineering ethics, then it provides context regarding their stance on licensing; that is, the ACM strongly opposes any movement toward licensure similar to that of other professions for software engineers. Specifically, the ACM council decided in 1999 that it could not support licensing of software engineers because the "state of knowledge and practice in software engineering is too immature to warrant licensing."[18] In 2000, the council strengthened its stance, further concluding that "the framework of a licensed professional engineer, originally developed for civil engineers, does not match the professional industrial practice of software engineering. Such licensing practices would give false assurances of competence even if the body of knowledge were mature; and would preclude many of the most qualified software engineers from becoming licensed."[19]

This reasoning is understandable but indefensible. Society has consistently and relentlessly demanded competency validation for professions that impact health, safety, or public welfare. At any given time in a software professional's life, he could impact all three individually, or sometimes, all three simultaneously. Professional licensing exists for barbers and cosmetologists, physicians, attorneys, accountants, security guards, fortune tellers, message therapists, and movie projector operators just to name a few of the hundreds of licensed occupations in the United States.[20] It is hard to imagine that occupations that have questionable impact on health, safety, or public welfare, such as a mule jockey, are licensed (I wish I were kidding), but developing software, which can greatly affect the public, remains unlicensed.

> *Society has consistently and relentlessly demanded competency validation for professions that impact health, safety, or public welfare.*

A valid counterargument to this line of reasoning made by both the ACM and a 2006 book by Professor Morris M. Kleiner titled *Licensing Occupations: Ensuring Quality or Restricting Competition* is that licensing does little to improve the quality of services provided to the public.[21] We all know good and bad doctors, good and bad accountants, and I guess if you're eccentric, good and bad mule jockeys. Licensing does not seem to sufficiently weed out the bad from the good, but this is a relative measurement and not absolute. A "bad" licensee may be unsatisfactory compared to the good licensee, but is preferable to one not licensed at all. The point is that licensing cannot and will not be perfect for lots of plausible reasons. For all its imperfections, licensing is primarily intended to fulfill society's mandate for protecting the public. The fact that some wonderfully talented software developers will unfairly be refused a license for one reason or another and a perfectly dreadful developer might get licensed by cruel luck is simply not a compelling argument against licensing. It is status quo for every other profession and opens and keeps open the necessary door for judging against a standard of care. Oddly, the software industry insists that developing perfect software is impossible but then demands that a licensing mechanism be perfect for it to be relevant. The irony is palpable.

As a counterargument, the lack of quality improvement through a licensing regime has some merit, but it is misleading. At present, the public is subject to the full spectrum of software—from high quality to life threatening. At any given moment, the type, quality, and safety of software an individual is subject to is unknown. This is far from fair. Arguably, buyers and users of software would much prefer to choose products from a group of imperfectly licensed software engineers than a group that is not licensed at all. At this time, consumers do not have a choice. More importantly, as software becomes a greater part of national infrastructure, the public's choice will be made for them without their direct consent through disparate contracting mechanisms and procurements. In this case, the public might care deeply who has been chosen to build their infrastructure and how accountable those selected might be. At present, the only U.S. State to impose licensing is Texas. As a bellwether state, the hope was that other states would eventually follow suit. However, since the program's inception in 1999, no other states have adopted software engineering licensing. This is a shame, but it also raises another bothersome aspect of licensing software engineers.

Regulation of the practice of engineering is performed by individual states. As a result, areas involving interstate commerce such as automotive engineering, aerospace engineering, and chemical engineering are essentially unregulated and can be specifically exempted from regulation via an "Industrial Exemption."[22] An industrial exemption can be granted for products created by these engineers that are sold or have the potential to be sold outside of the state in which the product is produced. In other words, automotive engineers do not need to be licensed; therefore, automobiles are one example of this industrial exemption. And, as the argument goes, so too should software.

Software is certainly a product like an automobile and is certainly a product involved in interstate commerce; however, software also creates the very freeways upon which other software applications communicate. Software manifests both the freeways and the cars. It is one thing to say that software is like a car and, like a car, is and has a high potential of being sold outside the state in which it is produced. But software also creates the freeway (the Information Super Highway analogy is quite helpful in solidifying this notion). Traditionally, freeways are not products to be exported like vehicles, but indeed, that is exactly the situation software just might be in. Software undeniably creates both infrastructure and the products that use infrastructure. Over half of civil engineers, those who build highways, bridges, and tunnels—the stuff of infrastructure that enables interstate commerce—are licensed. Software engineers are not.

Before we get ahead of ourselves and selectively choose which analogy—the freeway or the car—best satisfies possible pre-disposition regarding software engineering licensure, it is important to realize while automotive engineers may not need to be licensed to design and build automobiles, automobiles themselves are subject to federally mandated safety and fuel economy regulations. One way or the other, society has a way of discovering mechanisms for protecting the public, if not at the state level, then at a federal level or vice versa. On the issue of software, we just "aren't trying hard enough yet," as Bill Joy points out in the quote at the beginning of this chapter.

While the advantages of professional licensure for the software industry will continue to be contentious in the battle against low-quality and insecure software, a less bothersome matter of qualifying individuals might be certification.

Certification can be considered a light weight alternative to licensing. Like licensing, certification informs the public as to who is qualified to perform certain types of work. Certification still requires some modicum of requirements, such as level of education and years of experience, but certification does not carry the same market impact. For instance, certification does not preclude buyers from purchasing products or services from non-certified manufacturers as it does under a licensing regime. Certification is also voluntary and has few, if any, disciplinary mechanisms.

While multiple software manufacturers such as Microsoft, Sun Microsystems, Novell, and Red Hat have instigated certification programs over the past 10 years, these certifications largely ignore software development. The certifications that do address software development are limited to vendor perspectives and inconsistently value the notion of security in software development practices. After 50 years of software development, there is still no universally accepted certification for software development.

But whereas licensure may be objectionable to the software industry, certification is positively disdained among individual software developers. The argument goes something like this: "If everyone has a certification, how valuable could it be? I know plenty of people who passed a certification exam but have no clue as to what they're doing." The problem with certification is, in part, the same problem with licensing—only worse. While certification defines a basic threshold of qualification, the threshold is typically set so low that it does not clearly distinguish the smart from the lucky. As a rather egotistical crowd, individual software developers are understandably loath to kowtow to certification until, of course, they are compelled by project or job requirements.

Short of licensure and certification, the least politically contentious qualification, and therefore perhaps the most practical at this point in time, is not a qualification at all, but an assessment. The SANS Institute—an organization historically focused on network security—has taken on the issue of insecure software by supporting a national assessment program that rates software developers on their level of knowledge regarding software security issues. Whereas professional organizations such as ACM and IEEE have largely driven their programs from within their own ranks, the SANS Institute, in developing the assessment program, turned to those directly suffering from the problems of software: software buyers.

The Secure Programming Skills Assessment is a cooperative initiative involving more than 300 corporations, government agencies, and colleges. A majority of those surveyed during the assessment's development were focused on practical goals—namely, more than 80 percent of respondents stated they wanted to be able to identify where programmers have secure programming knowledge weaknesses so that efforts can be focused on improving those shortfalls. As such, the assessment program is not a pass/fail system, but a rating system that allows developers to determine their current state of knowledge and to progress up the ladder as their skills improve.

More importantly, a scaled rating system allows software buyers to negotiate in contract terms the desired level of software security expertise involved in their project. In addition to defining security requirements, then, procurement efforts can also focus on an objective measure of expertise for individuals building their desired software. This not only makes expertise more objective and transparent, as opposed to using "John who is a really talented developer," but also compels software manufacturers to meet clear and specific demands of software buyers.

Of course, even a collaboratively developed assessment program has difficulties. For one, agreement comes slowly, and not all members participate equally. Second, as with certification, participation among software developers is entirely voluntary. Third, a disciplinary mechanism for breach of conduct is not relevant since the program defines none. While more than 300 organizations back the assessment program, there are still millions of businesses that do not know of the program's existence. This means that as a voluntary program, it will be only as successful and as relevant as software buyers make it.

Whether public policy dictates licensure, certification, or assessment, the exponential growth of software usage and wide variety of ways software is employed poses challenges that simply do not have pleasant or satisfying responses. Licensure is perhaps the most heavy handed of the options, but it is, to date, the only reliable path for establishing a standard of care that might be used in determining malpractice and, therefore, negligence. On the far end of the spectrum, assessment is the most immediately practical of the options because it provides transparency to an otherwise opaque and subjective measurement of skill as well as establishes a clear pathway for individual improvement among software developers. That being said, it is too early to tell how successful the program will ultimately become or the impact the program will have. Nonetheless, some sort of immediate policy response is needed, and all three—licensure, certification, and assessment—should be kept on the table for discussion and debate.

In the end, as the software industry evolves and as the public becomes more educated regarding the impact and importance of software in their everyday lives, professional standards will be demanded. Whether with an iron ring or a knowledge rating, software manufacturers have a strong need to prove themselves—*transparently*—worthy of civilization's trust and confidence. As architects and engineers of modern civilization's foundation, the public should expect no less.

The Great Screw

A good scientist is a person with original ideas. A good engineer is a person who makes a design that works with as few original ideas as possible. There are no prima donnas in engineering.

—*Freeman Dyson*

Software engineers frequently violate this rule.

—*Martyn Thomas commenting on the above quote.*

There are no prima donnas in engineering; the software industry is full of them.[23] A vast majority of software remains handcrafted by extremely talented and innovative individuals that refuse, *refuse* to use the abysmal code of some other ignoramus developer, thank you very much. This tyranny of genius means that a vast majority of software projects are built from the ground up, employing as many original ideas and implementations within the project as possible, but in the end, duplicating for better or worse what others have done before. It also means the same mistakes are repeated project after project, year after year. Microsoft has been victim of this tyranny as have Google, Apple, Yahoo!, Sun Microsystems, and just about every software manufacturer in existence.

A non-generalized approach to software manufacturing requires a maximum of craftsmanship and results in minimal interchangeability; that is, modern software development is more akin to product manufacturing prior to Eli Whitney where each part within a product was handcrafted and unique. This is a problem. Even if professional standards become the norm in the software industry, software itself remains largely non-standardized. Eli Whitney's muskets, made under contract to the U.S. government in 1809, were the first muskets in the United States to have standardized, interchangeable parts.[24] This revolutionized how products could be made and is a hallmark of the industrial revolution. It is not the hallmark of software manufacturing.

This might seem an odd statement at first. If software is the closest thing to a universal tool we have, and software's radical malleability allows us to make of it what we will, then one would think that software could be made

> *Even if professional standards become the norm in the software industry, software itself remains largely non-standardized. Eli Whitney's muskets, made under contract to the U.S. government in 1809, were the first muskets in the United States to have standardized, interchangeable parts.[24] This revolutionized how products could be made and is a hallmark of the industrial revolution. It is not the hallmark of software manufacturing.*

into standardized and interchangeable parts quite easily. If Eli Whitney could do it with muskets, certainly brighter minds in the twenty-first century should prevail. As the argument goes, however, requiring software developers to abide by a particular construction standard stifles innovation and restricts creativity and talent. It denies them their craftsmanship. So while the radical malleability of software means you can do anything you want with software, apparently you cannot standardize it.

If a good engineer is a person who makes a design that works with as few original ideas as possible, software engineers are at a decided disadvantage if there are few pre-fabricated, interchangeable "ideas" lying around. The Internet is rife with standards and specifications from everything from how computers can talk to each other, to file formats, to how to find websites; yet, not a single standard addresses software manufacturing. What little guidance is provided regarding software construction is just that, guidance—non-binding, non-measurable guidance that is subject to personal judgments regarding what is best or most convenient. Without standardized, interchangeable "software parts," professional standards such as licensure and certification can do only so much to reduce weaknesses in software. It also means that software engineers are being limited by their own technology.

We live in a standardized world that is rapidly globalizing. Most industrial nations recognize that effective infrastructure includes, among other things, ready access to capital, energy, transportation, and information. Those "other things" are the systems and institutions that support standardization, testing, and quality.[25] It is surprising, then, that with more than 800,000 global standards, none apply to software construction.

Standardization allows a whole new range of functionality that is simply not possible with hand-made components. As malleable as software may be, this property comes at the cost of complexity and, at present, lack of interchangeability. Greater complexity makes security harder to accomplish, and without minimally defined boundaries on software's most exalted property, software manufacturers will repeatedly "re-invent the wheel" as well as "rediscover" previous defects along with some novel ones. This inflicts a tremendous amount of inefficiency on software production, hindering what software manufacturers could potentially accomplish. Sadly, software engineering is being limited by the very technology it employs along with the insistence on preserving an antiquated, pre-industrial era craftsmanship mentality.

Because we live in a standardized world, we often take standardization for granted. We should not. The battle for standardization was hard won and started with a man by the name of William Sellers in 1864.[26] His *cause celebre*: the screw. The similarities between software and screws are interesting.

At the time, screws, nuts, and bolts were custom-made with no guarantee of similarity between two different manufacturers even within the same city. Likewise, software is largely custom-made with no guarantee of interoperability even between different versions of software. In his speech, "On a Uniform System of Screw Threads," Sellers noted

---

In this country, no organized attempt has yet been made to establish any system, each manufacturer having adopted whatever his judgment may have dictated as best, or as most convenient for himself. So radical a defect should no longer exist.[27]

And so in 1864, Sellers set out to correct that defect. He rallied his substantial wealth, considerable technical skills, and enviable political connections to prosecute the first successful standardization battle in history. The conditions under which Sellers took on this fight sound very familiar to today's. In Sellers' time, America was fast-growing and rapidly industrializing—moving absolutely every relevant form of production to the factory floor. Today, America is quickly globalizing and rapidly "informationalizing"—connecting absolutely everything it can to the Internet. In Sellers' time, the machine-tools industry was the most significant driver of technological innovation, providing the infrastructure that allowed the Industrial Revolution to take off. Today, software fills that role, providing the infrastructure that makes the Information Age possible.

Sellers saw in the screw what others did not, a foundational element of civilization. Without a standardized screw, industrial might was impeded as was technological progress; parts could not be easily interchanged, interoperability was completely out of the question, and buyers would be bound to a particular manufacturer. If Sellers was focused on the common good, then what was needed was a common standard.

But not everyone shared Sellers' vision, particularly many within the machinist-tool industry itself. Naysayers saw standardization as a threat to their way of life, as a threat to their craftsmanship. This sounds familiar. Previously in this section, we noted the same hesitancy by software manufacturers toward "software parts"—namely, that standardization of software manufacturing stifles innovation and restricts developer creativity and talent. Standardization at the software level denies software developers their craftsmanship.

In reality, what was true of machinists in Sellers' day is true for software developers: Anything custom-made has the advantage of locking in customers. In economic terms this means whether someone buys a custom-made lathe, or an operating system comprised of custom-made parts, the buyer *must* come back for repairs, alterations, or upgrades. Even beloved open source software does not satisfactorily address this issue, given that "open" does not mean "standard." Open source software developers must extensively twiddle and whittle their own handmade software parts in order to get them to work with the custom-made parts of their colleagues. Software developers in proprietary ventures developing commercial off-the-shelf software do the same, only behind closed doors. Adopting open or closed source software simply means binding yourself to a given troupe of craftsmen, not to a standard of software production.

> *Adopting open or closed source software simply means binding yourself to a given troupe of craftsmen, not to a standard of software production.*

In short, if screws or software parts become interchangeable, the part becomes more important than the craftsmen; the craftsmen lose their relevancy, and therefore their influence over the market. The same-sized screw can be used in a Honda as easily as it can in a Toyota; it doesn't matter who put the screw in or even who made the screw, but it does matter that the screw fits, every time.

Members within the machine-tool industry had much to lose should Sellers prove successful. Members within the software industry have no less to lose should software standardization ever become reality. Software developers might fight hard, if not harder than their machinist predecessors, against standardization. A few lessons from Sellers might be helpful to illuminate the pathway ahead for software standardization.

First, Sellers recognized that interchangeability and mass production were inevitable. He focused his efforts, therefore, on selecting a screw design that was cheaper, easier, and faster to produce than current screws.[28] This was important. Sellers' "new economy" was no different than our new economy: Speed, volume, and cost were strategic issues. Any standardized software parts would need to show compelling evidence in this arena.

Second, Sellers recognized that momentum is everything in a standards battle. Rapid adoption by just a few key players lends the appearance of inevitability.[29] Before Sellers ever gave his speech, "On a Uniform System of Screw Threads," he had used his connections to persuade four of the biggest machine shops on the East Coast to adopt his screw. The railroads, rail cars, and eventually the U.S. Navy followed suit. By the close of World War II, Sellers' screw was accepted by a majority of industries on both sides of the Atlantic.

Third, setting standards is not without cost or bloodshed. A manufacturing standard, more than any other, threatens the existence of a majority of players within the market. Sellers recognized the market was best suited for establishing the standard, but the market does not always play along. Other players within the market have vested interests in the status quo.

In truth, software standardization remains far off. The software industry favors craftsmanship far more than any other mode of operation and will undoubtedly provide, as did machinists before them, a plethora of arguments why standardization is unachievable, unattainable, and unreasonable. This is detrimental to everyone. The next great security product will not be a product at all, but a revolution in software production. Perhaps mass production, interchangeability, and automation will eventually radically evolve the production techniques of the software industry to where the machine-tools industry was a hundred years ago. One can only hope for so much.

A Market for Weakness

Even if professional standards for software engineers and/or standards for software itself come to fruition, vulnerabilities in software will remain a concern, albeit hopefully a dramatically reduced concern. This appears to support the software industry's repeated assertion that perfect software—software completely devoid of defects—is impossible to create. The fact that perfect software is not possible to create in no way implies that improved software is not valuable. Certainly professional licensure creates incentives greater than those currently in effect for improving software quality and security—avoiding litigation is a considerable incentive indeed—and certainly software standardization reduces the craftsman's foibles from the production process, but in either case, significant software weaknesses may still be discovered "out in the wild" after a product has been released into the stream of commerce. Moreover, even if a majority of software manufacturers eventually aspire to building extremely reliable and secure software, this does not offset the problems created by low-quality software manufacturers or those who choose to use low-quality (and perhaps cheaper) software products. Due to the interconnectivity of software systems, those who invest in high-quality, secure software remain subject to the externalities created by those who manufacture and use bad software. Even copious amounts of dramatically improved software, it appears, might not be enough to change the story of software.

> *The fact that perfect software is not possible to create in no way implies that improved software is not valuable.*

Given the potential severity of current, and as yet unknown, future vulnerabilities, weaknesses in software will be a continual and foreseeable threat to civilization's newest foundation. Our inability to satisfactorily squeeze weaknesses out of software—even under the most optimal conditions—means vulnerabilities may be an unfortunate inevitability. In other words, we might just have to learn to live with the fact that someone out there can break into our computer systems or that low-quality software will "pollute" the Internet environment with vulnerabilities. But then again, this situation is not different from other industries that have environmental impacts and therefore does not mean our options are exhausted. We just need to try harder.

This book has argued that incentives are critical to understanding the story of software. It has also argued that weaknesses in software create significant costs both in monetary and social terms for users of software and for the global community at large. The burden of these costs, however, is not shared by software manufacturers even when offering free patches to the marketplace: Money the software industry directs toward offering free patching solutions is merely an investment in the continued supremacy of their licensing terms so the "cost" of free patching smells distinctly like a benefit. As pointed out repeatedly in this book, this imbalance is called a negative externality—when the self-interested behavior of one party detrimentally affects the well-being of another. In other words, the behavior of the software industry imposes costs on everyone but itself. The behavior is also economically inefficient.

In an ideal economic system, goods worth *more* than they cost to produce continue to be manufactured, whereas goods that are worth *less* than they cost to produce are not. For instance, if a restauranteur bought a few ingredients from the grocery store, mixed them expertly together, and was able to sell the delectable concoction at a higher price than the cost of the ingredients, the restauranteur makes a profit. As long as the restauranteur continues to make a profit, she should continue to sell her entrees. However, if the restauranteur is unable to sell entrees for more than the cost of the ingredients (she takes a loss), she should refrain from making them.

This is what economists mean by the term *economic efficiency*; the highest value is attained (profit) for the inputs (ingredients) involved. So entrees that should be produced are, and entrees that should not be produced are not. The ideal economic systems only work, however, when the manufacturer pays *all the costs* associated with production. In reality, manufacturers will only include in their calculations the costs they *must* pay, not the costs they *should* pay.

For example, consider a cement factory. Not only does the cement factory use limestone, calcium, silicon, iron, and so on, but coal-fired cement factories also "use" clean air; release hydrochloric acid into the atmosphere, which potentially causes throat irritation and more severe conditions like lung cancer; and release enormous amounts of carbon dioxide. In fact, cement manufacturing is one of the world's greatest polluters, releasing by itself upwards of 10 percent of the world's man-made greenhouse gases.[30] For every one ton of cement produced, as much as one ton of carbon dioxide is released into the atmosphere. For the sake of argument, let's say the cost of that one ton of carbon in the atmosphere is $100. If the cement industry does not pay directly for those costs, the cement manufacturer will not consider those costs in profit/loss calculations. This means not all the costs associated with cement production are considered resulting in economic *inefficiency*. In other words, some products might be produced even if their total cost (cost of ingredients along with environmental costs) is greater than their selling price. But the inefficiency goes deeper than this.

The cement factory might be able to reduce the amount of pollution by including magnesite in the manufacturing process (which absorbs carbon dioxide, making cement a "carbon sink" that removes CO_2 from the atmosphere). The cement factory might also use "capture and return" filters to reduce the amount of particulate levels in cement kilns, or even employ advances in nanotechnology that replicate cement's strength without the necessary energy requirements for production, but any of these or other abatement options only make sense if the cost of eliminating pollution is less than the damage prevented. In other words, it only makes sense for the cement manufacturer to pursue one or all of these options if for every one ton of cement created, the "solutions" cost less than $100 (the cost of one ton of carbon in the atmosphere).

Again, the cement manufacturer will only consider *required* costs in profit/loss calculations. If the cement manufacturer does not or is not made to pay the direct costs of pollution, it has no incentive to prevent it. Not only does this result in an inefficient level of cement production because all costs associated with production are not included in the selling price, but this also results in an inefficient level of pollution abatement considering that reasonable pollution controls that could be employed are not.

The similarities between cement manufacturing and software manufacturing are, once again, striking. As long as cement companies do not directly pay the costs imposed by greenhouse gases, they have no incentive to prevent their emissions. Likewise, as long as software manufacturers do not directly bear the costs of vulnerabilities, they do not have an incentive to prevent vulnerabilities. But there is another important aspect to manufacturing that might be helpful in addressing the software crisis.

Manufacturing *inevitably and unavoidably* causes pollution. Whether garbage from an organic restaurant, plastic remnants of toys, chemical solvents from batteries for hybrid cars, or carbon emissions from cement factories, manufacturing creates waste that imposes costs on others and the environment. *Inevitability and unavoid-ability* is central to the issue. Just as pollution-free manufacturing is not possible, neither is perfect software devoid of all latent defects. If environmental pollution is an inevitable consequence of manufacturing, then perhaps vulnerabilities are an inevitable consequence of software production. It is something we must most likely accept as reality but it does not mean we must forgo action.

If manufacturing products such as cars, lamps, and toasters inevitably causes pollution, and "imperfections" are inevitable in software manufacturing, a possible solution to the software crisis could be found in global warming or, more accurately, how world governments are addressing the issue of global warming.

The potential answer to pollution and to global warming in particular is not to stop manufacturing, as this is far from practical and would worsen everyone's lot, but to price pollution in such a way that market participants can account for these environmental costs in their profit/loss calculations. The same can be reasoned for software. The answer is not to stop manufacturing software, as this is far from practical and would worsen everyone's lot, but to price software vulnerabilities in such a way that market participants can account for these "environmental" costs in profit/loss calculations.

This pricing mechanism "internalizes" externalities by making companies account for a portion of costs associated with production that were previously ignored. The external cost is brought in-house, so to speak. Pricing pollution also encourages the use of abatement technologies given that pricing makes hidden costs more apparent. Each of these behaviors leads to greater economic efficiency and allows the market to more appropriately reflect the real costs of production. Governments have so far employed one of two pricing mechanisms for pollution and greenhouse gases in particular: a carbon tax and a cap-and-trade system.

A carbon tax is an emissions fee; that is, the company releasing a given pollutant must pay a fee based on how many units of the pollutant are released each year. The affected company will pay for the pollution—in the form of an emissions fee—along with other production costs. In deciding the extent to which they will control their emissions, the company balances the cost of abatement against its benefits and adjusts product prices accordingly. There is no upper ceiling to the carbon tax; that is, companies will each pay the amount of tax they believe optimal to their situation. However, market forces eventually start to prevail. Because producers are creating products or providing services under competitive pricing models, the more carbon a company produces, the greater the likelihood their prices will rise above their competitors. This puts high carbon emitters at a disadvantage compared to low carbon emitters because low carbon emitters pass on less of the tax to consumers. A carbon tax encourages reduction of emissions, which in turn reduces the size of the tax, which lowers the company's market prices thereby making them more competitive.

In contrast, the cap-and-trade system limits how much carbon-dioxide producers can emit and lets them buy and sell emissions credits. The more credits a company is willing to purchase, the more carbon they are allowed to produce. However, there is a finite number of credits available, so companies that sell credits to •

other companies wishing to purchase credits are forging their ability to emit carbon dioxide. In order to forgo their ability to emit carbon dioxide, companies must invest in green technologies or alter production techniques.

Each system has its drawbacks. The amount of pollution in the atmosphere and its effects on the environment, while generally agreed to be unacceptable, suffers to a large extent from considerable uncertainty. That is, how much carbon in the atmosphere is "bad" and how much will cause an irreversible rise in planetary temperatures is still open to debate. This makes the carbon tax the favored of the two pricing mechanisms because taxation is seen by economists to be the most efficient when uncertainty is greatest. It also is seen as a more stable pricing mechanism, allowing companies to plan their investments with longer vision. However, for most of its history, especially in the United States, "tax" has been considered a four-letter word. This resistance to taxation, which is completely understandable even in the most fair cases, almost guarantees painful battles in getting it established as a useful vehicle for battling climate change.

In contrast, the cap-and-trade system is relatively opaque and complex with potentially large price variations from year to year. This makes it difficult for companies to develop long-term investment strategies. Moreover, setting the right number of permits is difficult. Issue too few, and the price for permits rises dramatically. Issue too many, and reduction in emissions is less likely. Nonetheless, politicians appear to favor cap and trade for its convenient lack of transparency and because it doesn't appear like a tax even though it is.

In the end either system, if implemented properly, should discourage carbon emission and in doing so, encourage the development and adoption of cleaner-energy technologies. In this way, either system is also bound to raise consumer prices, but this is the point: to more equally share the costs of production with all those (or a healthy majority of those) who are affected by our behaviors, not just those within the market. It's only fair.

In the same manner that world governments constrain carbon emissions, a possible solution to the software crisis entails using the same pricing mechanisms, such as a vulnerability tax or cap-and-trade system, to manage the inevitability of software vulnerabilities. In essence, reported software vulnerabilities would be equivalent to measured carbon-dioxide emissions. By pricing software vulnerabilities in the cyber environment, just as carbon is priced in the natural environment, this should discourage vulnerabilities and in doing so, encourage the development and adoption of "cleaner" software manufacturing technologies, including even, standardization of software parts.

The similarities between global warming and the software crisis are debatable but interesting. Like climate, software is tremendously complex with literally thousands of variables affecting it, not all of which are known. Also predicting how much hotter a particular level of carbon dioxide will make the world is as daunting as predicting how "secure" a particular amount of vulnerabilities will make the Internet.

While technologies certainly exist to solve both the climate and software problem, adoption of "cleaner" technologies is frustratingly slow due primarily to political and economic issues. Because climate change affects everyone on the planet, it is in the best interest of everyone to share the burden as equally as possible. Likewise, because a majority of software is networked across a global Internet, and software creates the network itself, it is in everyone's interest to share the burden of securing the global infrastructure. Also no one owns the planet, but we each own our little parts of it. Likewise, no one owns the Internet, but we each have oversight over our own little sections, which immediately leads to a complication.

Because the problem of climate change is global, but the precise effect of greenhouse gases on temperature is uncertain, responsibility of a particular nation for contributing to carbon emissions can be easily shirked. Likewise, because software use is so widespread, and the risk of software vulnerabilities so difficult to nail down empirically, it is relatively easy to blame somebody else for cyberspace's woes.

In the end, if implemented properly, and having learned the lessons the world has already learned in pricing carbon emission, a vulnerability tax on manufacturers should discourage production of insecure, poorly written software as well as encourage the development and adoption of "cleaner" software development technologies. This is perhaps the most powerful incentive (and one that is far more pleasant than litigation) to changing the status quo in the story of software.

This tax need not solely apply to software manufacturers, however. A vulnerability tax could be imposed on both vendors *and* consumers—not only those who are content to *manufacture* products with vulnerabilities, but those who choose to *purchase* insecure, poorly written software. This has the same effect as does incentivizing the purchase of hybrid cars in America. Consumers would be rewarded for choosing products that are "cleaner" and less risky for the Internet.

But the similarities between climate change and software vulnerabilities are not always so clear cut. As it turns out, there are a few problems with a software vulnerability taxation model. The first problem is where to set the threshold. With carbon emissions, targets are set for carbon levels at a given point in time. For instance, the Kyoto protocol tried to get the world's big polluters to commit to cutting emissions to 1990 levels. The "rise" in the Internet's "temperature"—the count of vulnerabilities per year—is consistently on the up tick. But are previous levels of vulnerabilities acceptable? Small rises in global temperature are a cause for concern, but we are uncertain in the cyber realm what impact the magnitude of dips or rises in the number of vulnerabilities may have.

A second major problem is measuring the number and severity of vulnerabilities. Unlike carbon-dioxide, which can be objectively measured, software vendors have historically had a tendency to disclaim or minimize vulnerabilities or, at minimum, declare that a "bug" is actually a feature. With the introduction of a tax on vulnerabilities, vendors are much more likely to contest reported vulnerabilities to avoid taxation. In fact, as hackers realize the power they wield in discovering and exploiting software vulnerabilities, it is reasonable to speculate that hackers might eventually forgo publicly reporting software vulnerabilities. This means while the number of vulnerabilities might go down, the "temperature" of the Internet might indeed go *up*. Exploits will exist that we will not know about, yet we will be subject and susceptible to their use. The count of vulnerabilities could be far too erratic a measurement to reliably determine the level of risk we encounter because of software vulnerabilities.

The third problem, and a significant problem indeed, is the aggressiveness with which vulnerability discovery can be undertaken. Unlike in the carbon emissions scheme where a given company cannot "discover" more carbon in a competitor's factory than actually exists and therefore unexpectedly increase the tax on the competitor, aggressive companies in the software industry could foreseeably invest a significant amount of effort in discovering vulnerabilities in a competitor's product. This would cause competing companies to pay more tax and, in effect, be driven out of business not by their lack of effort to reduce vulnerabilities, but by the concerted effort of aggressive companies to discover vulnerabilities before the competitor had a chance to improve their development efforts. The larger and wealthier the aggressive company, the more likely the wealthier company could drive smaller less prepared companies unfairly from the market.

For instance, under the traditional carbon taxation scheme, if company A produced 10 units of carbon, and company B produced 5 units of carbon, company B cannot "force" company A to produce more carbon. Company A will produce whatever amounts of carbon their production process creates. There are no hidden carbon emissions—no latent carbon compounds—in manufacturing that can be unexpectedly discovered; carbon levels for different manufacturing processes can be measured quite readily and objectively. So company A would pay a certain amount of taxes, and company B would pay less than A because it produced less carbon. Under a vulnerability taxation mechanism, this scenario might be quite different.

If software manufacturer A, which for the sake of argument is a large, wealthy software manufacturer, produced on average 10 vulnerabilities a year, and software manufacturer B, which is a smaller, up-and-coming manufacturer, produced on average 5 vulnerabilities a year, under a vulnerability taxation scheme, each would pay taxes proportional to the number of vulnerabilities released into the stream of commerce. If vulnerabilities were priced at, say $100 each, manufacturer A would pay $1000 in taxes and manufacturer B would pay $500 in taxes.

Because manufacturer B produced less vulnerability "emissions" than manufacturer A, B's taxation would be lower and it could therefore sell its product at a lower cost than manufacturer A. This is the ideal situation.

However, if software manufacturer A were directly competing with software manufacturer B, software manufacturer A might invest additional resources (because it is wealthier) to "discover" vulnerabilities in software manufacturer B's product over and above what software manufacturer B invests in testing and quality control. Because perfect software is impossible to create, manufacturer A is likely to find a vulnerability manufacturer B was unable to avoid. This means software manufacturer A can "target" software manufacturer B and any other potential competitor by specifically investing additional funds (such as hiring third-party "security researchers") with the intent of looking for undiscovered latent defects in the products of competitors.

In this situation, instead of manufacturer B producing 5 vulnerabilities on average, all of a sudden software manufacturer B could now have 15 vulnerabilities or more, far higher than what was expected. The effect is software manufacturer B must unexpectedly pay more taxes than manufacturer A, driving up the cost of B's product and making the product more expensive and less competitive in the marketplace. This gives manufacturer A a distinct advantage because it can invest in finding vulnerabilities in competitors' products potentially driving smaller competitors from the market while doing nothing to reduce its own level of vulnerabilities. This is but one possible distortion of the vulnerability taxation model.

A final challenging aspect of imposing a price on vulnerabilities is correctly sizing a vulnerability tax. Economists, information security professionals, and software companies all are in wild disagreement about the real cost of software. Pricing vulnerabilities would require extensive research that to date has only been applied to global climate change and is subject to far more debate than even the heated, often ideological arguments regarding the extent, impact, and causes of global warming. Software vulnerabilities, unlike carbon atoms, come with different severities and impacts on the environment. Basing a price on different severities therefore may prove difficult, even unworkable. One possible avenue is simply separating obviously critical software vulnerabilities (vulnerabilities that give unrestricted access to a computer system regardless of how the system is attacked) from all other lesser vulnerabilities. Still, the actual price of a vulnerability might be difficult to establish, but is certainly worthy of further investigation.

A vulnerability taxation scheme is tempting since it, among all other incentives, allows market participants to define what is acceptable regarding software and what is not with very little external involvement of government and possibly, the courts. In reality, a vulnerability taxation scheme will be wrought with the same, if not more contentious, problems as those surrounding global warming. One thing is fairly clear, however; the world's viewpoint on global climate change has only recently come clearly into focus. Just over 30 years ago in 1975, *Newsweek* magazine ran a cover story about potentially cooler planetary temperatures in the following decades. It was feared another Ice Age might ensue, causing dramatic reduction in food production, among other calamities. In contrast, since the late 1960s, software security experts and luminaries in the software industry have relentlessly, unwaveringly, and loudly pronounced the dangers of insecure, poorly manufactured software. What has been relatively unclear for climate change until recently has never been in question for software. One might hope that momentum to resolve the thornier issues of "Internet pollution" would build more quickly.

Global warming might begin to irreversibly alter the planet's climate in 10, 15, or even 20 years. This much might be hyperbole espoused by over zealous environmentalists, but insecure, poorly manufactured software is affecting you now and as such threatens the very foundation upon which you build your life, your hopes, and your future. While an unexpectedly warm winter or a cool summer might be indicative of global climate change, the Earth's weather has been capricious even in its best moods. Nature may be cantankerous, but software exploitation is downright vicious. It is the immediacy of the software crisis that is so dramatic after the turn of the century and the quickness by which it has gained momentum that is so worrisome. Do not expect organized crime or foreign nation states to voluntarily shun the opportunities set before them by insecure software. The fact that the software crisis remains opaque to the general populace, even though more and more people are feeling its impacts, is unfortunate.

It is not too late. I believe we have not gone too far down the path to alter course, but we aren't trying hard enough yet. The last chance to assert control—the fail-safe point—might be rapidly approaching, but it is up to us to decide our future. Which is to be master? Software or ourselves?

Whatever our choices, the software crisis will be hugely expensive, either in the cost of ignoring it or in the cost of mitigating its impacts. It is up to us to determine what cost we are willing to bear and the results we are willing to accept. Nothing in this story is pre-ordained—not the dominance of software manufacturers, not the willful supremacy of attackers, not the purchasing power of the consumer, and not government's inaction. Something will happen, but what will it be?

Closure

The challenges of insecure software are hard to solve and easy to disagree about. Those who fear letting government into the business of software manufacturing are rightly suspicious: government is not always to be trusted. Nor, sadly, are some software manufacturers.

Those who fear legal action against software companies might lead to an overwhelming number of frivolous lawsuits are duly cautious; yet, software manufacturers, like many corporate entities, are far from hapless victims of an unfair legal system. Though some lawsuits may certainly test the bounds of Reason, not all cases will be frivolous or unfounded, nor might the expense of these legal proceedings be extraordinarily different from previous ground-breaking civil actions.

Significant technical hurdles may indeed exist that makes high-quality, secure software difficult to design and thoroughly test and therefore easy to avoid manufacturing if software buyers do not demand it. But none of these technical hurdles are unsolvable, or even impossible to overcome. For a group of manufacturers known for and who freely espouse the value of innovation, innovation is simply all that is asked on this matter.

While disagreement about solving the software crisis may be inevitable, failure is not. Markets do not necessarily create the products we *need*, simply the products *we are willing to buy*. In reality, the world is not ruled by engineers, software or otherwise, focusing on creating elegant, robust structures, or by business people focusing primarily on profits, though both groups' influence are inarguably high. The world is ruled by a wide diversity of humans. And those humans are ruled in their totality by incentives.

This book has argued, no matter how imperfectly, that incentives are key to changing the story of software. In light of this, technology is ancillary. The story has been, and always will be, about us. Change the incentives, and the story changes.

E P I L O G U E

"You can't possibly analyze things properly within a couple of minutes. All you can rely on is your intuition. I had two arguments to fall back on. First, missile attacks do not start from just one base. Second, the computer is, by definition, brainless. There are lots of things it can mistake for a missile launch."

—Lieutenant Colonel Stanislav Petrov

"The Russians saw a U.S. government preparing for a first strike, headed by a President capable of ordering a first strike...I think that this is the closest we've come to accidental nuclear war."

—Bruce Blair, Nuclear strategy expert, Dateline NBC

The world as we know it almost ended on September 26, 1983.[1] Lieutenant Colonel Stanislav Petrov was standing watch at Serpukhov-15, a command post for the Soviet Union's ballistic missile early warning system. Three weeks earlier the Soviets had accidentally shot down Korean Airlines Flight 007, killing all 269 people on board. NATO countries, including the United States, were preparing to engage in operation Able Archer, a military exercise spanning the whole of continental Europe that simulated a coordinated nuclear release. Worse, both General Secretary Brezhnev and KGB Chairman Yuri Andropov were convinced (more through their own paranoia than by any hard facts) the United States was preparing to launch a surprise nuclear strike against the Soviet Union. The KGB had just sent flash messages warning its operatives to prepare for a possible nuclear outbreak. According to Bruce Blair, relations between the United States and the Soviet Union "had deteriorated to the point where the Soviet Union as a system—not just the Kremlin, not just Andropov, not just the KGB—but as a system, was geared to expect an attack and to retaliate very quickly to it. It was on hair-trigger alert. It was very nervous and prone to mistakes and accidents...."

Amongst all these tensions and undercurrents, on the night of September 26 the warning systems within Serpukhov-15 alerted. "An alarm at the command and control post went off with red lights blinking on the terminal. It was a nasty shock," said Petrov. The computer systems that watched and monitored the United States heartland for Minutemen missile launches had detected one, then two, then three, then four, then five missile launches from the same American base. Five missiles were on their way, but no more. Petrov went on to say, "We checked the operation of all systems—on 30 levels, one after the other. Reports kept coming in: All is correct; the probability factor [of a U.S. nuclear attack] is two [at its highest]."

The United States was attacking, or so it appeared, but not as the Soviets expected. A handful of nuclear missiles certainly fell under the rubric of nuclear attack since one well-placed missile could level the whole of the Kremlin and most of Moscow, but so few missiles from a single American base was simply not the all-out first strike needed to gain any hope of surviving a retaliatory second strike by the Soviets. In the philosophical madness of nuclear strategy, either all missiles were launched, or none at all. The American "attack" was a trickle, when it should have been a flood.

> In the philosophical madness of nuclear strategy, either all missiles were launched, or none at all.

Petrov had just a few minutes to determine whether to "push the button" and respond to the American attack or report up the chain of command. Within 15 minutes of the alert U.S. missiles, if they had been indeed launched, would be entering into Soviet airspace. Delay too long, and Soviet missiles would not leave their silos in time.

Petrov decided to report up the chain of command. His superiors told him to launch. Petrov hesitated. Attacks from a single U.S. base did not make sense. As a software engineer he was also aware the software used in the Soviet monitoring system had weaknesses. In the end, Petrov reported it was a false alarm despite what the screens and the monitoring systems were displaying and despite the procedures he himself had written for just this situation. "I had a funny feeling in my gut. I didn't want to make a mistake." In 15 minutes he would know for sure.

The fact that I am writing this story, and you are reading it, means Petrov's funny feeling proved correct. Humans, as I mentioned in the beginning of this book, are perceptive creatures. We live, and even thrive, in a world full of ambiguity, paradox, and uncertainty. Computers are not nearly so lucky. Computers are stupid and will do exactly as they are instructed by software. No more, no less. Stripped of all the technical reasons and detailed explanations, the false alarm generated by the Soviet ballistic missile monitoring system was caused by this: computer error...a software bug.

> *Computers are stupid and will do exactly as they are instructed by software. No more, no less. Stripped of all the technical reasons and detailed explanations, the false alarm generated by the Soviet ballistic missile monitoring system was caused by this: computer error...a software bug.*

As an author, one hopes to keep the conversation tightly scoped to one critical aspect; a simple, easily digestible message for which the reader can repeat the mantra to their friends, colleagues, and family. Software does not lend itself easily to such distillation. My hope, now that we are at the end of this book, is that to some extent you understand the full scope and consequence of software's impact on modern civilization and that it is not a topic that should be left only to the experts. As software becomes more common in every aspect of our lives, its composition becomes more important. The more we depend on software, the more we need to care about who creates it, how it is used, and what it is used for. The genius of software developers needs a better story than the one being written right now. Our lives depend on it. The real cost of software just might be us.

N O T E S

Preface

[1] This number is estimated based on the cost of cyber crime in 2007 ($117 billion, GAO) and the cost of insufficient software testing in 2002 ($60 billion, NIST). This NIST estimate has not been recently updated, but inarguably has not reduced in any significant manner since then. The problem with all these numbers is an acknowledged difficulty with under-reporting by victims and the intermixture of different causes for said losses. As such, the problem with the estimate given here is that not only may it be "soft," but significantly lower than actual costs if reporting levels among victims was higher. This estimate also tends to conflate numbers that may be unrelated to insecure software directly. that said, I still feel comfortable quoting $180 billion for two primary reasons. First, insecure software communicates a message of disorder into cyberspace. It invites greater elements of disorder, even crime (as Chapter 3 illuminates). *But for* insecure software, many costs (both direct and indirect) might not need to be borne by software buyers. The message of disorder is prevalent in cyberspace and imposes a substantial cost on its inhabitants (not just in crime, but other misbehavior). Second, the cost of insecure software appears somewhere above $100 billion annually although I was unable in my interviews to confirm just how far above $100 billion this estimate might be. The number was felt to be "about right." Arguably, it may not be. Regardless, the real cost of something is not always measured in dollars, but dollars sure can help. The greater upset (to me) is not so much that $180 billion might be uncomfortably inaccurate, but that we, at this moment in time, have no idea by how much. This is a shame. The U.S. Department of Defense budget for calendar year 2007 is estimated at $439 billion. "Katrina Could Cost Economy $100B, Estimated figure could make hurricane the costliest to hit the United States, topping Andrew," CNNMoney.com, September 2, 2005.

[2] *The Jungle* is a famous book that described, in nauseating detail, the practices of the American meat packing industry at the turn of the twentieth century. President Roosevelt was so disturbed by the book he called on Congress to create the Food and Drug Administration.

Chapter 1

[1] Peter Ackroyd, *The Great Stink of London* (Sutton Publishing, 1998), p. xi.

[2] Ibid., p. 152.

[3] Makers Gallery, http://www.makersgallery.com/concrete/tech.html. Accessed August 3, 2006.

[4] Ackroyd, p. 152. The tests required a significant amount of time. To quote Bazalgette directly, "It is to be brought on to the works in a state fit for use, and is not to be used therein, until it shall have been upon the ground for three weeks at the least, nor until it has been tested by taking samples out of every tenth sack, at the least, gauging these samples in moulds, and by apparatus similar to those heretofore in use by the said Board, placing the cement at once in water, in which it is to remain for seven clear days, and testing it at the end of that time by the application of a weight or lever. All cement that shall not bear, without breaking, a weight of five hundred pounds, at the least, when subjected to this test, shall be peremptorily and forthwith removed from the works."

[5] Ibid., p. 152. There were three drainages for the project: Northern, Western, and Southern.

[6] The difference between concrete and cement is subtle but distinct. Concrete contains cement plus other additives such as aggregates like sand, rocks, or gravel. Cement is the binding agent that holds aggregates together.

[7] Ackroyd, p. 137. In 1866, another cholera epidemic erupted in the East End of London—the only section of the city not connected to Bazalgette's sewer network. This provided further evidence that cholera was a waterborne and not an airborne pathogen.

[8] *United States Geological Survey*, Mineral Commodity Summaries, January 2006.

[9] Thomas, Martyn, "Engineering Judgment," *Australian Computer Society Inc.*, 2004.

[10] A Collection of Well-Known Software Failures, http://www.cs.bc.edu/~gtan/bug/softwarebug.html, A Collection of Software Bugs, http://www5.in.tum.de/~huckle/bugse.html.

[11] "Facts About Childhood Drowning," Safe Kids Worldwide, 2004, http://www.cpsc.gov/cpscpub/pubs/5097.html.

[12] Drucker, Peter, *The Effective Executive*, New York: Collins, 1960, p. 159.

[13] Zollers, Frances, and McMullin, Andrew, and others, "No More Soft Landings for Software: Liability for Defects in an Industry That Has Come of Age," *Santa Clara Computer and High Technology Journal*, May 1, 2005.

[14] McMillan, Robert, "Two Charged with Hacking LA Traffic Lights," *Computerworld*, January 10, 2007.

Chapter 2

[1] General Motors Corp. V. Johnston, 592 So.2d 1054 (Ala. 1992).

[2] "Computer Failure Puzzling In Peruvian Crash," CNN World News, October 3, 1996.

[3] "A Collection of Well-Known Software Failures," http://www.cs.bc.edu/~gtan/bug/softwarebug.html.

[4] Poulsen, Kevin, "Known Hole Aided T-Mobile Breach," *Wired Magazine*, February 2005.

[5] "A Collection of Well-Known Software Failures," http://www.cs.bc.edu/~gtan/bug/softwarebug.html.

[6] *CNN Money*, "Prius Hybrids Dogged by Software," May 16, 2005.

[7] This is a 2003 estimate and does not include or forecast losses in later years.

[8] Jacky, Jonathan, "Safety-Critical Computing: Hazards, Practices, Standards, and Regulation," 1994, http://staff.washington.edu/jon/pubs/safety-critical.html.

[9] Pinkney, Kevin, "Putting Blame Where Blame is Due: Software Manufacturers and Customer Liability for Security-related Software Failure," *Albany Law Journal of Science and Technology*, 2002.

[10] Rustad, Michael and Thomas Koenig, "The Tort of Negligent Enablement of Cybercrime," *Berkley Law Journal*, Fall 2005.

[11] Barnes, Douglas, "Deworming the Internet," *Texas Law Review*, 83 Tex. L. Rev. 279.

[12] "Crappy Software," http://crappysoftware.home.comcast.net/.

[13] "The Economic Impacts of Inadequate Infrastructure for Software Testing," *NIST*, May 2002.

[14] In fact, the software is offered as free, but the vendor will then sell services around just getting the software to work in the first place. This software is only "free" if purchasers do not value their time.

[15] Thurrott, Paul, "Most Users Do Not Trust Microsoft," *Windows IT Pro*, August 1, 2003.

[16] http://www.nhtsa.gov/cars/rules/import/FMVSS/index.html.

[17] Nader, Ralph, *Unsafe at Any Speed*, Knightsbridge Publishing Co., 1965.

[18] Chrysler Corporation v Department of Transportation, United States Court of Appeals for the Sixth Circuit, 472 F.2d 659 (6th Cir. 1972).

[19] NHTSA VRTC Pedestrian and Applied Biomechanics Division, http://www-nrd.nhtsa.dot.gov/vrtc/bio/adult/hybIII50dat.htm.

[20] Mello, Tara, "What Crash Test Scores Mean," http://www.edmunds.com/ownership/safety/articles/43804/article.html.

[21] Ibid.

[22] "Stars on Cars Could Spotlight Safety," Cathy Nikkel, http://www.automedia.com/Stars/on/Cars/to/Spotlight/Safety/dsm20050601sc/1.

[23] "Five Star Crash Ratings," *Associated Press*, March 2007.

[24] White, Joseph, "Do Five Star Ratings Really Matter?" *The Wall Street Journal*, February 26, 2007.

[25] Brooks, Frederick, *No Silver Bullet: Essence and Accidents of Software Engineering*, 1986.

[26] The "Mom and Pop Software Tinkershop" does not exist and has no relation to any company imagined or actual. This is a placeholder name for any software company comprised of a few entrepreneurs, or, as the Brits like to say, "a man and his dog."

[27] Ricciuti, Mike, "Oracle: Unbreakable No More?" *CNET News*, July 28, 2005.

[28] Ibid.

[29] Evers, Joris, "Oracle Dragging Heels on Unfixed Flaws, Researcher Says," CNET News.com, July 19, 2005.

[30] Common Criteria Introduction, Apple web site, http://www.apple.com/support/security/commoncriteria/ and Wikipedia, http://en.wikipedia.org/wiki/Common_Criteria.

[31] The Common Criteria does specify that "penetration testing" must be accomplished, but again, this is after the fact when all the design mistakes have already been made.

[32] Odlyzko, Andrew, "Economics, Psychology, and Sociology of Security," Digital Technology Center, University of Minnesota, 2003.

[33] Robert, Jaques, "2006 'The Year of Cybercrime,'" VNUNET.COM, July 17, 2006.

[34] Chrysler Corporation v Department of Transportation, United States Court of Appeals for the Sixth Circuit, 472 F.2d 659 (6th Cir. 1972).

[35] Vijayan, Jaikumar, "Breach Notification Laws: When Should Companies Tell All," Computerworld, March 2006 http://www.computerworld.com/action/article.do?command=viewArticleCoverage&articleId=109161&continuingCoverageId=1019.

[36] Pinkney, Kevin, "Putting Blame Where Blame is Due: Software Manufacturers and Customer Liability for Security-related Software Failure," *Albany Law Journal of Science and Technology*, 2002.

[37] Mello, John, "Cybercrime Costs US Economy at Least $117 Billion Each Year," *E-Commerce Times*, July 26, 2007.

[38] Ibid.

[39] Ibid.

[40] Wolinsky, Howard, "Resolution Due in Medical Software Regulation," http://www.annals.org/cgi/content/full/127/10/953.

[41] Curtis, Polly, "Brushing Teeth Could Prevent Heart Attacks and Strokes," *The Guardian*, March 2007.

[42] Baum, Sandy, "Education Pays 2004: The Benefits of Higher Education for Individuals and Society," *College Board*, 2005.

[43] Kawasaki, Guy, "Rule No. 4: Get Going," http://www.alwayson-network.com/comments.php?id=11965_0_11_0_C.

[44] Barron, Cheryll, "High Tech's Missionaries of Sloppiness," Salon.com, 2000.

[45] "Estimates say XBOX 360 Failure Rate as High as 33%," GamePro Staff, *PCWorld*, July 3, 2007.

[46] Pan, Jiantao, "Software Reliability," http://www.ece.cmu.edu/~koopman/des_s99/sw_reliability/.

[47] Reliability League Table, 2007. Extract from Ford website. http://media.ford.com/newroom/release_display.cfm?release=25480.

[48] Kawasaki, Guy, "The Art of Bootstrapping," http://blog.guykawasaki.com/2006/01/the_art_of_boot.html.

[49] Microsoft Announces "People Ready" Business Vision, http://www.microsoft.com/presspass/press/2006/mar06/03-16PeopleReadyPR.mspx.

[50] http://www.apple.com/support/switch101/.

[51] Net Applications: Apple's Mac "market share" continues to rise, http://www.macdailynews.com/index.php/weblog/comments/net_applications_apples_mac_market_share_continues_rise1/.

[52] In the course of writing this book, Apple has started to release non-copy protected music files.

[53] Broersma, Matthew, "iPod's 'Dirty Secret' Wins Web Fans, CNET News, http://news.com.com/iPod's+'dirty+secret'+wins+Web+fans/2100-1027_3-5112066.html.

[54] http://www.ipodbatteryfaq.com/#1.

[55] http://www.boingboing.net/2006/06/09/antiitunes_drm_demon.html.

[56] "Apple Hit by Swedish Anti-iTunes Pressure," http://www.engadget.com/2006/06/11/apple-hit-by-swedish-anti-itunes-pressure/.

[57] "Where Would Jesus Queue," *The Economist*, July 5, 2007.

[58] "The Economic Impacts of Inadequate Infrastructure for Software Testing," *NIST*, May 2002.

[59] Mossberg, Walter, "How to Protect Yourself From Vandals, Viruses If You Use Windows," *The Wall Street Journal*, September 16, 2004.

[60] Naraine, Ryan, "Zero-day Firefox Exploit Sends Mozilla Scrambing," *EWeek*, May 9, 2005.

[61] Achohido, Byron, "Cybercrooks constantly find new ways into PCs," *USAToday* August 2006, http://www.usatoday.com/tech/news/computersecurity/hacking/2006-08-02-black-hat_x.htm.

[62] Google: Security Mishaps and User Trust, Michael Arrington, October 18, 2006.

[63] McAlearney, Shawna, "Yankee says Patching Costs Companies Milllions," http://searchsecurity.techtarget.com/originalContent/0,289142,sid14_gci951006,00.html.

[64] Barnes, Douglas, "Deworming the Internet," *Texas Law Review*. The following paragraphs are a summarization of Douglas' exceptional paper on issues precipitating failure in the software market.

[65] Barnes, Douglas, "Deworming the Internet," *Texas Law Review*, 83 Tex. L. Rev. 279.

[66] Bott, Ed, "Microsoft's Licensing Mess," June 7, 2007 http://blogs.zdnet.com/Bott/?p=250.

[67] Jacky, Jonathan, "Safety-Critical Computing: Hazards, Practices, Standards, and Regulation," http://staff.washington.edu/jon/pubs/safety-critical.html.

[68] Barron, Cheryll, "High Tech's Missionaries of Sloppiness," Salon.com, 2000.

[69] Ibid.

[70] Bagchi, Kallol, "An Analysis of the Growth of Computer and Internet Security Breaches," *Communications of the Association for Information Systems*, December 2003.

Chapter 3

[1] Zeller, Tom, "Black Market in Stolen Credit Card Data Thrives on Internet," *New York Times*, June 21, 2005; Horn, Paul, "It's Time to Arrest Cyber Crime," *Business Week Online*, November 12, 2006. In December 2006, I spoke directly with Dr. James Lewis regarding this statistic. Dr. Lewis was the originator of the McAfee study where this number is cited. He confirms five percent is "about right," but there is a significant gray area since under-reporting by victims makes these numbers difficult to nail down. While the following cites from Zeller and Horn use the Federal Trade Commission as the source, Dr. Lewis believes he derived these numbers from the FBI and Secret Service statistics, not the FTC. Dr. Lewis' estimate is also supported by Mary Calkins in her paper "They Shoot Trojan Horses, Don't They?" in the November 2000 issue of *Georgetown Law Journal*. This article cites two percent.

[2] Reuters, "Cybercrime Becoming More Organized," September 15, 2006.

[3] In fact, it is believed only two percent of all intrusions ever reach the initial attention of law enforcement. Calkins, Mary, "They Shoot Trojan Horses, Don't They? An Economic Analysis of Anti-hacking Regulatory Models," *Georgetown Law Journal*, November 2000.

[4] To start, about 1000 cases are brought before the courts, but a majority are thrown out on insufficient grounds (about 800 or so). Only the most clear cut cases go to trial, and even then it's a crap shoot depending on what expert testimony has to say. Granick, Jennifer and Hernandez, Carmen, "Commission's request for public comment about how the Commission should respond to Section 225(b) of the Homeland Security Act of 2002," *Letter by The National Association of Criminal Defense Lawyers*, February 2003.

[5] Symantec Internet Security Threat Report, September 2004.

[6] Knapp, Kenneth and Bolton, William R. "Cyber-Warfare Threatens Corporations: Expansion into Commercial Environments," *Information Systems Management* (ISM-Journal.com), 23, Spring, 2006.

[7] Weber, Amelie, "CYBERCRIME: The Council of Europe's Convention on Cybercrime," *Berkeley Technology Law Journal & Berkeley Center for Law and Technology*, 18 Berkeley Tech. L.J. 425

[8] Morin, Monte, "U.S. Indicts Russian Citizen in Hacking Case," *Los Angeles Times*, June 21, 2001.

[9] Paller, Alan, *SANS Newsbites*, August 14, 2006.

[10] Statement made in Visa CISP Compliance meeting, Visa Headquarters, 2003.

[11] Glaessner, Thomas, Tom Kellermann and Valerie McNevin, "Electronic Security: Risk Mitigation in Financial Transactions," *The World Bank*, June 2002.

[12] Ibid.

[13] Lemos, Robert, "Vulnerability Tallies Surged in 2006," *SecurityFocus*, January 1, 2007.

[14] CSI/FBI Cyber crime Survey 2005 and 2006.

[15] Skibell, Reid, "Cybercrimes and Misdemeanors: A Reevaluation of the Computer Fraud and Abuse Act," *Berkley Technology Law Journal*, Summer 2003.

[16] Morin, Monte, "U.S. Indicts Russian Citizen in Hacking Case," *Los Angeles Times*, June 21, 2001. "Russian Hacker Gets Three Years in US," Out-law.com, October 2002, http://www.out-law.com/page-3000.

[17] Department of Justice website, Computer Crime and Intellectual Property Section, http://www.usdoj.gov/criminal/cybercrime/intl.html.

[18] Electronic Privacy Information Center, The Council of Europe's Convention on Cybercrime Overview, http://www.epic.org/privacy/intl/ccc.html.

[19] Notable Hacks, http://www.pbs.org/wgbh/pages/frontline//shows/hackers/whoare/notable.html.

[20] Biever, Celeste, "Murky Trade in Bugs Plays into the Hands of Hackers," *New Scientist*, June 16, 2007.

[21] Ibid.

[22] Ibid.

[23] Sutton, Michael and Nagle, Frank, "Emerging Economic Models for Vulnerability Research," paper presented at the Workshop on the Economics of Information Security 2006.

[24] Naraine, Ryan, "Hackers Selling Vista Zero-Day Exploit," eweek.com, December 15, 2006, http://www.eweek.com/article2/0,1895,2073611,00.asp.

[25] Emerging Economic Models for Vulnerability Research, Workshop on the Economics of Information Security, 2006. http://weis2006.econinfosec.org/docs/17.pdf

[26] At the time of Sumudra's activities in 2002, gold was roughly $282 USD per ounce. The price of gold in 2002 varied between a low of $278 and a high of $286 USD. The price calculated in the text is selected at $282 USD. At this price, five pounds of gold is roughly $16,900 USD. If you bothered to do the calculation, your number was probably larger than the one stated in the text. This is because gold is measured on the troy system of measurement in which there are 12 ounces in a pound. The everyday weight system used in the United States is the avoirdupois system in which a pound consists of 16 ounces.

[27] Sipress, Alan, "An Indonesian's Prison Memior Takes Holy War Into Cyberspace," *Washington Post*, December 14, 2004, p. A19.

[28] Paller, Allan, "Testimony of Alan Paller before the House Committee on Homeland Security," October 18, 2005, http://www.american.edu/radiowave/CII%20SITE/paller.pdf.

[29] Sipress, Alan, "An Indonesian's Prison Memoir Takes Holy War Into Cyberspace," *Washington Post*, December 14, 2004, p. A19.

[30] Krebs, Brian, "Three Worked the Web to Help Terrorists," *The Washington Post*, July 6, 2007.

[31] Ibid.

[32] Lewis, James, "Assessing the Risks of Cyber Terrorism, Cyber War, and Other Cyber Threats," *Center for Strategic and International Studies*, December 2002, http://www.shaneland.co.uk/ewar/docs/dissertationsources/institutionalsource1.pdf.

[33] Knapp, Kenneth, "Cyber-Warfare Threatens Corporations: Expansion into Commercial Environments," *Information Systems Journal* (ISM-Journal.com), Spring 2006.

[34] Poteat, Eugean, "The Attack on America's Intellectual Property, Espionage After the Cold War," *The Bent of Tau Beta Pi*, Winter 2001.

[35] Ibid.

[36] Ibid.

[37] Cohen, William, "Former Defense Secretary Cohen's Remarks at the 2001 Summit," March 6, 2001.

[38] Ibid.

[39] A Case Study in French Espionage: Renaissaince Software, October 2000, http://www.hanford.gov/oci/maindocs/ci_r_docs/frenchesp.pdf.

[40] Warren, Peter, "Smash and Grab, the Hi-tech Way," *Guardian Unlimited*, January 2006.

[41] Winkler, Ira, "Guard Against Titan Rain Hackers," *ComputerWorld*, October 20, 2005.

[42] Ibid.

[43] Onley, Dawn and Wait, Patience, "Red Storm Rising," *Government Computer News*, August 2006.

[44] Knapp, Kenneth and Boulton, William, "Cyber-warfare Threatens Corporations: Expansion Into Commercial Environments," *ISM Journal*, Spring 2006.

[45] Cohen, William, "Former Defense Secretary Cohen's Remarks at the 2001 Summit," March 6. 2001.

[46] Lesk, Michael, "How Much Information Is There In The World," http://www.lesk.com/mlesk/ksg97/ksg.html.

[47] Winkler, Ira, "Guard Against Titan Hackers," *Computer World*, October 20, 2005.

[48] Pinkney, Kevin R., "Putting the Blame Where Blame Is Due: Software Manufacturer and Customer Liability for Security-related Software Failure," *Albany Law Journal of Science and Technology*, 43, 2002.

[49] Calkins, Mary, "They Shoot Trojan Horses, Don't They?" *Georgetown Law Journal*, November 2000.

[50] Wilson and Kelling wrote an article describing the Theory of Broken Windows for *The Atlantic Magazine* in 1982.

[51] Kelling, George and Coles, Catherine, *Fixing Broken Windows*, Simon and Schuster, New York, 1996, p. 25.

[52] Ibid., p. 114.

[53] A graffiti writer's tag is his or her personalized signature that stipulates, "I was here. I did this." In the late 1970s the amount of graffiti exploded, particularly in New York City. The goal of many artists was to draw as many tags in as many places as possible, an act known as "getting up." Artists began to break into subway yards in order to tag as many trains as they could.

[54] Kelling, George, "Reclaiming the Subway," *City Journal*, Winter 1991.

[55] Kelling, George and Coles, Catherine, *Fixing Broken Windows*, Simon and Schuster, New York, 1996, p. 118.

[56] Ibid., p. 134.

[57] Ibid., p. 152.

[58] Ibid., p. 24.

[59] Skogan, Wesley, *Disorder and Decline: Crime and the Spiral of Urban Decay in American Neighborhoods*, New York, Free Press, 1990, p. 75.

[60] Ibid.

[61] This comes from part of a discussion with fellow security professionals I was involved in during a Visa Payment Card Industry conference.

[62] My notes on Vladimir are incomplete, and therefore I do not have his full name. However, the facts of the case are represented to the best of my ability.

[63] Weiss, Gus, *The Farewell Dossier*.

[64] Reed, Thomas, *At The Abyss: An Insider's History of the Cold War*, New York, Presidio Press, 2004.

[65] Ibid.

[66] Safire, William, "The Farewell Dossier," *New York Times*, February 2, 2004. http://seclists.org/isn/2004/Feb/0011.html.

Chapter 4

[1] O'Niel, Don, "Competitiveness versus Security," *The Journal of Defense Software Engineering*, June 2004.

[2] Kelly, Kevin, "New Rules for a New Economy," *Wired Magazine*, September 1997, http://www.wired.com/wired/archive/5.09/newrules_pr.html.

[3] White House, A Framework for Global Electronic Commerce, July 1, 1997.

[4] Landwehr, Carl, "Improving Information Flow in the Information Security Market," *University of California at Berkley*, May 2002.

[5] SANS Newsbytes, Vol. 9, Num 61, August 3, 2007.

[6] http://archives.openflows.org/hacktivism/hacktivism00019.html. Original article in *Washington Post*, but no longer available online. Babington, Charles, "Clinton Declares War on Cyber-Terrorism," *Washington Post*, January 7, 2000.

[7] The National Strategy to Secure Cyberspace, February 2003, p. 32.

[8] A detailed account is given by Nancy Leveson from the University of Washington, summarized in part here. Leveson, Nancy, *Safeware: System Safety and Comptuers, Appendix A: Medical Devices: The Therac-25*," Addison-Wesley: 1995.

[9] The conversion between rads (radiation absorbed dose) and rem (roetnger equivalent man) gets very complicated and complex, and these are rough estimations based on a quality factor of 1; that is, a rem and a rad are considered equivalent in these calculations. Also exposure time must be taken into account. Chronic exposure (over a long period) and acute exposure (over a short period) had different effects. Special thanks to Dr. Robert Gardner for giving me guidance on rough estimations. The exposure values for Nagasaki were acquired from Chapter 6 of the "Pediatric Terrorism and Disaster Preparedness" manual. http://www.ahrq.gov/research/pedprep/pedchap6.htm.

[10] Vesely, Rebecca, "Since When Does the FDA Regulate Software?," *Wired Magazine*, September 24, 1997.

[11] Volokh, Alexander, "Software Pirates," *ReasonOnline*, November 1997.

[12] U.S. Department of Health and Human Services, Food and Drug Administration, "General Principles of Software Validation," January 11, 2002.

[13] Gage, Deborah, and McCormick, John, "We Did Nothing Wrong," *Baseline Magazine*, March 4, 2004.

[14] FDA News, "FDA Seeks Injunction Against Multidata Systems International," May 7, 2003. http://www.fda.gov/bbs/topics/NEWS/2003/NEW00903.html

[15] http://www.baselinemag.com/article2/0,1540,1543569,00.asp.

[16] supra 13.

[17] http://en.wikipedia.org/wiki/Commercial_off-the-shelf.

[18] Ibid.

[19] U.S. Department of Health and Human Services, Food and Drug Administration, "Off-The-Shelf Software Use in Medical Devices," September 9, 1999.

[20] supra 13.

[21] Scalet, Sarah, "Navigating the PCI Standard," *CSOOneline.com*, April 20, 2007.

[22] Ibid.

[23] TJX refers to the company which operates the TJ Maxx and Marshalls chains. Abelson, Jenn, "Breach of data at TJX is called biggest ever," *The Boston Globe*, March 29, 2007.

[24] Krim, Jonathan, and Barbaro, Michael, "40 Million Credit Cards Hacked," *The Washington Post*, June 18, 2005.

[25] Litan Avivah, "Changes Will Improve PCI Security, But Not Enough," *Gartner Research*, September 2006.

[26] Section 6.5.a of PCI version 1.1, PCI DSS Security Audit Procedures, https://www.pcisecuritystandards.org/tech/supporting_documents.htm.

[27] Hines, Matt, "Security Alliance Pitches Government Incentives," *InfoWorld*, April 11, 2007.

[28] Ibid.

29 Cyber Security Industry Alliance, "Talking Points for Cyber Security, Preventing Identity Theft, Protecting Intellectual Property and Critical Infrastructure, Increasing Accountability," 2004.

30 In fact, the Defense Information Systems Agency (DISA) has a few checklists for evaluating software that can be used in part for FISMA and DITSCAP requirements.

31 Cox, Wendell and Love, Jean, "40 Years of the U.S. Interstate Highway System: An Analysis The Best Investment a Nation Ever Made," June 1996. http://www.publicpurpose.com/freeway1.htm.

32 "Dream Machines," *The Economist*, June 2, 2005.

33 "WHO report highlights traffic safety in China," *China Daily* October 12, 2004.

34 "Dream Machines," *The Economist*, June 2, 2005.

35 Status of the Nation's Highways, Bridges, and Transit: 2002 Conditions and Performance Report, http://www.fhwa.dot.gov/policy/2002cpr/ch2.htm.

36 "WHO report highlights traffic safety in China," *China Daily*, October 12, 2004.

37 Ibid.

38 Yidong, Yang, "Road Traffic Safety Plan in China," Ministry of Communications of People's Republic of China.

39 CNN Money, "Survey ranks states with dumbest drivers," May 2005. http://money.cnn.com/2005/05/26/Autos/drivers_study/

40 Cox, Wendell, and Love, Jean, "40 Years of the US Interstate Highway System: An Analysis The Best Investment A Nation Ever Made," June 1996. http://www.publicpurpose.com/freeway1.htm.

41 Ibid.

42 Ibid.

43 https://www.csialliance.org/news/newsletters/may2006/may_dcisurvey.html

44 Keizer, Gregg, "Most Consumers Don't Trust Their Security Software" http://www.informationweek.com/security/showArticle.jhtml;jsessionid=JCP4XTSI-IJX22QSNDLOSKHSCJUNN2JVN?articleID=196800396.

45 Multiple quotes drawn from the text. Cox, Wendell, and Love, Jean, "40 Years of the US Interstate Highway System: An Analysis. The Best Investment A Nation Ever Made," June 1996.

46 Technically, the definition of engineering includes "art," but in this discussion I am more concerned with the systematic and repeated processes associated with modern engineering. While there is certainly a component of engineering that relies on "art" in the sense of using intuition and creativity, the work of an artist is not easily repeatable by others. Engineering, in the sense that I am using it, is focused on repeatable and systematic processes that engineers use to build bridges, buildings, and so on.

47 Gudrias, Elizabeth, "Artful Engineering," *Harvard Magazine*, May-June, 2007, http://www.harvardmagazine.com/2007/05/artful-engineering.html.

48 Gibbs, Wayt, "Software's Chronic Crisis," *Scientific American*, 1994.

49 ACM Panel of Professional Licensing in Software Engineering, Report to Council, May 15, 1999, http://www.acm.org/serving/se_policy/report.html.

50 Storey County, Nevada, "Laws Governing Legal Prostitution," http://www.sex-in-nevada.com/Bashful/THE_LAW/Storey_County_Laws.html.

51 Nevada State Law, NRS 41.1397a, "Actions for Personal Injuries by Wrongful Act, Neglect, or Default," http://www.leg.state.nv.us/nrs/NRS-041.html#NRS041Sec1397.

52 "Prius Hybrids Dogged by Software," *CNN Money*, May 16, 2005.

Chapter 5

[1] http://www.wired.com/wired/archive/2.01/flux.html.

[2] Rustad, Michael, and Koenig, Thomas, "The Tort of Negligent Enablement of Cyber crime," *Berkley Law Journal*, Fall 2005.

[3] Feinman, Jay, "The Economic Loss Rule and Private Ordering," *Arizona Law Review*, Volume 48.

[4] A rather funny juxtaposition of law and order on comic book heroes by Stephen Bates: Superman liable for negligently failing to use X-ray vision to detect acquaintance's tumor. Bates, Stephen, "How Law Destroys Order," *National Review*, February 11, 1991. http://www.encyclopedia.com/doc/1G1-10330563.html.

[5] Smith, Neville, "Insurers May Be Hit By a Bad Idea Whose Time Has Come," *Lloyd's List International*, Issue 58751, September 23, 2004.

[6] Pinkney, Kevin, "Putting Blame Where Blame is Due: Software Manufacturers and Customer Liability for Security-related Software Failure," *Albany Law Journal of Science and Technology*, 2002.

[7] Ibid.

[8] Rustad, Michael, and Koenig, Thomas, "The Tort of Negligent Enablement of Cyber crime," *Berkley Law Journal*, Fall 2005.

[9] Zollers, Frances, and McMullin, Andrew, and others, "No More Soft Landings for Software: Liability for Defects in an Industry That Has Come of Age," *Santa Clara Computer and High Technology Journal*, May 1, 2005.

[10] Reagan, Ronald, "Inaugural Address," West Front of the U.S. Capitol, January 20, 1981, http://www.reaganfoundation.org/reagan/speeches/first.asp.

[11] Kaner, Cem, "Background on UCITA," http://www.badsoftware.com/uccindex.htm.

[12] Ibid.

[13] Ibid.

[14] McMahon, David, "Consumers Still Opposed to UCITA," 2003, http://www.consumerlaw.org/action_agenda/e_commerce/ucita/index.shtml.

[15] Rustad, Michael, and Koenig, Thomas, "The Tort of Negligent Enablement of Cyber crime," *Berkley Law Journal*, Fall 2005.

[16] Pinkney, Kevin, "Putting Blame Where Blame is Due: Software Manufacturers and Customer Liability for Security-related Software Failure," *Albany Law Journal of Science and Technology*, 2002.

[17] Shaw v. Toshiba Am. Info. Sys., 91 F. Supp. 2d 926 (D. Tex. 1999)

[18] Ibid.

[19] North Tex. Preventive Imaging v. Eisenberg, 1996 U.S. Dist. LEXIS 19990 (D. Cal. 1996)

[20] Ibid.

[21] Ibid.

[22] Rasch, Mark, "Vista's EULA Product Activation Worries," *SecurityFocus*, November 21, 2006, http://www.securityfocus.com/print/columnists/423.

[23] Pinkney, Kevin, "Putting Blame Where Blame is Due: Software Manufacturers and Customer Liability for Security-related Software Failure," *Albany Law Journal of Science and Technology*, 2002.

[24] Ibid.

[25] Krebs, Brian, "Federal Data Breach Bills Clear Senate Panel," http://blog.washingtonpost.com/ securityfix/ 2007/05/federal_data_breach_bills_adva.html.

[26] Symantec Internet Security Threat Report, Trends for January 1, 2004 – June 30, 2004, Volume VI, September 2004. Critical Infrastructure Protection, Efforts of the Financial Services Sector to Address Cyber Threats, United States Government Accounting Office, GAO-03-173, January 2003.

[27] Rustad, Michael, and Koenig, Thomas, "The Tort of Negligent Enablement of Cyber crime," *Berkley Law Journal*, Fall 2005.

[28] Rustad, Michael and Koenig, Thomas, "Cybertorts and Legal Lag: An Empirical Analysis," *Southern California Interdisciplinary Law Journal*, 2003.

[29] Ibid.

[30] Ibid.

[31] Ibid.

[32] Rustad, Michael, and Koenig, Thomas, "The Tort of Negligent Enablement of Cyber crime," *Berkley Law Journal*, Fall 2005.

[33] Rustad, Michael and Koenig, Thomas, "Cybertorts and Legal Lag: An Empirical Analysis," *Southern California Interdisciplinary Law Journal*, 2003.

[34] Ibid.

[35] Ibid.

[36] Ibid.

[37] Ibid.

[38] Ibid.

[39] Ibid.

[40] Common Law, Wikipedia, http://en.wikipedia.org/wiki/Common_law.

[41] Ibid.

[42] Feinman, Jay, "The Economic Loss Rule and Private Ordering," *Arizona Law Review*, Volume 48.

[43] Ibid.

[44] Ibid.

[45] Ibid.

[46] Ibid.

[47] Rustad, Michael and Koenig, Thomas, "Cybertorts and Legal Lag: An Empirical Analysis," *Southern California Interdisciplinary Law Journal*, 2003.

[48] Ibid.

[49] "Information Technology: An Important Tool for More Effective Government," Legislative Analysts Office, State of California, June 16, 1994.

[50] Tort Law, http://www.answers.com/topic/tort.

[51] Adapted from *Stanford Encyclopedia of Philosophy*. Coleman, Jules, "Theories of Tort Law," *Stanford Encyclopedia of Philosophy*, 2003.

[52] Feinman, Jay, "The Economic Loss Rule and Private Ordering," *Arizona Law Review*, Volume 48.

[53] Elliott v. Laboratory Specialists, Inc., 588 So. 2d 175, 176 (La. Ct. App. 1991).

[54] Ibid.

[55] Ibid.

[56] Coleman, Jules, "Theories of Tort Law," *Stanford Encyclopedia of Philosophy*, 2003.

[57] Ibid.

[58] Law.com, Legal Dictionary, http://dictionary.law.com/default2.asp?selected=1314&bold=.

[59] MacPherson v. Buick Motor Co., 217 N.Y. 382, 391 (N.Y. 1916).

[60] Henningsen v. Bloomfield Motors, Inc., 32 N.J. 358 (N.J. 1960).

[61] Greenman v. Yuba Power Products, Inc., 59 Cal. 2d 57 (Cal. 1963).

[62] Ibid.

[63] Elements in this section and the next were adapted from "An Economic Analysis of Alternative Standards of Liability in Accident Law," Legal Theory, Law and Economics, Harvard Law School, http://cyber.law.harvard.edu/bridge/LawEconomics/neg-liab.htm.

[64] http://www.lexjet.com/lexjet/newsletter/2006/December_Expand/ExpandingCompanies.asp.

[65] Zollers, Frances, and McMullin, Andrew, and others, "No More Soft Landings for Software: Liability for Defects in an Industry That Has Come of Age," *Santa Clara Computer and High Technology Journal*, May 1, 2005.

[66] Ibid.

[67] Ibid.

[68] Aetna Casualty & Surety Co. v. Jeppesen & Co., 642 F.2d 339 (9th Cir. 1981).

[69] Ibid.

[70] Ibid.

[71] Ibid.

[72] Ibid.

[73] Saloomey v. Jeppesen & Co., 707 F.2d 671, 677 (2d Cir. 1983).

[74] Ibid.

[75] Ibid.

[76] Brocklesby v. United States, 767 F.2d 1288, 1295 (9th Cir. 1985).

[77] Ibid.

[78] Ibid.

[79] Ibid.

[80] Ibid.

[81] Fluor Corp. v. Jeppesen & Co., 170 Cal. App. 3d 468 (Cal. Ct. App. 1985).

[82] Ibid.

[83] Ibid.

[84] Ibid.

[85] Zollers, Frances, and McMullin, Andrew, and others, "No More Soft Landings for Software: Liability for Defects in an Industry That Has Come of Age," *Santa Clara Computer and High Technology Journal*, May 1, 2005.

[86] Ibid.

[87] Ibid.

[88] Ibid.

[89] Ibid.

[90] Ibid.

[91] Ibid.

[92] Ibid.

[93] Ibid.

[94] Ibid.

[95] Rustad, Michael, and Koenig, Thomas, "The Tort of Negligent Enablement of Cyber crime," *Berkley Law Journal*, Fall 2005.

[96] Ibid.

[97] Ibid.

[98] Ibid.

[99] Ibid.

[100] Ibid.

[101] Ibid.

[102] Ibid.

[103] Tort Reform, Perception versus Reality, Minnesota Trial Lawyer, Winter 2003.

[104] Ibid. In fact, the rise in insurance premiums has less to do with claims against manufacturers and more to do with investment earnings of insurance companies. "During the booming economy of the 1990s, insurance companies in fierce competition for new territories sold coverage for less than the cost of claims. When the economy went bust, and investment earnings dwindled profit reserves, the insurance industry found itself in crisis. The only way out was to raise premiums."

[105] Robins, Kaplan, Miller & Ciresi, "Tort Reform: Perception versus Reality," *Minnesota Trail Lawyer*, Winter 2003.

Chapter 6

[1] Evers, Joris, "Homeland Security Helps Secure Open Source Code," *CNET News.com*, January 12, 2006.

[2] In fact, Portland cement was once under patent, so when it was first created, *who* could make Portland cement was restricted to the patent holder. The formula was not a secret, however, since it was disclosed in the patent itself. But once the patent expired after 20 years, Portland cement became the dominant element in infrastructure projects.

[3] "Portland Cement," U.S. Department of Transportation, Federal Highway Administration, Infrastructure Materials Group, http://www.fhwa.dot.gov/infrastructure/materialsgrp/cement.html.

[4] Ibid.

[5] The original formula for making Coca-Cola was patented in 1893. When the formula changed, the company chose not to patent the formula again. If Coca-Cola were to patent its formula, the formula would become known to others, and once the patent expired (in 20 years), anyone could use it.

[6] Weber, Harry, "Coca-Cola to Buy Vitamin Water Maker," *ABC News*, May 25, 2007, http://abcnews.go.com/Business/wireStory?id=3211909.

[7] "Open, but not as Usual," *The Economist*, May 16, 2006.

[8] This touches on a bifurcation in the "free software" and "open software" distinction. Truly free software means that software, once released to the public, can never be restricted; that is, free software cannot become part of a proprietary software application. Open software, on the other hand, does not have this restriction. Open software may be used in proprietary software applications and therefore may lose its "freedom" so to speak. However, this does not preclude the original source code from being used by other software developers.

[9] "Open, but not as Usual," *The Economist*, May 16, 2006.

[10] "A Brief History: The Bell System," http://www.corp.att.com/history/history3.html. Elements of this story line were also derived from Steven Weber's excellent historical recounting of the evolution of open source in his book, *The Success of Open Source*, Harvard University Press, 2004.

[11] Sullivan, Lawrence and Hertz, Ellen, "The AT&T Antitrust Consent Decree: Should Congress Change the Rules?," http://www.law.berkeley.edu/journals/btlj/articles/vol5/Sullivan/html/text.html.

[12] "A Brief History: The Bell System," http://www.corp.att.com/history/history3.html.

[13] "The International Telegraph Union," http://bnrg.eecs.berkeley.edu/~randy/Courses/CS39C.S97/regulation/regulation.html.

[14] http://www.swtech.com/server/os/unix/.

[15] "A Brief History: The Bell System," http://www.corp.att.com/history/history3.html.

[16] Excerpt from the GNU website.

[17] Stallman, Richard, "The GNU Operating System and the Free Software Movement," *Open Sources*, p 70.

[18] Weber, Steven, *The Success of Open Source*, Harvard University Press, Cambridge, Massachusetts: 2004, p. 7.

[19] Sterling, Bruce, "A Contrarian View of Open Source," *O'Reilly Network*, September 2002.

[20] Levesque, Michelle, http://www.firstmonday.org/issues/issue9_4/levesque/.

[21] "Open, but not as Usual," *The Economist*, May 16, 2006.

[22] Nichols, David, and Twidale, Michael, "Usability and Open Source Software," University of Waikato, Hamilton, New Zealand, 2003, http://www.cs.waikato.ac.nz/~daven/docs/oss-wp.html.

[23] Ibid.

[24] http://www.anecdotage.com/index.php?aid=11812.

[25] Evers, Joris, "Homeland Security Helps Secure Open Source Code," *CNET News.com*, January 12, 2006.

[26] Ibid.

[27] Ibid.

[28] Ibid.

[29] Ibid.

[30] Levesque, Michelle, http://www.firstmonday.org/issues/issue9_4/levesque/.

[31] Espiner, Tom, "Linux Guru Argues Against Liability," ZDNet.co.uk, January, 2007.

[32] Ibid.

[33] Weber, Steven, *The Success of Open Source*, Harvard University Press, Cambridge, Massachusetts: 2004, p. 7.

Chapter 7

[1] "Life 2.0," *The Economist*, August 31. 2006.

[2] Ibid.

[3] Genetic Weapons Alert, *BBC News*, January 21, 1999. http://news.bbc.co.uk/2/hi/health/259222.stm.

[4] Burns, Enid, "The Deadly Duo: Spam and Viruses," November 2006, http://www.clickz.com/showPage.html?page=3624278.

[5] Calkins, Mary, "They Shoot Trojan Horses, Don't They? An Economic Analysis of Anti-Hacking Regulatory Models," *Georgetown Law Journal*, November 2000.

[6] Camp, Jean, and Wolfram, Catherine, "Pricing Security," *Economics of Information Security*, Vol. 12, 2004 http://papers.ssrn.com/sol3/papers.cfm?abstract_id=894966.

[7] "Critical Foundations, Protecting America's Infrastructures," *The Report of the President Commission's on Critical Infrastructure Protection*, October 1997, p. 31.

[8] Landwehr, Carl, "Improving Information Flow in the Information Security Market," Workshop on Economics and Information Security, May 2002 http://www2.sims.berkeley.edu/resources/affiliates/workshops/econsecurity/.

9 Common Criteria, Wikipedia, http://en.wikipedia.org/wiki/Common_Criteria.

10 Montalbano, Elizabeth, "Update: Microsoft Windows earns Common Criteria certification," December 2005, InfoWorld Online, http://www.infoworld.com/article/05/12/15/HNwindowscertification_1.html?SECURITY%20STANDARDS.

11 NIST, Wikipedia, http://en.wikipedia.org/wiki/NIST.

12 "Requiring Software Independence in VVSG 2007: STS Recommendations for the TGDC," November 2006 http://vote.nist.gov/DraftWhitePaperOnSIinVVSG2007-20061120.pdf.

13 NIST, Wikipedia, http://en.wikipedia.org/wiki/NIST.

14 The Iron Ring, The Calling of an Engineer, http://www.ironring.ca/.

15 Iron Ring, Wikipedia, http://en.wikipedia.org/wiki/Iron_Ring. Elements of this story line were also derived from Steve McConnel's wonderful book *After the Gold Rush, Creating a True Profession of Software Engineering*, Microsoft Press, 1999.

16 "Requiring Software Independence in VVSG 2007: STS Recommendations for the TGDC," November 2006, pp. 8 and 10.

17 "Software Engineering Code of Ethics and Professional Practice," ACM website, http://www.acm.org/serving/se/code.htm.

18 "A Summary of the ACM Position on Software Engineering as a Licensed Engineering Profession," July 17, 2000.

19 Ibid.

20 Krueger, Alan, "Do You Need a License to Earn a Living? You Might be Surprised at the Answer," *New York Times*, March 2006.

21 Ibid.

22 Professional Engineer, Wikipedia, http://en.wikipedia.org/wiki/Professional_Engineer.

23 Thomas, Martyn, "Engineering Judgment," *Australian Computer Society*, 2004.

24 The Eli Whitney Museum and Workshop, http://www.eliwhitney.org/factory.htm.

25 "Profiles of National Standards-Related Activities," NIST, April 1997.

26 Surowiecki, James, "Turn of the Century," *Wired Magazine*, January 2002. The following paragraphs in this book provide a summary of Mr. Surowiecki's excellent article.

27 Ibid.

28 Ibid.

29 Ibid.

30 "Nanoengineered Concrete Could Cut Carbon Dioxide Emissions," *Massachusetts Institute of Technology Tech Talk*, February 2007.

Chapter 8

1 This story line was adapted from multiple sources including "On the Brink" from *The Moscow News*, Wikipedia entries for Petrov and Able Archer, as well as the website Bright Star Sound, http://www.brightstarsound.com/world_hero/insight.html.

INDEX

BOOKS ONLINE

ENABLED

Addison
Wesley

Reclaim the Internet from Hackers and Thieves

Phillip Hallam-Baker
ISBN 0-321-50358-9

Ever since the Internet became a mass medium over a decade ago, everyone connected with it; users, administrators, and developers have consistently ranked "security" as their number one priority. Despite the advances in Internet security technology, the problem of criminal activity on the Internet has only become worse. As the world goes digital, so does crime. Phillip Hallam-Baker sets out a manifesto for addressing Internet crime. The key principle of the manifesto is that Internet crime should be approached in the manner of a public health problem rather than the "command and control" approach that has dominated the academic approach to the field.

Hallam-Baker works closely with law enforcement and understands from those interactions that even though the police might only ever catch the stupid criminals, the stupid criminals turn out to be responsible for a staggering amount of crime. *The dotCrime Manifesto* is arranged into four sections providing a rough narrative from problem to solution and from people issues to technology issues. It discusses how some of the oldest scams are now the new cybercrimes, discusses issues around spam, phishing, and botnets, and looks at measures that can deployed in the short term with minimal changes to the existing Internet infrastructure.

Dr. Philip Hallam-Baker is VeriSign's first Principal Scientist and has been at the center of Internet security for more than a decade. A frequent speaker at international conferences with over 100 appearances over the past four years and numerous media interviews, Hallam-Baker is known for his passionate advocacy of what he calls technology for real people. Hallam-Baker gave testimony at the Federal Trade Commission workshop on authentication based approaches to stopping spam.

For more information on this title please visit www.informit/title/978032150358